Nepal Rising

Journey from Monarchy to Democracy

DR. TC RAO

An Initiative of Gramin Uthaan - Bharat Nirman

BlueRose ONE.com
Stories Matter
NewDelhi • London

BLUEROSE PUBLISHERS
India | U.K.

BlueRose ONE.com
Stories Matter
NewDelhi • London

For permissions requests or inquiries regarding this publication, please contact:

BLUEROSE PUBLISHERS
www.BlueRoseONE.com
info@bluerosepublishers.com
+91 8882 898 898
+4407342408967

ISBN: 978-93-5989-360-0

Cover design: Tahira
Typesetting: Tanya Raj Upadhyay

First Edition: February 2024

Acknowledgement

I would like to express my heartfelt gratitude to the individuals and organizations who have played a significant role in the completion of my book, "**Nepal Rising - Journey from Monarchy to Democracy.**" Their support, encouragement, and assistance have been invaluable throughout this journey.

First and foremost, I would like to dedicate this book to my wife, Mrs. Kamlesh Rao. Her unwavering moral support and encouragement have been the driving force behind my work. Her belief in my capabilities has been a constant source of motivation.

I am indebted to my sons, Navneet Pratap Singh and Navdeep Pratap Singh, for their understanding and patience during the long hours I spent researching and writing. Their encouragement and understanding have been instrumental in my endeavours.

I would also like to express my gratitude to my daughters-in-law, Sayali Bhagat and Kinni Pratap Singh, for their support and understanding throughout the process. Their encouragement and positivity have been a constant source of inspiration.

To my granddaughters, Ivanka and Naveera, I offer my heartfelt thanks for their love and joy, which have brought a smile to my face even during the most challenging times. Their innocent presence has been a constant reminder of why I embarked on this journey.

I would like to acknowledge the management and members of Gramin Uthaan - Bharat Nirman, Martyrs Families' Welfare Foundation, Delhi Cantonment Development Committee, and Skylark Group of companies for their generous help and cooperation. Their contributions and assistance have been invaluable in shaping this book.

I cannot forget to mention my parents, who may no longer be with me physically but have blessed me from the heavens. Their love and guidance continue to inspire me every day. I am also grateful to my brothers and sister for their unconditional love, support, and affection.

Finally, I extend my gratitude to all those who have supported me in various ways, directly or indirectly, during the creation of this book. Your contributions, whether big or small, have made a significant impact, and I am truly grateful for your involvement.

Thank you all once again for being an integral part of this endeavour and for your unwavering support.

Dr TC Rao

Foreword

It is with great pleasure that I introduce the book titled ***"Nepal Rising - Journey from Monarchy to Democracy"*** authored by Dr TC Rao. This remarkable piece of work provides a comprehensive account of the transformative journey undertaken by the Republic of Nepal during a crucial period in its history. As a witness and observer of the events that unfolded between 1989 and 1993, Dr Rao's firsthand experience, coupled with his expertise as a research scholar and military historian, lends a unique perspective to this significant period of Nepal's evolution.

The transition from monarchy to democracy is a pivotal phase in any nation's history, marking a profound shift in the socio-political landscape. Dr Rao delves into the pre and post events surrounding Nepal's transition, meticulously documenting the circumstances, challenges, and transformations that shaped the nation. The book provides invaluable insights into the factors that influenced this transition, shedding light on the political, social, and economic changes that took place during this period.

One cannot discuss Nepal's transition without acknowledging the substantial financial aid provided by neighbouring countries, particularly India and China. Dr Rao's analysis encompasses the impact of this aid, exploring the dynamics and implications for Nepal's development. Furthermore, the book explores the role played by the armed forces of Nepal in this transition, examining their influence and contributions to the process.

A significant aspect of Nepal's transition is the fate of the ex-servicemen who are Nepalese domiciled Gorkhas and have settled in Nepal. My exposure as, the former Director General of Assam Rifles, and Pension Paying Officer at PPO Pokhra from 1990 to 1993, bring my own unique perspective to this narrative. Having witnessed and closely engaged with the activities during this period, I provide invaluable insights into the role of the Government of India, particularly the military wing of the Indian Embassy in Kathmandu, in ensuring the welfare and support of the three lakh ex-servicemen.

The book also sheds light on the significant contributions of various United Nations agencies in the development of Nepal. The role of these agencies in supporting Nepal's transition and their ongoing efforts to foster growth and progress are examined, offering readers a comprehensive understanding of the collaborative endeavors that have shaped the nation.

"Nepal Rising - Journey from Monarchy to Democracy" by Dr TC Rao is an exceptional and timely contribution to the literature on Nepal's history. The author's depth of knowledge and personal experience, combined with my insights, provide readers with a comprehensive and nuanced understanding of the complexities involved in Nepal's transformative journey. This book will undoubtedly serve as a valuable resource for scholars, researchers, policymakers, and anyone interested in Nepal's history and its path toward democracy.

As I reflect upon the contents of this book, I am reminded of the profound significance of transitions in the course of a nation's destiny. Nepal's transition from monarchy to democracy was a momentous undertaking, marked by numerous challenges, aspirations, and aspirations. Dr TC Rao's meticulous research and insightful analysis provide readers with a deep understanding of the intricacies and complexities associated with such a transformative period.

The author's comprehensive examination of the events leading up to Nepal's transition serves as a reminder of the importance of historical context in understanding the present. By tracing the pre-transition era, Dr Rao sets the stage for a profound exploration of the forces that shaped Nepal's political landscape. His examination of the post-transition period highlights the enduring impact of this monumental shift and the subsequent changes that unfolded within the Republic of Nepal.

One cannot discuss the transition without acknowledging the role played by external actors. Dr Rao's exploration of the financial aid provided by India and China offers valuable insights into the geopolitical dynamics at play during this period. The book meticulously examines the motivations, interests, and implications of this aid, shedding light on the intricate web of regional relationships and their impact on Nepal's development.

The armed forces of Nepal, as an integral component of the nation's transition, also come under scrutiny in this book. Dr Rao's analysis underscores the critical role played by the armed forces in safeguarding the transition process and maintaining stability during this period of change. The book offers a unique perspective on the military's contributions and sheds light on their challenges and successes in navigating this transformative period.

Furthermore, my firsthand experience as the Pension Paying Officer at PPO Pokhra from 1990 to 1993 adds a valuable dimension to the narrative. His insights into the role of the Government of India and the military wing of the Indian Embassy in Kathmandu in supporting the welfare of the three lakh ex-servicemen, who are Nepalese domiciled Gorkhas, provide a glimpse into the complexities of managing and addressing the needs of this significant demographic.

The inclusion of the role played by United Nations agencies in Nepal's development further enriches the narrative. Dr Rao's examination of their contributions underscores the importance of international cooperation and collaboration in fostering sustainable development. The book highlights the multifaceted efforts of these agencies and their ongoing commitment to supporting Nepal's progress.

"Nepal Rising - Journey from Monarchy to Democracy" by Dr TC Rao is a comprehensive and illuminating piece of work that captures the essence of a pivotal period in Nepal's history. The author's meticulous research, coupled with my firsthand experience, offers readers a unique insight into the multifaceted aspects of Nepal's transition. This book is a valuable resource for anyone seeking a deeper understanding of the challenges, changes, and future prospects of Nepal as it embarked on its path towards democracy.

Lt. Gen. KS Yadav, PVSM, AVSM, SM, VSM
Former Director General, Assam Rifles

Disclaimer

This book *"Nepal Rising - Journey from Monarchy to Democracy"* contains material that has been sourced from various Web Portals, Books, Periodicals, Newspapers, Extracts of Interviews, TV programmes, Government Publications, Records of Events, Government Bulletins, Notification and from other relevant sources. The content in this book may include text, ideas or other material that has been generated or assisted by AI algorithms. AI-generated material may not reflect the opinions, beliefs or experiences of any specific individual or group. While efforts have been made to ensure the accuracy and reliability of the material, we cannot guarantee its absolute correctness or completeness. Readers should exercise their own judgement when interpreting and relying on the content within this book. We have made reasonable efforts to verify and validate the content, but errors and inaccuracies may still exist. We are committed to adhering to ethical and legal standards in the use and presentation of AI-Generated material. Any identifiable information or sensitive content has been handled with appropriate care and consideration. We have made every effort to ensure that the material used in this book is used in accordance with the fair-use policy and to the best of our knowledge, all the material used is free from any copyright restrictions. However, we acknowledge that there may be instances where we have unintentionally used copyright material, despite our best efforts to avoid it. In such cases, we apologize to the copyright owners and are open to discuss any concerns they may have. While every effort has been made to ensure the accuracy of the information, the author or publishers makes no guarantees, either express or implied, about the completeness, accuracy, reliability, suitability, or availability of the information contained in this book. The author assumes no responsibility or liability for any errors or omissions in the contents of this book. The material used in this book is intended for educational and informational purposes only and should not be construed as professional advice. Readers are advised to seek the advice of qualified professionals before making any decisions based on the information contained in this book.

Author

Preface

"Nepal Rising - Journey from Monarchy to Democracy"

In the annals of history, there are few narratives as captivating and transformative as the journey of Nepal from a Monarchy to a thriving Democracy. It is a story of resilience, struggle, and the indomitable spirit of the Nepalese people. Driven by a desire for change, Nepal underwent a remarkable transformation that upended centuries of tradition, and this book seeks to chronicle that extraordinary transition. The book has been divided into 14 sections and 60 chapters. The sections namely are from Introduction, Historical Context, Factors Leading to Democratic movements, The People's Movement of 1990, Challenges & setbacks, The Interim Period & the constituent assembly, Writing the new constitution, Consolidation of Democracy, Inclusion & social transformation, Economic Development & Democracy, International Perspectives & Relations, Reflections & Future Prospectus, Potential of a Gorkha Soldier and Author's Experiments with Nepal.

In the following pages, Dr TC Rao, a seasoned diplomat and scholar, takes us on a captivating journey through Nepal's history, from the era of Hindu monarchy to its eventual evolution into a secular democracy. Drawing upon his extensive experience as a diplomat in the Indian embassy in Kathmandu, Dr Rao provides an insider's perspective on the administrative and sociopolitical changes that have shaped the nation.

The story begins with an exploration of Nepal's rich historical tapestry, where Hinduism played a central role in shaping the country's identity for centuries. Dr Rao delves into the intricacies of the monarchy, detailing its power dynamics, cultural influences, and the profound impact it had on the lives of the Nepalese people. With a keen eye for detail and a deep understanding of the region, he paints a vivid picture of a bygone era, setting the stage for the monumental changes that were about to unfold.

The book then takes us through the tumultuous period of transition that Nepal experienced in the late 20th century. It was a time of great political upheaval, as the Nepalese people clamored for democratic reforms and an end to the autocratic rule. Dr Rao provides a comprehensive account of the political movements, protests, and negotiations that eventually led to the dismantling of the monarchy and the establishment of a democratic system.

What sets this book apart is the author's ability to seamlessly interweave personal anecdotes with historical facts. Through his own experiences, Dr Rao offers readers a unique perspective on the challenges and triumphs faced by both Nepal and its people. His tenure in the Indian embassy in Kathmandu provided him with a front-row seat to the unfolding drama, and he shares his observations with great candor and insight. From engaging with Nepalese officials to interacting with ordinary citizens, Dr Rao's encounters offer a glimpse into the diverse tapestry of Nepali society and its inherent resilience.

Education emerges as a recurring theme in the narrative, as Dr Rao reflects on the role it played in Nepal's journey toward democracy. He explores the challenges faced by the education system and the efforts made to empower the Nepalese youth with the tools they needed to shape their nation's future. With a deep appreciation for the transformative power of education, Dr Rao celebrates the triumphs and acknowledges the hurdles that Nepal faced in this critical domain.

Furthermore, the author delves into the social fabric of Nepal, unravelling the cultural nuances, traditions, and personal traits that define the Nepalese people. His admiration for the Nepali language shines through his writing, as he eloquently describes its beauty and significance in shaping the national identity.

The latter part of the book focuses on the post-democracy era and the remarkable growth and development witnessed in Nepal. Dr Rao explores the economic reforms, infrastructure projects, and social initiatives that have propelled Nepal forward on its path to progress. He examines the challenges that still persist and offers insights into the opportunities that lie ahead, urging readers to reflect on Nepal's journey and its implications for other nations grappling with similar transitions.

As we turn the pages of this book, we embark on a journey through time, witnessing the transformation of a nation and the indomitable spirit of its people. Dr TC Rao's meticulous research, combined with his personal experiences and keen observations, offers a comprehensive and nuanced account of Nepal's transition from monarchy to democracy.

In documenting Nepal's shift from a Hindu state to a secular format, Dr Rao presents a balanced exploration of the religious and cultural dynamics at play. He delves into the complexities of this transition, examining the implications for Nepal's diverse communities and the challenges faced in forging a new national identity. Through his thoughtful analysis, he reveals the delicate balance required to accommodate the aspirations and beliefs of a multicultural society.

This book is not merely a historical account or a political analysis; it is a testament to the author's deep affection for Nepal and its people. Dr Rao's words resonate with admiration for the resilience, determination, and warmth of the Nepalese population. He paints a vivid portrait of a nation that has overcome immense challenges and stands poised to embrace a brighter future.

In writing this preface, I am reminded of the profound impact Nepal's journey has had on the global stage. It serves as a beacon of hope for nations grappling with political upheaval and social transformation. Nepal's transition from monarchy to democracy offers valuable lessons in resilience, unity, and the power of collective action.

As readers delve into the rich tapestry of Nepal's history, they will not only gain a deeper understanding of the nation but also be inspired by the remarkable achievements of its people. Dr TC Rao's expertise, combined with his genuine passion for Nepal, makes this book an invaluable resource for scholars, policymakers, and anyone seeking to understand the complexities of political and societal change.

Finally, I would like to express my gratitude to Dr TC Rao for his tireless efforts in researching and documenting Nepal's transition. His dedication to capturing the essence of this pivotal period in Nepal's history shines through every page, and his commitment to fostering understanding and dialogue is commendable.

In closing, I invite readers to embark on this captivating journey, to immerse themselves in the rich history and vibrant culture of Nepal, and to draw inspiration from a nation that has triumphed over adversity. May this book serve as a reminder that the pursuit of democracy is a constant endeavour, one that requires unwavering dedication, resilience, and the unwavering belief in the power of the human spirit.

Dr TC Rao

Table of Contents

1. INTRODUCTION

"The transition from monarchy to democracy in Nepal symbolizes the power of the people to shape their own destiny"

Purpose of Writing the Book

Writing a comprehensive book on *"**Nepal Rising - Journey from Monarchy to Democracy**"*, with a specific focus on India's role, serves multiple purposes. Firstly, it provides a detailed historical account of the events, actors, and factors that influenced Nepal's journey towards democracy. Secondly, it underscores the significance of regional dynamics and bilateral relations in shaping the political destiny of a nation. Lastly, it contributes to a deeper understanding of the intricate relationship between Nepal and India, and the impact of external factors on a country's democratization process.

By documenting and analyzing the role of India in Nepal's transition, this book will serve as a valuable resource for academics, researchers, policymakers, and anyone interested in understanding the complexities of democratic transitions, regional dynamics, and the interplay of domestic and external factors in shaping the political landscape of a nation. It will provide a nuanced perspective on the challenges, successes, and lessons learned from Nepal's transition, highlighting the role of India as a key player.

Furthermore, the book aims to foster a deeper appreciation for the importance of diplomatic relations and cooperation between neighboring countries during times of political change. It will examine how India's engagement with Nepal went beyond mere assistance and support, encompassing diplomatic negotiations, mediation, and the sharing of democratic values and practices. By highlighting these aspects, the book seeks to promote dialogue and collaboration among nations facing similar transitions or grappling with democratic reforms.

The book will also address the implications of Nepal's transition for the broader South Asian region. As a country that shares borders with India, China, and other countries, Nepal's political transformation has broader geopolitical implications. By examining India's role in Nepal's transition, the book will shed light on the complexities of regional dynamics, power struggles, and the interests of various actors involved. This analysis will provide valuable insights for policymakers and scholars seeking to understand the broader impact of democratization processes within a regional context.

In addition, the book will delve into the socio-political factors within Nepal that influenced the transition. It will explore the role of civil society organizations, political parties, student movements, and other grassroots initiatives that contributed to the momentum for change. By examining the domestic forces at play, the book will provide a comprehensive understanding of the multifaceted nature of Nepal's transition, moving beyond the external factors and highlighting the agency of Nepalese actors in shaping their own political destiny.

Moreover, the book will critically examine the challenges and shortcomings of Nepal's transition from monarchy to democracy. It will analyze the obstacles faced in consolidating democratic institutions, addressing issues of social inclusion, and promoting political stability. By identifying these challenges, the book will contribute to a more nuanced understanding of the complexities involved in democratic transitions, enabling policymakers and scholars to draw important lessons for future endeavors.

Finally, the purpose of this book is to document and preserve the history of Nepal's transition from monarchy to democracy, with India's role as a central theme. It will serve as a lasting record of a significant period in Nepal's history and the collaborative efforts between Nepal and India in shaping the political landscape. By providing an in-depth analysis and comprehensive account, the book will ensure that future generations have access to the knowledge and insights necessary to understand the context and dynamics of Nepal's democratic transition.

The purpose of writing a book on Nepal's transition from monarchy to democracy, highlighting the role of India, is multifaceted. It aims to provide a comprehensive account of the historical events, actors, and factors that shaped Nepal's journey towards democracy. The book will explore India's multifaceted role, including its inspiration, diplomatic relations, economic assistance, mediation, and security concerns. It will contribute to a deeper understanding of the complexities of democratic transitions, regional dynamics, and the interplay of domestic and external factors. Furthermore, the book will address the implications of Nepal's transition for the broader South Asian region and examine the domestic forces within Nepal that influenced the transition. By critically analyzing the challenges and shortcomings, the book will provide valuable insights for policymakers and scholars. Ultimately, the book aims to document and preserve the history of Nepal's transition, ensuring that future generations have access to the knowledge and insights necessary to understand this transformative period.

"In the heart of the Himalayas, Nepal rises as a beacon of democracy."

Overview of Nepal's Historical Background and Monarchy

Nepal, nestled in the Himalayas, is a land of rich cultural heritage and a fascinating historical background. Throughout its history, Nepal has been shaped by various dynasties and rulers, with the monarchy playing a significant role. This chapter aims to provide an overview of Nepal's historical background and its monarchy, tracing the country's evolution from ancient times to the present day.

- ***Ancient Nepal:*** Nepal's history stretches back thousands of years, with evidence of human habitation dating back to prehistoric times. The ancient period saw the emergence of various tribes and kingdoms, including the Kiratis, Licchavis, and Mallas. These kingdoms laid the foundation for the cultural, political, and religious traditions that continue to thrive in Nepal today.
- ***The Monarchy Takes Shape:*** By the 18th century, Nepal had become a collection of small kingdoms and principalities, and the Shah dynasty rose to prominence. King Prithvi Narayan Shah, considered the founder of modern Nepal, embarked on a campaign to unify these fragmented territories into a single nation. His conquests led to the establishment of the Kingdom of Nepal in 1768 and the beginning of the Shah dynasty's rule.
- ***The Rana Era:*** Following the Shah dynasty's ascension, Nepal entered a period of Rana rule, referred to as the Rana era, which lasted from the mid-19th century until the early 1950s. During this time, the Rana prime ministers held real power, while the monarchy took on a largely ceremonial role. The Ranas maintained a tight grip on governance, limiting political freedoms and suppressing dissent.
- ***The End of Rana Rule:*** The early 1950s marked a turning point in Nepal's history as the country underwent a series of political changes. Inspired by democratic movements worldwide, Nepali citizens began demanding greater political participation and an end to Rana rule. In 1951, a popular uprising led to the overthrow of the Rana regime and the restoration of power to the monarchy.
- ***The Shah Monarchy:*** With the Ranas out of power, Nepal experienced a period of relative political openness. King Tribhuvan Bir Bikram Shah, the

reigning monarch at the time, played a crucial role in the transition to democracy. He sought to modernize Nepal and initiated reforms that paved the way for a constitutional monarchy. However, the monarchy's role remained influential, with the king acting as a unifying figure for the nation.

- ***Democracy and Political Change:*** In 1990, Nepal witnessed another significant political shift. Following widespread protests and demands for democratic reforms, King Birendra Bir Bikram Shah introduced a new constitution that established a multi-party system. This move marked the end of the Panchayat system, which had been in place since 1962. Nepal transitioned to a parliamentary monarchy, with the king serving as the head of state.
- ***The Palace Massacre and Aftermath:*** Tragedy struck Nepal in 2001 when King Birendra, along with several members of the royal family, was assassinated in the Narayanhiti Palace massacre. The incident shocked the nation and plunged Nepal into a period of uncertainty. Crown Prince Dipendra, who was also injured in the incident and later declared king, died a few days later. King Gyanendra Bir Bikram Shah assumed the throne, but his reign was marked by political turmoil. The monarchy faced growing criticism, and calls for the establishment of a republic gained momentum.
- ***The End of the Monarchy:*** In 2006, Nepal witnessed a historic turning point with the signing of the Comprehensive Peace Agreement between the government and Maoist rebels. This agreement ended the decade-long Maoist insurgency and paved the way for a transitional period. As part of the peace process, an interim constitution was promulgated, which stripped the king of his powers and declared Nepal a federal democratic republic.
- ***Nepal as a Federal Democratic Republic:*** In 2008, Nepal held its first Constituent Assembly elections, leading to the abolition of the monarchy and the declaration of Nepal as a federal democratic republic. The monarchy, which had played a central role in Nepal's history for centuries, came to an end. The declaration of a republic marked a significant milestone in Nepal's political evolution.
- ***Post-Monarchy Nepal:*** Since the transition to a federal democratic republic, Nepal has experienced a series of political and constitutional changes. The country has seen the adoption of a new constitution in 2015, which established Nepal as a secular, federal democratic republic. Political parties, civil society, and the people continue to shape the country's democratic institutions and processes.

Nepal's historical background is intertwined with the monarchy, which played a central role in the country's governance for many centuries. From the ancient kingdoms to the Shah dynasty and the Rana era, the monarchy shaped Nepal's political landscape. However, political changes, popular uprisings, and demands for democracy eventually led to the end of the monarchy and the establishment of a federal democratic republic. Today, Nepal stands as a vibrant and diverse nation, striving to navigate the challenges of democracy and build a prosperous future for its people.

"The winds of change in Nepal echo the voices of the people longing for democracy."

---

2. HISTORICAL CONTEXT

"In Nepal, the shift from monarchy to democracy heralds a new era of inclusivity and empowerment"

Map of Nepal

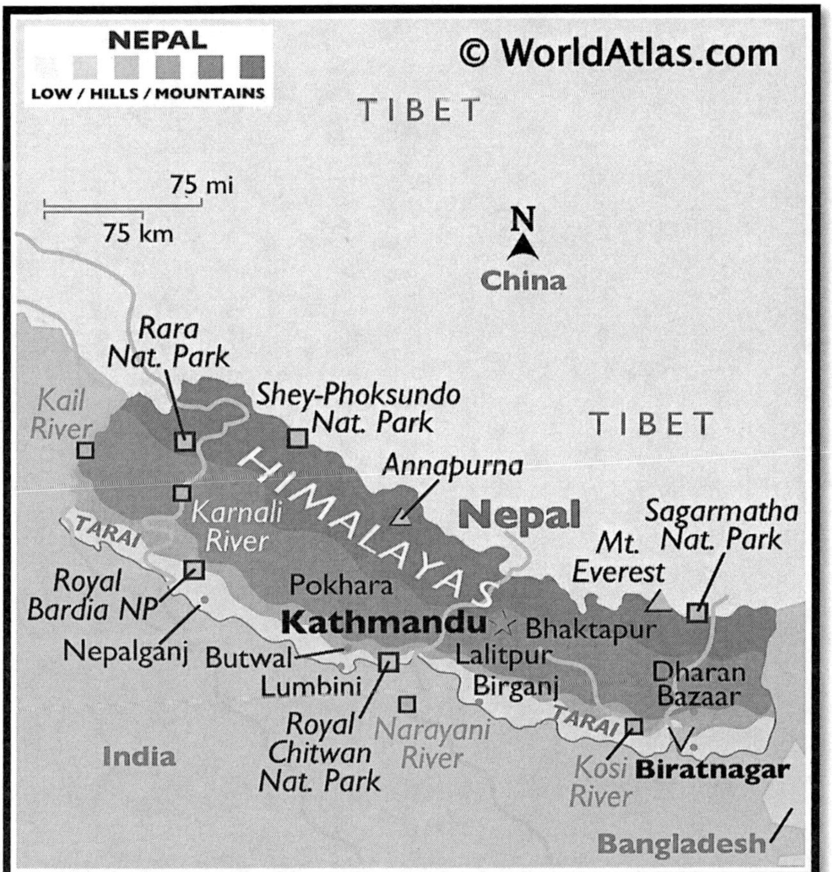
NEPAL
LOW / HILLS / MOUNTAINS
© WorldAtlas.com
TIBET
75 mi
75 km
N
China
Rara
Nat. Park
Shey-Phoksundo
Nat. Park
Kail
River
TIBET
HIMALAYAS
Annapurna
Karnali
River
Nepal
Sagarmatha
Nat. Park
TARAI
Mt.
Everest
Royal
Bardia NP
Pokhara
Kathmandu
Bhaktapur
Nepalganj
Butwal
Lalitpur
Lumbini
Birganj
Dharan
Bazaar
Royal
Chitwan
Nat. Park
Narayani
River
TARAI
India
Kosi
River
Biratnagar
Bangladesh

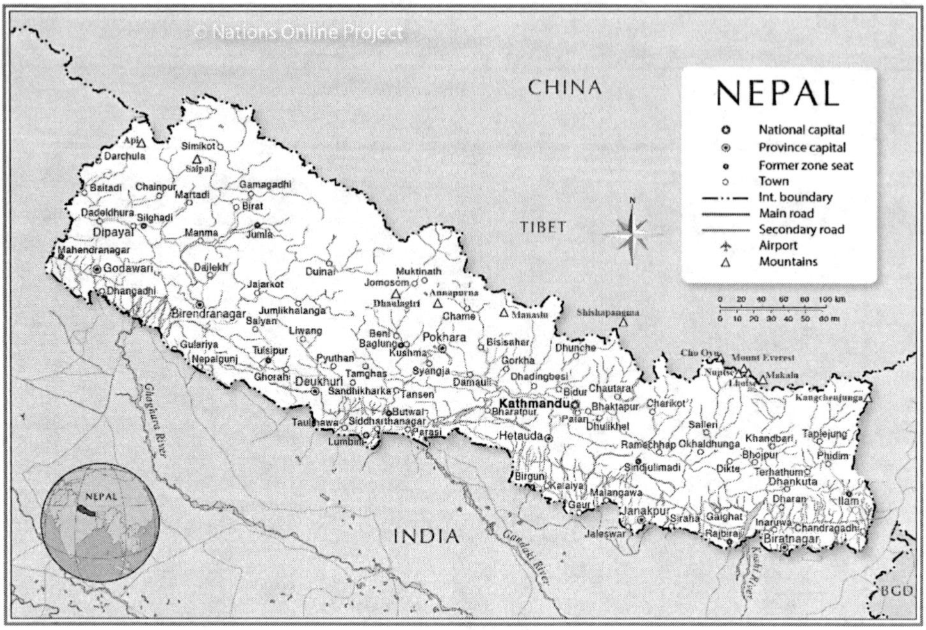
© Nations Online Project
NEPAL
National capital
Province capital
Former zone seat
Town
Int. boundary
Main road
Secondary road
Airport
Mountains
CHINA
TIBET
INDIA
BGD
Api
Darchula
Simikot
Saipal
Baitadi
Chainpur
Martadi
Gamagadhi
Dadeldhura
Silghadi
Birat
Dipayal
Manma
Jumla
Mahendranagar
Godawari
Dailekh
Dunai
Muktinath
Jomosom
Dhangadhi
Jajarkot
Dhaulagiri
Annapurna
Manaslu
Shishapangma
Birendranagar
Jumlikhalanga
Salyan
Chame
Liwang
Beni
Baglung
Pokhara
Bisisahar
Dhunche
Gulariya
Tulsipur
Kushma
Gorkha
Nepalgunj
Pyuthan
Ghorahi
Deukhuri
Tamghas
Syangja
Damauli
Dhadingbesi
Sandhikharka
Tansen
Bidur
Chautara
Kathmandu
Bharatpur
Bhaktapur
Charikot
Patan
Dhulikhel
Butwal
Taulihawa
Siddharthanagar
Parasi
Lumbini
Hetauda
Ramechhap
Okhaldhunga
Salleri
Khandbari
Taplejung
Bhojpur
Phidim
Sindhulimadi
Dikte
Terhathum
Dhankuta
Birgunj
Kalaiya
Malangawa
Gaur
Janakpur
Siraha
Gaighat
Dharan
Ilam
Inaruwa
Chandragadhi
Jaleswar
Rajbiraj
Biratnagar
Cho Oyu
Mount Everest
Nuptse
Lhotse
Makalu
Kangchenjunga
Ghaghara River
Gandaki River
Koshi River

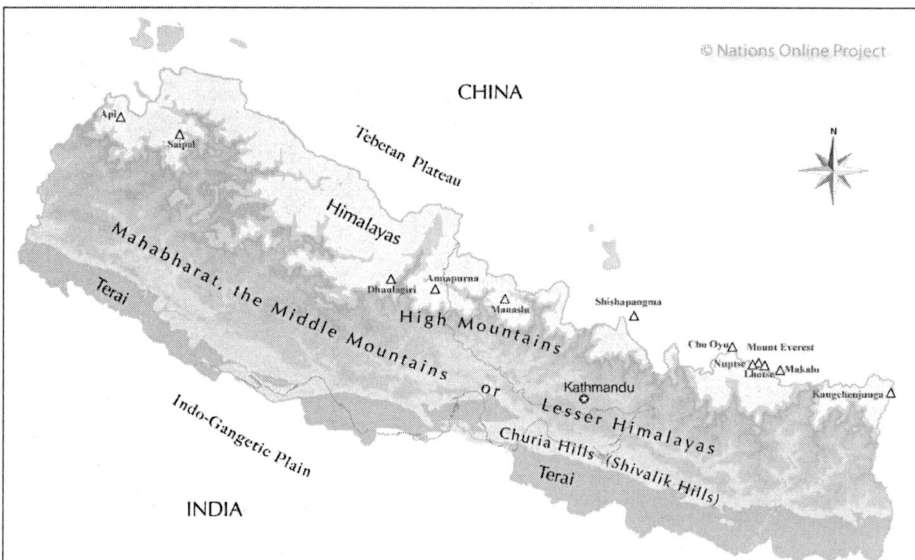
© Nations Online Project
CHINA
Tebetan Plateau
Himalayas
Mahabharat, the Middle Mountains or Lesser Himalayas
High Mountains
Churia Hills (Shivalik Hills)
Terai
Terai
Indo-Gangetic Plain
INDIA
Api
Saipal
Dhaulagiri
Annapurna
Manaslu
Shishapangma
Cho Oyu
Mount Everest
Nuptse
Lhotse
Makalu
Kangchenjunga
Kathmandu
N

The Pre-Democracy Era in Nepal: A Historical Perspective

Nepal's pre-democracy era represents a crucial phase in the country's history, characterized by autocratic rule, political instability, and limited civic participation. This chapter aims to provide a comprehensive exploration of the pre-democracy era in Nepal, examining key historical events, the role of the monarchy, and the socio-political landscape of the time. By delving into the pre-democracy era, we can gain a deeper understanding of the factors that led to the demand for democratic reforms and set the stage for the transition to a democratic system.

- ***The Monarchy and the Shah Dynasty:*** The pre-democracy era in Nepal was dominated by the Shah Dynasty, which ruled the country for over two centuries. The monarchy held significant power and authority, shaping the political and social structures of the nation. We delve into the origins of the Shah Dynasty, the consolidation of power, and the centralization of authority under the monarchy.
- ***Feudalism and Social Hierarchy:*** Nepal's pre-democracy era was characterized by a feudalistic system, where power and wealth were concentrated in the hands of a few elites. We explore the social hierarchy prevalent during this time, highlighting the privileges enjoyed by the ruling class and the challenges faced by the marginalized sections of society.
- ***Rana Rule and Autocracy:*** One of the defining features of the pre-democracy era was the Rana regime, which emerged in the mid-19th century. The Ranas, a powerful oligarchic family, held de facto power in Nepal for more than a century. We examine the Rana rule, the centralization of power, and the suppression of political dissent during this period.
- ***Emergence of Pro-Democracy Movements:*** The pre-democracy era witnessed the emergence of pro-democracy movements that challenged the autocratic rule of the monarchy and the Rana regime. We delve into the early signs of dissent, the role of influential figures, and the growing demands for political reforms and democratic governance.
- ***The Nepali Congress and the People's Movement of 1951:*** The Nepali Congress played a pivotal role in the struggle for democracy during the pre-democracy era. We discuss the formation of the Nepali Congress, its

objectives, and the significant People's Movement of 1951, which marked a turning point in Nepal's political landscape.

- ***Political Parties and Intellectual Movements:*** The pre-democracy era saw the emergence of various political parties and intellectual movements advocating for democratic reforms. We explore the contributions of key political leaders and intellectuals who played a crucial role in shaping public opinion and mobilizing support for democratic ideals.
- ***Suppression and Repression:*** The pre-democracy era was also marked by instances of suppression and repression by the ruling authorities. We examine the measures taken by the monarchy and the Rana regime to stifle dissent, curtail civil liberties, and maintain their grip on power.
- ***Socio-Political Awakening and Public Awareness:*** Despite the challenges and restrictions, the pre-democracy era witnessed a growing socio-political awakening among the Nepalese population. We discuss the role of civil society, student organizations, and the media in raising awareness, promoting democratic values, and challenging the status quo.
- ***International Influences and External Factors:*** The pre-democracy era in Nepal was not isolated from global events and international influences. We explore the impact of external factors such as the end of colonial rule in neighboring countries, the spread of democratic movements worldwide, and the role of international actors in advocating for democratic reforms in Nepal.
- ***Cultural and Intellectual Shifts:*** The pre-democracy era also witnessed significant cultural and intellectual shifts that contributed to the demand for democratic reforms. We examine the influence of literature, arts, and cultural movements in shaping public consciousness and fostering a sense of national identity and democratic aspirations.
- ***Challenges and Resistance:*** The struggle for democracy in the pre-democracy era was not without challenges. We delve into the obstacles faced by pro-democracy activists, including political repression, imprisonment, and exile. Additionally, we explore the resilience and determination of individuals and groups in their quest for democratic rights and freedoms.
- ***Legacy and Lessons:*** The pre-democracy era left a lasting impact on Nepal's political landscape. We reflect on the legacy of the pro-democracy movements, the sacrifices made by activists, and the lessons learned from this era. Furthermore, we analyze the significance of preserving historical memory and the role it plays in shaping the present and future of Nepal's democracy.

- ***Transition to Democracy:*** The pre-democracy era set the stage for the eventual transition to a democratic system in Nepal. We highlight the key milestones and events that paved the way for the establishment of a democratic government, including the People's Movement of 1990 and the subsequent adoption of a multiparty system.

The pre-democracy era in Nepal was a critical period marked by autocratic rule, political suppression, and socio-political awakening. Through the struggles and resistance of pro-democracy activists, the groundwork for democratic reforms was laid, shaping Nepal's path towards a democratic system. As Nepal continues its democratic journey, it is essential to reflect on the pre-democracy era, its challenges, and the sacrifices made by those who fought for democratic ideals. By understanding this era, we can gain insights into the significance of democracy in Nepal and the importance of safeguarding and strengthening democratic institutions for the future.

The pre-democracy era in Nepal was characterized by autocratic rule, political suppression, and socio-political awakening. The monarchy and the Rana regime held significant power, leading to a concentration of authority and limited civic participation. However, the emergence of pro-democracy movements, the persistence of activists, and external influences contributed to the demand for democratic reforms. The legacy of the pre-democracy era continues to shape Nepal's democratic journey, highlighting the importance of preserving historical memory and the ongoing commitment to democratic principles.

"As the monarchy fades, Nepal rises to embrace the dawn of democracy."

The Rise and Consolidation of Monarchy in Nepal: A Historical Perspective

Nepal, a landlocked country nestled in the heart of the Himalayas, has a rich and vibrant history that spans several centuries. Throughout its past, Nepal has experienced various forms of governance, including kingdoms, republics, and even foreign rule. This chapter delves into the rise and consolidation of monarchy in Nepal, exploring key historical events, influential monarchs, and the factors that contributed to the establishment and endurance of monarchy in the country.

- ***Early History and the Shah Dynasty:*** Nepal's monarchy traces its roots back to the mid-18th century when Prithvi Narayan Shah, a visionary leader, unified several small principalities to form a cohesive kingdom. Prithvi Narayan Shah laid the foundation of the Shah dynasty, which would reign over Nepal for the next two and a half centuries. Under the Shah dynasty, Nepal witnessed territorial expansion, cultural growth, and the preservation of national identity.
- ***Rana Regime and the Shah Monarchy:*** In the mid-19th century, a powerful oligarchy emerged within the monarchy known as the Ranas. The Rana regime, led by a hereditary prime minister known as the Rana Maharaja, held absolute power for more than a century. During this period, the Shah monarchy existed as a symbolic institution, with the Ranas controlling political affairs. However, the Shah kings played a crucial role in maintaining national unity and identity, even amidst the Rana autocracy.
- ***Democracy Movement and the Palace Massacre:*** In the mid-20th century, Nepal witnessed a wave of democratic movements that sought to challenge the Rana regime's dominance. These movements, led by political parties and activists, culminated in the 1951 revolution, which led to the overthrow of the Rana oligarchy and the restoration of power to the Shah monarchy. King Tribhuvan, the then-monarch, played a pivotal role in this movement, and his reign marked the beginning of a new era for Nepal.

However, tragedy struck in 2001 when King Birendra and most of the royal family were assassinated in the infamous Palace Massacre. This event sent shockwaves throughout Nepal and raised questions about the future of the monarchy. Crown Prince Dipendra, the alleged perpetrator, also died in the massacre, leaving his uncle, Gyanendra, to ascend the throne.

- ***The Shah Monarchy's Challenges and Reforms:*** The Palace Massacre and subsequent events brought significant challenges for the Shah monarchy. The monarchy faced growing criticism and demands for a more inclusive and democratic system. In response, King Gyanendra attempted to consolidate power, assuming direct control of the government in 2005. However, his reign was marked by political instability, civil unrest, and a Maoist insurgency, which ultimately led to the downfall of the monarchy.
- ***The End of Monarchy and the Republic Era:*** In 2008, Nepal held its first Constituent Assembly elections, which resulted in the declaration of Nepal as a federal democratic republic, effectively ending the Shah monarchy. The monarchy's demise marked a significant turning point in Nepal's history, as the country embarked on a new era of democratic governance, with a president as the head of state.
- ***Legacy and Reflections:*** The rise and consolidation of monarchy in Nepal left an indelible mark on the country's history and culture. Despite the challenges and controversies surrounding the monarchy, it played a vital role in shaping Nepal's identity and fostering a sense of national unity. The Shah dynasty's contributions in terms of territorial expansion, cultural preservation, and diplomatic relations cannot be overlooked.

The monarchy served as a unifying symbol for the diverse ethnic and religious groups within Nepal, providing a sense of stability and continuity during times of political upheaval. The kings of Nepal were also seen as patrons of art, literature, and spirituality, contributing to the rich cultural heritage of the country.

However, the monarchy also faced criticism for its autocratic tendencies, lack of inclusivity, and widening disparities between the ruling elite and the general population. The Rana regime, in particular, was notorious for its oppressive rule and suppression of democratic aspirations. This led to the rise of democratic movements, demanding greater political representation and social equality.

The Palace Massacre in 2001 was a tragic event that shook the foundations of the monarchy and raised questions about its relevance and future. The incident exposed internal divisions within the royal family and eroded public trust in the institution. The subsequent reign of King Gyanendra was marked by further discontent, as he attempted to consolidate power and suppress dissent, leading to widespread protests and a resurgence of the Maoist insurgency.

Ultimately, the decision to transform Nepal into a federal democratic republic reflected the aspirations of the Nepalese people for a more inclusive and accountable form of governance. The monarchy, as an institution, was seen as an impediment to these aspirations, and the Constituent Assembly elections of 2008 marked a significant milestone in Nepal's transition towards a republican system.

The rise and consolidation of monarchy in Nepal is a complex and multifaceted chapter in the country's history. While the monarchy played a crucial role in the unification and preservation of Nepal, it also faced criticism for its autocratic tendencies and lack of inclusivity. The Palace Massacre and subsequent events highlighted the challenges and controversies surrounding the monarchy, ultimately leading to its downfall and the establishment of a federal democratic republic. The legacy of the monarchy, with its cultural contributions and symbolic significance, continues to shape Nepal's national identity and collective memory.

"The Himalayan spirit soars higher as Nepal embraces the principles of democracy."

Nepal Under Monarchy: A Comprehensive Analysis of Administrative, Judicial, Armed Forces, Education, Health, Economic, Political, and Power Conditions

Nepal, a landlocked nation nestled in the heart of the Himalayas, experienced a prolonged period of monarchy until sweeping political changes in recent decades transformed the nation into a federal democratic republic. This chapter delves into the various aspects of Nepal's administrative, judicial, armed forces, education, health, economic, political, and power conditions during the era of monarchy, providing insights into the strengths and shortcomings of the system.

- ***Administrative System:*** Under the monarchy, Nepal operated under a centralized administrative structure with the king at the helm. The king held absolute power and controlled the government machinery. The bureaucracy, comprising civil servants, implemented policies and regulations. However, corruption and bureaucratic inefficiency were persistent challenges, hindering effective governance and public service delivery.
- ***Judicial System:*** The judiciary in Nepal during the monarchy was characterized by a hierarchical structure. The Supreme Court, the highest judicial body, had the authority to interpret the constitution and pass verdicts. However, the independence of the judiciary was often compromised due to political interference and executive influence, impeding the fair administration of justice. Access to justice and the timely disposal of cases were significant concerns during this period.
- ***Armed Forces:*** The Nepalese Armed Forces, consisting of the Nepalese Army, Nepal Police, and Armed Police Force, played a crucial role in maintaining law and order and safeguarding national security. The king served as the supreme commander of the armed forces. While the military remained disciplined and professional, concerns of human rights violations were raised, particularly during periods of political unrest and the Maoist insurgency.
- ***Education System:*** During the monarchy, the education system in Nepal faced several challenges. Access to quality education was limited, especially

in rural areas. The curriculum and teaching methods were often outdated, focusing primarily on rote learning. The government's investment in education was insufficient, resulting in inadequate infrastructure and teacher shortages. As a result, literacy rates remained low, particularly among marginalized communities.

- ***Healthcare System:*** Nepal's healthcare system under the monarchy struggled to provide adequate medical services to the population. Access to quality healthcare, especially in rural areas, was limited. Healthcare infrastructure, including hospitals and clinics, was inadequate and poorly equipped. The government's investment in the health sector was insufficient, leading to a lack of essential medical supplies and a shortage of healthcare professionals. As a result, the overall health indicators of the population remained below the desired standards.
- ***Economic Condition:*** Nepal's economy during the monarchy was primarily agrarian, with agriculture forming the backbone of the country's economic activities. The government focused on promoting subsistence farming and small-scale industries. However, economic development remained sluggish due to limited access to capital, inadequate infrastructure, rampant corruption, and political instability. Poverty and income inequality were prevalent, especially in rural areas, exacerbating socio-economic disparities.
- ***Political Landscape:*** Under the monarchy, Nepal experienced a highly centralized political system. The king held absolute power and governed through appointed officials. Political parties were allowed, but their activities were closely monitored and restricted. Dissent and opposition were suppressed, leading to limited political freedom and the curtailment of civil liberties. The lack of a participatory political system resulted in widespread disillusionment among the populace.
- ***Power Structure:*** The monarchy wielded significant power in Nepal's governance structure. The king, as the head of state, had the authority to appoint key government officials, including the prime minister, cabinet ministers, and ambassadors. The king's decisions and decrees were considered final and binding. This concentration of power in the monarchy often led to a lack of checks and balances, undermining democratic principles and fostering a culture of authoritarianism.

The era of monarchy in Nepal witnessed a variety of conditions across administrative, judicial, armed forces, education, health, economic, political, and power sectors. While the monarchy provided stability and a sense of national identity, it also exhibited numerous shortcomings. Widespread corruption, lack of political freedom, limited access to quality education and healthcare, and economic challenges hindered the overall progress of the nation.

The transition from monarchy to a federal democratic republic in Nepal marked a significant turning point in the country's history. It opened up avenues for greater political participation, improved governance, and enhanced respect for human rights. However, the challenges inherited from the monarchy era continue to impact Nepal's journey towards a more inclusive and prosperous future.

Today, Nepal is striving to build a more inclusive society, strengthen democratic institutions, and address the socio-economic disparities that persist. Efforts are being made to reform the administrative and judicial systems, improve access to quality education and healthcare, and promote sustainable economic development. The country is also working towards ensuring equal political representation and empowering marginalized communities.

By critically analyzing the conditions prevalent during the monarchy, Nepal can learn valuable lessons and overcome historical challenges. It is through sustained efforts, political will, and inclusive policies that Nepal can forge a brighter future, where the principles of democracy, justice, and equality are upheld, and the well-being of all its citizens is prioritized.

"The journey from monarchy to democracy is Nepal's declaration of freedom and self-determination."

Nepal's Transition from Monarchy to Democracy: The Role of India

The transition from monarchy to democracy is a significant turning point in the history of any nation. Nepal, a landlocked country nestled in the Himalayas, embarked on this transformative journey in recent decades. This chapter aims to explore the purpose of writing a comprehensive book on Nepal's transition from monarchy to democracy, with a specific focus on the role played by India. By delving into the socio-political dynamics, historical context, and diplomatic relations between the two nations, we can gain insights into the intricate processes that shaped Nepal's democratization and the external influences that contributed to this transition.

- ***Historical Background:*** To establish a solid foundation for understanding Nepal's transition to democracy, it is crucial to delve into its historical background. Nepal was ruled by a monarchical system for centuries, with the Shah dynasty reigning supreme. However, the late 20th century witnessed a surge in demands for political reforms and the establishment of a more inclusive and democratic governance structure. This period was characterized by political unrest, student protests, and calls for change.

The Role of India:

India, as Nepal's neighboring country, has played a pivotal role in shaping its political landscape throughout history. The book aims to shed light on the multifaceted role of India during Nepal's transition from monarchy to democracy. India's assistance and influence were instrumental in several key aspects:

- ***Democratic Movements:*** The book will analyze how India's own democratic framework served as an inspiration for Nepal's democratic movements. The Indian democratic experience and its success in fostering inclusive governance provided a roadmap for Nepal's political activists and intellectuals.
- ***Diplomatic Relations:*** The book will explore the complex diplomatic relations between India and Nepal during this period. It will examine the interactions between leaders of both countries, the exchange of

ideas, and the negotiations that took place to facilitate Nepal's transition.

- ***Economic Assistance:*** India's economic assistance to Nepal played a crucial role in bolstering the country's democratic aspirations. The book will delve into the various developmental projects, aid packages, and trade agreements that India extended to Nepal to support its transition.
- ***Mediation and Facilitation:*** As a regional power, India acted as a mediator and facilitator between the Nepalese monarchy and the democratic forces. The book will highlight India's efforts to bridge the gap between different stakeholders, encourage dialogue, and facilitate negotiations to ensure a peaceful transition.
- ***Security Concerns:*** Given the shared border and historical ties, India had legitimate security concerns during Nepal's transition. The book will discuss India's role in maintaining stability, preventing spillover effects of political turmoil, and addressing security challenges arising from the transition.

"In the shadow of the peaks, Nepal rises with the sun of democracy."

Historical Perspective of India-Nepal Relations

India and Nepal share a unique bond that is built on a foundation of historical, cultural, and socio-economic ties. The relationship between these two South Asian neighbors has evolved over centuries, shaped by a complex interplay of factors such as geography, religion, politics, and diplomacy. This chapter delves into the historical perspective of India-Nepal relations, tracing their journey from ancient times to the present day.

- ***Ancient Ties:*** The roots of India-Nepal relations can be traced back to ancient times when the Indian subcontinent was characterized by a vibrant tapestry of kingdoms and empires. Nepal, situated on India's northern border, was an integral part of the broader Indian civilization. The ties between the two regions were strengthened by the spread of Buddhism from India to Nepal, establishing cultural and religious connections that endure to this day. The Mauryan and Gupta empires played a crucial role in shaping these early interactions.
- ***Medieval Period:*** During the medieval period, Nepal witnessed the rise of various Hindu dynasties, and its connections with India deepened. The Malla dynasty, which ruled over Kathmandu Valley, maintained close ties with the Rajput kingdoms of North India. Medieval Nepal also saw the emergence of influential religious figures such as Guru Gorakhnath, whose teachings had a profound impact on both Nepali and Indian society.
- ***Colonial Era:*** The arrival of European powers in the Indian subcontinent during the colonial era had a significant impact on India-Nepal relations. The British East India Company gradually expanded its influence in the region, which led to a series of treaties between Nepal and the British. The Treaty of Sugauli in 1816, following the Anglo-Nepalese War, marked a turning point in the relationship, as it delineated the borders between the two nations and established British control over certain territories. This treaty laid the foundation for the modern boundaries between India and Nepal.
- ***Post-Independence:*** The post-independence era witnessed the transformation of India-Nepal relations as both nations sought to redefine their identities in a rapidly changing global landscape. India's independence in 1947 and Nepal's subsequent emergence as a constitutional monarchy in 1951 set the stage for a new era of bilateral cooperation. The 1950 Treaty of

Peace and Friendship between India and Nepal was a landmark agreement that established a unique relationship between the two nations. It emphasized close cooperation and mutual respect, including open borders, trade facilitation, and cultural exchanges.

- ***Kingdom to Republic:*** Nepal underwent a significant political transformation in the 21st century. The abolition of the monarchy in 2008 and the establishment of a federal democratic republic signaled a new chapter in Nepal's history. This transition had implications for India-Nepal relations, as the new government sought to redefine its foreign policy priorities. While the relationship remained strong, occasional strains surfaced due to differences in political ideologies and perceptions.
- ***Border Disputes and Challenges:*** Over the years, India and Nepal have faced occasional border disputes and challenges. These issues primarily revolve around the demarcation of the boundary and the interpretation of historical agreements. The border blockade in 2015, triggered by protests against Nepal's new constitution, strained relations between the two countries. However, both nations have consistently engaged in diplomatic dialogues to address these challenges and maintain their long-standing ties.
- ***Strategic Cooperation and Economic Partnership:*** India and Nepal have recognized the importance of strategic cooperation and economic partnership in their bilateral relations. India has been a major development partner for Nepal, providing financial assistance, infrastructure development projects, and technical expertise. The two countries have collaborated on various initiatives, including cross-border connectivity, hydropower projects, and trade facilitation measures. The Indian government's "Neighborhood First" policy and the "Act East" policy have further emphasized the significance of strengthening ties with Nepal.
- ***Cultural Exchanges and People-to-People Contacts:*** Cultural exchanges and people-to-people contacts have been integral to India-Nepal relations. Given their shared history and cultural heritage, there is a natural affinity between the people of both countries. Nepali culture, language, and traditions have significantly influenced various regions of India, particularly in the Himalayan states and the northeastern part of the country. Similarly, Indian films, music, and spiritual practices have found a dedicated audience in Nepal. These cultural exchanges and interactions have fostered a deep sense of mutual understanding and friendship.

• ***Challenges and Opportunities:*** While India-Nepal relations have generally been characterized by warmth and cooperation, they have also faced challenges and occasional strains. Geopolitical dynamics in the region, border disputes, and differences in political ideologies have at times created tensions between the two nations. However, both countries have demonstrated a commitment to resolving these issues through dialogue and diplomatic channels.

The Belt and Road Initiative (BRI), China's ambitious infrastructure development project, has also presented both challenges and opportunities for India-Nepal relations. Nepal's participation in the BRI has raised concerns in India regarding its strategic implications. However, it has also opened up avenues for enhanced connectivity and economic cooperation between Nepal, India, and China.

The historical perspective of India-Nepal relations reveals a rich tapestry of shared cultural, religious, and historical ties. From ancient times to the present day, the relationship between these two nations has evolved, adapting to changing political and social landscapes. Despite occasional challenges, India and Nepal have consistently sought to strengthen their ties through strategic cooperation, economic partnership, and people-to-people contacts. The future of India-Nepal relations holds immense potential for further collaboration, mutual growth, and regional stability. By nurturing their historical bonds and addressing the challenges constructively, India and Nepal can continue to build a strong and enduring partnership in the years to come.

• ***The Way Forward:*** As India and Nepal navigate the complexities of the modern world, it is crucial to prioritize open communication, mutual respect, and understanding. Both nations must continue to engage in bilateral dialogues, diplomatic negotiations, and cultural exchanges to foster stronger ties and address any remaining challenges. Here are a few key areas that deserve attention for the way forward:

- *Strengthening Economic Cooperation:* India and Nepal should explore avenues to enhance economic cooperation. This includes promoting trade and investment, developing cross-border infrastructure, and harnessing the potential of sectors such as tourism, agriculture, and renewable energy. Special economic zones and joint ventures can facilitate economic growth and create employment opportunities for both countries.

- *Addressing Border Disputes:* Resolving outstanding border disputes and clarifying the demarcation of the boundary is essential for maintaining peace and stability in the region. Both countries should engage in constructive dialogue, considering historical agreements, legal frameworks, and the aspirations of the affected communities. Bilateral mechanisms, such as boundary commissions and joint survey teams, can be established to facilitate this process.
- *Strengthening People-to-People Contacts:* Cultural exchanges, educational programs, and tourism play a vital role in promoting people-to-people contacts. Encouraging greater mobility of students, artists, scholars, and tourists between India and Nepal can foster deeper understanding and forge lasting bonds. Scholarships, exchange programs, and cultural festivals can serve as platforms for promoting cross-cultural interactions.
- *Collaborating on Regional Issues:* India and Nepal should collaborate closely on regional issues of mutual interest, such as climate change, disaster management, and regional security. Joint efforts can be undertaken to address common challenges, share best practices, and coordinate responses to emerging threats. Regional forums, such as the South Asian Association for Regional Cooperation (SAARC), provide a platform for such collaboration.
- *Harnessing Technological Advancements:* Embracing technological advancements can unlock new opportunities for India-Nepal relations. Cooperation in areas such as digital connectivity, e-governance, and innovation can drive inclusive growth and socio-economic development. Joint research and development initiatives can also be pursued to address shared challenges, such as healthcare, agriculture, and environment.

"Democracy's embrace in Nepal is the melody of freedom sung by its people."

India Nepal Friendship Treaty of 1950

The India-Nepal Friendship Treaty of 1950 is a significant agreement that has played a crucial role in shaping the relationship between these two neighboring countries. Signed on July 31, 1950, this treaty has laid down the foundation for a strong and enduring friendship, establishing a framework for cooperation and collaboration across various sectors. Over the years, this treaty has evolved and faced its share of challenges, but it continues to serve as a cornerstone for bilateral relations between India and Nepal. In this chapter, we will delve into the various aspects of the India-Nepal Friendship Treaty of 1950, its historical context, key provisions, and its impact on the two nations.

To understand the significance of the treaty, it is essential to examine the historical backdrop against which it was signed. Nepal, a landlocked country located between India and China, has a long-standing history of independence and sovereignty. Despite its geographic proximity to India, Nepal managed to maintain its independence and autonomy throughout history. However, the early 1950s marked a period of political instability in Nepal, with the country facing internal conflicts and a struggle for modernization. During this time, King Tribhuvan sought India's support to restore stability and strengthen the democratic aspirations of the Nepalese people.

Recognizing the importance of stability in Nepal and its strategic interests in the region, India responded positively to Nepal's appeal. The India-Nepal Friendship Treaty of 1950 was the outcome of this bilateral engagement. The treaty aimed to foster a long-term friendship, mutual trust, and cooperation between the two nations. It recognized Nepal's sovereignty, territorial integrity, and independence, while also emphasizing the principles of non-interference and non-aggression.

One of the key provisions of the treaty was the establishment of an open border between India and Nepal. This provision allowed for the free movement of people and goods across the border without the need for passports or visas. The open border has facilitated cultural, economic, and social exchanges between the two countries, fostering a sense of closeness and interdependence. Nepalese citizens have benefited from employment opportunities in India, while Indian tourists and traders have been able to explore and invest in Nepal. This provision has undoubtedly contributed to the deepening of people-to-people contacts and the overall integration of the two societies.

Another important aspect of the treaty was the provision for national treatment and equal opportunities for the citizens of both countries. It ensured that Indian and Nepalese citizens residing in each other's territories would enjoy the same rights and privileges as the nationals of the host country. This provision has been instrumental in protecting the interests of Nepalese migrant workers in India and Indian businesses operating in Nepal. It has also facilitated the movement of students, scholars, and professionals between the two countries, promoting educational and cultural exchanges.

The treaty also recognized the need for economic cooperation and development between India and Nepal. It emphasized the importance of promoting trade, commerce, and transit facilities to enhance economic ties. India committed to providing technical and financial assistance to Nepal for its developmental projects, while Nepal agreed to grant India the right to use its territory for trade with third countries. This provision has played a vital role in promoting economic cooperation and enhancing connectivity between the two nations.

In addition to economic cooperation, the treaty also laid the foundation for defense and security cooperation between India and Nepal. It recognized the security concerns of both nations and emphasized the importance of maintaining peace and stability in the region. The treaty allowed for close cooperation in matters of defense and security, including the exchange of information, training, and joint exercises. This provision has been particularly significant in the context of regional security challenges and the shared border between India and Nepal. It has facilitated cooperation in areas such as border security, counter-terrorism, and disaster management, ensuring the safety and well-being of both nations.

The India-Nepal Friendship Treaty of 1950 also addressed the issue of water resources, which holds great importance for both countries. Nepal is home to numerous rivers and streams that originate in the Himalayas and flow into India. The treaty acknowledged the equitable utilization of water resources and emphasized the need for joint development and management of these shared water bodies. It paved the way for future agreements and projects related to water sharing and hydropower generation, promoting sustainable development and cooperation in this crucial sector.

Over the years, the India-Nepal Friendship Treaty of 1950 has faced its share of challenges. Some sections of the Nepalese society have criticized the treaty, arguing that it infringes upon Nepal's sovereignty and perpetuates an unequal relationship with India. There have been calls for its revision or even abrogation to address these concerns. These sentiments have been fueled by various factors, including perceived interference by India in Nepal's internal affairs and issues related to the implementation of the treaty's provisions.

In response to these concerns, both India and Nepal have engaged in discussions and negotiations to address the evolving dynamics of their bilateral relationship. Several agreements and protocols have been signed between the two countries to update and reinforce the provisions of the 1950 treaty. These agreements have sought to address the concerns of Nepal while also recognizing India's legitimate security and developmental interests.

It is important to note that the India-Nepal Friendship Treaty of 1950 cannot be viewed in isolation. It is part of a broader historical, geopolitical, and socio-cultural context that shapes the dynamics between the two nations. India and Nepal share deep-rooted historical, cultural, and familial ties that go beyond the legal framework of any treaty. These ties have been nurtured and strengthened through centuries of interactions, religious pilgrimage, and cultural exchanges.

In recent years, both countries have demonstrated their commitment to renewing and revitalizing their friendship. High-level visits, exchange programs, and joint initiatives have been undertaken to promote understanding, trust, and cooperation. Furthermore, India has reiterated its respect for Nepal's sovereignty and territorial integrity, emphasizing the principles of non-interference and equality in their bilateral relations.

The India-Nepal Friendship Treaty of 1950 has played a pivotal role in shaping the relationship between these two neighboring countries. It has laid down the foundation for a strong and enduring friendship, promoting cooperation and collaboration in various sectors. The treaty's provisions regarding an open border, equal treatment of citizens, economic cooperation, defense and security, and water resources have contributed to the deepening of bilateral ties and the overall development of both nations. While challenges and concerns have emerged over time, both India and Nepal have shown a willingness to address these issues through dialogue and negotiation. The treaty's significance extends beyond its legal framework, encompassing the historical, cultural, and emotional bonds that connect India and Nepal. As the two countries continue to navigate their evolving relationship, the spirit of friendship and cooperation embedded in the 1950 treaty will undoubtedly remain a guiding principle for their future endeavors.

"From the crown to the people: Nepal's journey signifies the empowerment of the masses."

Indo-Nepal Relations in 1988-1989: Turmoil and the Path to Normalcy

Indo-Nepal relations have witnessed various ups and downs throughout history. The year 1988 marked a significant period of turmoil, as India's decision to block ten out of twelve entry points between the two countries strained bilateral ties. This chapter delves into the reasons behind the turmoil and examines how the situation was eventually tackled, leading to the restoration of normalcy in Indo-Nepal relations.

- ***Historical Background:*** Indo-Nepal relations have long been characterized by a unique blend of cultural, economic, and political ties. The 1950 Treaty of Peace and Friendship laid the foundation for close cooperation between the two nations. However, underlying issues and occasional differences have occasionally strained this relationship.
- ***Rising Tensions in the Late 1980s:*** By the late 1980s, several factors contributed to souring relations between India and Nepal. Nepal's growing political aspirations were met with apprehension in India, which feared a potential threat to its security. Additionally, the issue of Nepal's transit rights through India became a contentious matter, with Nepal demanding more autonomy and diverse transit routes.
- ***The 1988 Trade and Transit Treaty:*** In 1988, India and Nepal signed the Trade and Transit Treaty, aimed at promoting bilateral trade and transit through Indian territory. However, disagreements soon emerged regarding the treaty's implementation, leading to the blockade of ten out of twelve entry points between the two countries by India. This move severely affected Nepal's economy and led to widespread discontent and protests.
- ***Economic Impact on Nepal:*** The blockade had a devastating impact on Nepal's economy. The country heavily relied on Indian transit routes for imports and exports, including essential commodities like fuel and medicines. The scarcity of these goods resulted in widespread inflation, black market activities, and a decline in public morale.
- ***Political Ramifications:*** The political ramifications of the blockade were significant. Nepal's citizens viewed India's actions as a breach of trust and an infringement on their sovereignty. Anti-India sentiments escalated, and

political parties capitalized on the public's frustration, demanding a more assertive stance against India.

- ***Diplomatic Efforts and Mediation:*** To address the escalating crisis, diplomatic efforts were initiated by both India and Nepal. Mediation attempts were made by various international actors, including the United Nations and neighboring countries. These efforts aimed to find a mutually agreeable solution that would restore normalcy in bilateral relations.
- ***Negotiations and the Path to Resolution:*** Amid mounting pressure and public outrage, negotiations between India and Nepal gained momentum. Both sides engaged in discussions to address the underlying issues and find a way forward. Key concerns included Nepal's demand for alternative transit routes and guarantees of uninterrupted supplies.
- ***The Role of International Community:*** The international community played a significant role in facilitating dialogue and encouraging a resolution. Neighboring countries, particularly China and Bangladesh, offered support to Nepal, providing alternative transit routes and essential supplies, mitigating the impact of the blockade.
- ***Restoring Normalcy:*** Gradually, as negotiations progressed, India began reopening the blocked entry points, easing the economic strain on Nepal. Confidence-building measures, such as the resumption of high-level visits and cultural exchanges, were also implemented to restore trust and normalcy in bilateral relations.
- ***Rebuilding Trust and Strengthening Cooperation:*** Following the resolution of the crisis, both India and Nepal recognized the importance of rebuilding trust and strengthening cooperation. Efforts were made to enhance people-to-people contacts, foster cultural exchanges, and promote tourism between the two countries. Additionally, joint initiatives in areas such as infrastructure development, energy cooperation, and water resource management were undertaken to deepen economic ties.
- ***Lessons Learned:*** The turmoil in Indo-Nepal relations in 1988-1989 highlighted the need for open and honest dialogue, mutual respect, and understanding between the two nations. It served as a wake-up call for both India and Nepal to address underlying issues and work towards a more balanced and equitable relationship. The crisis underscored the importance of diversifying transit routes and reducing dependency on a single route for trade and supplies.

- ***Sustaining Normalcy and Future Prospects:*** After the resolution of the crisis, sustained efforts were made to maintain normalcy in Indo-Nepal relations. Regular high-level diplomatic engagements, bilateral meetings, and joint commissions were established to ensure ongoing dialogue and cooperation. The two countries also worked towards resolving other outstanding issues, such as border disputes and water-sharing agreements.
- ***Regional Integration and Cooperation:*** The turmoil in Indo-Nepal relations in 1988-1989 served as a catalyst for greater regional integration and cooperation. It highlighted the need for South Asian nations to address common challenges and explore avenues for collective growth. Efforts were made to strengthen regional organizations such as the South Asian Association for Regional Cooperation (SAARC) and promote economic integration through initiatives like the South Asian Free Trade Area (SAFTA).

The turmoil in Indo-Nepal relations in 1988-1989 was a challenging period that strained the ties between the two countries. However, through diplomatic negotiations, international mediation, and the resilience of the people, the situation was eventually tackled, and normalcy was restored. The crisis served as a lesson for both nations to address underlying issues, diversify transit routes, and work towards a more balanced and equitable relationship. The events of that period also highlighted the importance of regional integration and cooperation in South Asia. Today, India and Nepal continue to build on the lessons learned from that tumultuous time, striving for stronger ties and mutual prosperity.

3. FACTORS LEADING TO DEMOCRATIC MOVEMENTS

Democracy in Nepal is a testament to the indomitable spirit of its citizens and their desire for self- governance"

Factors Leading to Democratic Movements: A Comprehensive Analysis

Democratic movements have played a pivotal role in shaping the political landscape across the globe. These movements are characterized by the collective efforts of individuals and groups advocating for democratic principles and institutions, often in the face of authoritarian regimes or oppressive systems. While the specific circumstances and triggers may vary, several common factors have consistently emerged as catalysts for democratic movements. Understanding these factors is vital to comprehend the dynamics behind the rise of democratic movements and their impact on societies. This chapter aims to explore and analyze the key factors that contribute to the emergence and growth of democratic movements.

- ***Historical Context and Legacy:*** Examining the historical context is crucial to understanding the factors leading to democratic movements. Historical events such as the American and French Revolutions, the abolition of slavery, and the suffrage movements have left a lasting legacy that continues to inspire individuals and groups fighting for democratic ideals. These historical milestones have demonstrated the power of collective action, civil rights, and the ability to challenge oppressive systems, providing a blueprint for future democratic movements.
- ***Socioeconomic Factors:*** Socioeconomic factors play a significant role in shaping democratic movements. Economic inequality, poverty, and lack of opportunities often fuel discontent and frustration among marginalized populations. When individuals and communities feel disenfranchised and excluded from the benefits of society, they are more likely to mobilize and demand democratic reforms. Economic crises, corruption, and the concentration of wealth in the hands of a few elites can trigger widespread protests and movements aimed at achieving greater economic justice and democratic governance.
- ***Political Repression and Authoritarianism:*** The presence of political repression and authoritarian regimes is a potent catalyst for democratic movements. When people's basic rights and freedoms are infringed upon, they tend to mobilize against oppressive regimes. Authoritarian governments, characterized by limited political freedoms, censorship, and restrictions on

civil liberties, often face strong opposition from those who seek democratic governance. The desire for political participation, freedom of speech, and the right to choose their leaders drives individuals and groups to fight for democratic reforms.

- ***Technological Advancements and Global Connectivity:*** Technological advancements, particularly in communication and social media, have revolutionized the way democratic movements emerge and spread. The ease of access to information, the ability to organize and mobilize online, and the power to expose government abuses have empowered individuals and groups in their pursuit of democratic ideals. Social media platforms have become powerful tools for organizing protests, raising awareness, and mobilizing support domestically and globally. The interconnectedness fostered by technological advancements has enabled democratic movements to transcend geographical boundaries, inspiring and influencing others across the world.
- ***Youth Activism and Social Change:*** The role of youth activism in democratic movements cannot be overstated. Young people often bring fresh perspectives, idealism, and a willingness to challenge the status quo. With increased access to education, exposure to diverse ideas, and a desire for a better future, young activists become catalysts for change. Their energy, creativity, and ability to mobilize through social media platforms have been instrumental in many democratic movements, as seen in the Arab Spring, the Hong Kong protests, and climate change activism.
- ***Civil Society and Non-Governmental Organizations:*** The presence of a vibrant civil society and active non-governmental organizations (NGOs) are essential factors in driving democratic movements. Civil society encompasses a wide range of organizations, including human rights groups, labor unions, grassroots movements, and advocacy organizations. These entities serve as platforms for mobilization, advocacy, and the protection of citizens' rights. NGOs, in particular, play a crucial role in promoting democratic values, providing resources, and advocating for policy changes. Their efforts in raising awareness, monitoring elections, and holding governments accountable contribute significantly to the development and sustainability of democratic movements.
- ***International Support and Solidarity:*** International support and solidarity have proven to be influential factors in the success of democratic movements. When democratic movements gain global attention and receive support from international actors, it strengthens their legitimacy and increases their

chances of success. International organizations, such as the United Nations and regional bodies like the European Union, often play a vital role in promoting democratic governance and providing assistance to democratic movements. Additionally, international media coverage and diplomatic pressure on repressive regimes can create a favorable environment for democratic reforms.

- ***Cultural and Identity Movements:*** Cultural and identity movements have emerged as significant drivers of democratic change, particularly in diverse societies. These movements often seek to challenge discrimination, inequality, and the marginalization of specific cultural or ethnic groups. They advocate for inclusive policies, recognition of cultural rights, and the promotion of diversity within the democratic framework. By mobilizing around shared identities and cultural heritage, these movements contribute to the broader struggle for democratic values and equal representation.
- ***Transitional Processes and Democratic Openings:*** Transitional processes following the collapse of authoritarian regimes or the end of armed conflicts provide fertile ground for democratic movements to thrive. During these periods, there is often a window of opportunity to establish democratic institutions, draft new constitutions, and initiate political reforms. Transitional justice mechanisms, such as truth commissions and accountability measures, serve to address past human rights abuses and contribute to the establishment of democratic norms. The desire for justice, reconciliation, and a fresh start can galvanize democratic movements and lead to lasting democratic transformations.

Democratic movements arise from a complex interplay of various factors, each contributing to the desire for political change, freedom, and inclusive governance. Socioeconomic factors, political repression, technological advancements, youth activism, civil society engagement, international support, cultural movements, and transitional processes all play vital roles in driving democratic movements.

"Nepal's rising democracy is a symphony composed by the voices of the people."

Social, Economic, and Political Factors that Fueled Demands for Democracy

Democracy, as a form of governance, has been sought after by societies worldwide. The desire for democratic systems has been driven by various social, economic, and political factors throughout history. This chapter aims to delve into these factors and explore how they have fueled demands for democracy. By examining the social aspirations for freedom and equality, the economic conditions that shape societal demands, and the political circumstances that call for participatory governance, we can gain a comprehensive understanding of the multifaceted nature of democratic movements.

- ***Social Aspirations for Freedom and Equality:*** One of the fundamental factors that fuel demands for democracy is the human desire for freedom and equality. Societies yearn for a system that upholds their basic rights, ensures equal opportunities, and respects individual liberties. Throughout history, individuals and communities have challenged authoritarian regimes and advocated for democratic principles. The Enlightenment period, for example, saw the rise of thinkers who promoted concepts such as popular sovereignty, individual rights, and social contract theory. The desire for self-determination and the belief in the inherent worth of every individual have been powerful drivers of demands for democratic governance.
- ***Economic Conditions and Democratic Demands:*** Economic factors play a significant role in shaping demands for democracy. Socioeconomic disparities and grievances often fuel unrest and mobilize citizens to demand political change. Inequality, poverty, and economic exclusion can create social unrest and drive marginalized groups to seek democratic systems that prioritize social welfare and economic justice. Economic crises and downturns can also erode trust in autocratic regimes, as citizens hold them accountable for mismanagement and corruption. Conversely, economic prosperity and a vibrant middle class can create a conducive environment for democratic demands, as citizens aspire for political representation and protection of their economic interests.
- ***Political Circumstances and Calls for Participation:*** Political factors are crucial in driving demands for democracy. Authoritarian regimes,

characterized by repression, censorship, and lack of political freedoms, often face opposition from citizens yearning for a more participatory system. Suppression of civil liberties, electoral fraud, and lack of accountability can lead to mass protests and movements calling for democratic reforms. The Arab Spring, for instance, saw widespread demands for democracy across the Middle East and North Africa, as citizens challenged autocratic regimes and demanded political freedoms. Political transitions and the fall of oppressive regimes often create opportunities for democratic movements to emerge.

- ***Information and Communication Technologies (ICT) and Democratic Demands:*** The advent of information and communication technologies has significantly influenced demands for democracy. The internet and social media platforms have provided unprecedented avenues for citizens to express their opinions, mobilize, and coordinate actions. Online platforms have revolutionized political activism, enabling the rapid dissemination of information, organizing protests, and exposing human rights abuses. The Arab Spring and the Occupy Wall Street movement are examples of how social media platforms facilitated the mobilization of citizens demanding democratic change. The free flow of information and the ability to connect with like-minded individuals have empowered citizens and challenged autocratic regimes.
- ***Globalization and Democratic Aspirations:*** Globalization has also played a role in fueling demands for democracy. Increased interconnectedness and the spread of democratic ideas across borders have created expectations of political freedoms and participatory governance. As individuals become more exposed to democratic systems and the values they uphold through travel, media, and international interactions, they develop aspirations for similar rights and freedoms in their own societies. Global human rights movements and international organizations advocating for democratic principles have further amplified demands for democracy worldwide. The desire to align with global norms and be part of the international community has pushed societies to demand democratic reforms and institutions.
- ***Historical Events and Democratic Awakening:*** Historical events have served as catalysts for democratic demands. Moments of political upheaval, such as revolutions and independence movements, have often sparked calls for democratic governance. The American Revolution, the French Revolution, and the struggles for independence in various regions have infused societies with the spirit of democracy and the belief in the power of

self-governance. These historical events have inspired subsequent generations to fight for democratic rights and challenge oppressive regimes.

- ***Demographic Shifts and Democratic Demands:*** Demographic changes can also influence demands for democracy. The rise of educated and politically aware youth populations has been a driving force behind democratic movements in many regions. Young people, driven by aspirations for a better future, often lead protests and demand political change. Their access to education, exposure to diverse ideas, and connectivity through technology empower them to challenge autocracy and demand democratic reforms. The Arab Spring and the recent pro-democracy protests in Hong Kong exemplify the role of young people in shaping democratic demands.
- ***Economic Interdependence and Democracy:*** Economic interdependence between countries can foster demands for democracy. In an interconnected global economy, trade relations and international investments create dependencies that can influence political dynamics. Democracies often provide a more stable and predictable environment for economic activities, attracting foreign investments and fostering economic growth. Consequently, societies may demand democratic reforms to attract economic opportunities and ensure stability in an increasingly interdependent world.
- ***Challenges and Counterforces against Democratic Demands:*** While social, economic, and political factors have fueled demands for democracy, there are challenges and counterforces that hinder its realization. Authoritarian regimes often employ repressive tactics, such as censorship, propaganda, and violence, to suppress democratic movements. External actors, driven by geopolitical interests, may support autocratic regimes, impeding democratic aspirations. Socioeconomic inequalities, ethnic tensions, and religious divisions can also undermine democratic demands by fueling social unrest and undermining societal cohesion.
- ***The Role of Leadership and Institutions in Meeting Democratic Demands:*** Leadership and the strength of democratic institutions are crucial in meeting the demands for democracy. Effective leadership that embraces democratic values, respects human rights, and promotes inclusive governance can address societal aspirations and foster democratic reforms. Strong and independent institutions, including the judiciary, media, and civil society organizations, play a vital role in upholding democratic principles and holding those in power accountable. The presence of checks and balances,

transparency, and mechanisms for citizen participation are essential for the sustainable advancement of democratic systems.

- ***The Importance of Democratic Education and Civic Engagement:*** Education and civic engagement are vital in sustaining and deepening democratic demands. A well-informed and engaged citizenry is crucial for the functioning of democratic systems. Education systems that prioritize civic education, critical thinking, and democratic values can empower individuals to actively participate in political processes, advocate for their rights, and hold their leaders accountable. Civil society organizations, grassroots movements, and platforms for public discourse foster civic engagement and the exchange of ideas, strengthening democratic demands and ensuring the voice of the people is heard.
- ***International Support and Solidarity for Democratic Movements:*** International support and solidarity play a significant role in fueling and sustaining democratic demands. The global community, including international organizations, democratic nations, and human rights advocates, can provide moral and material support to societies struggling for democracy. Diplomatic pressure, economic sanctions, and conditional aid can be leveraged to encourage autocratic regimes to respect democratic principles and engage in democratic reforms. International assistance in strengthening democratic institutions, promoting human rights, and fostering inclusive governance can contribute to the realization of democratic aspirations.
- ***The Evolving Nature of Democratic Demands:*** It is important to recognize that the nature of democratic demands continues to evolve in response to changing societal, economic, and political contexts. As societies face new challenges and opportunities, their expectations from democratic systems may shift. Emerging issues such as climate change, technological advancements, and global health crises may shape the demands for democracy in the future. Adapting democratic institutions to effectively address these evolving demands is essential for the continued relevance and success of democratic governance.

"As the monarch steps aside, Nepal's democracy steps forward."

The Role of Activists, Intellectuals, and Civil Society Organizations in Democratic Movements

Democratic movements across the world have often been driven by the active participation of individuals and groups who are committed to advocating for human rights, social justice, and political reform. The role of activists, intellectuals, and civil society organizations in these movements cannot be understated. Their contributions have been instrumental in challenging oppressive regimes, promoting democratic values, and fostering a culture of civic engagement. In this chapter, we will explore the multifaceted roles played by activists, intellectuals, and civil society organizations in democratic movements, highlighting their impact and significance.

- ***Activists:*** Activists are individuals who passionately advocate for a cause, often working on the ground to raise awareness, mobilize communities, and bring about social and political change. In democratic movements, activists play a crucial role in challenging authoritarian regimes and pushing for democratic reforms. They engage in various activities such as organizing protests, demonstrations, and civil disobedience campaigns to demand accountability and justice. Activists also leverage social media platforms and other communication channels to amplify their message and build networks of support. Their relentless efforts often expose human rights abuses, corruption, and other injustices, raising public consciousness and galvanizing support for democratic ideals.
- ***Intellectuals:*** Intellectuals, including academics, writers, artists, and thinkers, have historically played a vital role in democratic movements. They provide critical analysis, theoretical frameworks, and intellectual discourse that help shape public opinion and challenge oppressive ideologies. Intellectuals contribute by generating new ideas, envisioning alternative futures, and providing intellectual legitimacy to democratic aspirations. Through their writings, speeches, and public engagements, they articulate the values and principles that underpin democratic societies, inspiring and guiding both activists and the broader public. Intellectuals also act as a bridge between grassroots movements and policymakers, translating complex ideas into accessible language and influencing policy debates.

- ***Civil Society Organizations:*** Civil society organizations, including non-governmental organizations (NGOs), community groups, and grassroots movements, form the backbone of democratic movements. These organizations operate independently of the state and are driven by a shared commitment to promoting social justice, human rights, and democratic governance. They provide a platform for collective action, facilitating coordination, collaboration, and capacity-building among activists and citizens. Civil society organizations engage in a range of activities, including advocacy, research, education, and service delivery, to address societal challenges and promote democratic values. They monitor elections, promote transparency and accountability, and provide support to marginalized communities, empowering them to participate meaningfully in democratic processes.

Moreover, the collaboration between activists, intellectuals, and civil society organizations is a powerful force in democratic movements. Activists bring the passion, energy, and grassroots mobilization needed to drive change on the ground. Intellectuals provide the intellectual rigor, analysis, and vision necessary to shape the discourse and inspire new ideas. Civil society organizations offer the infrastructure, networks, and expertise to facilitate coordination and sustained action. When these actors work together in a coordinated manner, their impact is amplified, and their collective influence becomes greater than the sum of their individual contributions.

One of the key roles of activists, intellectuals, and civil society organizations in democratic movements is to raise awareness and mobilize public support. They play a crucial role in informing and educating the public about the importance of democratic values, human rights, and political participation. By highlighting social injustices, abuses of power, and violations of rights, they create a sense of urgency and galvanize public opinion. Through various channels such as social media, public demonstrations, and community outreach, they engage with citizens, encouraging them to become active participants in the democratic process.

Another significant contribution of these actors is their ability to hold governments accountable. Activists, intellectuals, and civil society organizations act as watchdogs, monitoring the actions of those in power and exposing corruption, human rights abuses, and violations of democratic principles. They play a crucial role in advocating for transparency, accountability, and good governance. Through research, investigations, and advocacy campaigns, they shed light on issues that might otherwise go unnoticed or unaddressed. Their efforts often lead to policy reforms, institutional changes, and the prosecution of those responsible for wrongdoing.

Furthermore, activists, intellectuals, and civil society organizations serve as a voice for marginalized and vulnerable communities. They work tirelessly to amplify the voices of those who are often excluded or oppressed, advocating for their rights, dignity, and inclusion in the democratic process. By providing platforms for marginalized groups to express their concerns, they ensure that the democratic movement is inclusive and representative of all segments of society. They also work towards eliminating discrimination, promoting social justice, and addressing structural inequalities that hinder democratic development.

In addition to their immediate impact on democratic movements, these actors also contribute to long-term societal change. By fostering a culture of civic engagement, critical thinking, and active citizenship, they nurture the values and behaviors necessary for a thriving democracy. They promote democratic education, civic literacy, and youth empowerment, ensuring that future generations are equipped with the knowledge and skills to participate meaningfully in democratic processes. Through their work, they cultivate a sense of collective responsibility, encouraging citizens to be actively involved in shaping the future of their societies.

However, it is important to acknowledge the challenges faced by activists, intellectuals, and civil society organizations in their pursuit of democratic change. They often encounter resistance from authoritarian regimes, face censorship, surveillance, and repression, and are subjected to threats, harassment, and violence. Governments may enact restrictive laws, impede their activities, or even label them as enemies of the state. In such circumstances, the international community plays a crucial role in advocating for their protection, providing support, and exerting diplomatic pressure on repressive governments.

To strengthen the impact of activists, intellectuals, and civil society organizations in democratic movements, several measures can be taken. Governments should create an enabling environment that upholds the principles of freedom of expression, assembly, and association. They should repeal restrictive laws and regulations that hinder the work of these actors and actively promote an inclusive and participatory democracy. International organizations and donor agencies should provide financial and technical support to civil society organizations, enabling them to enhance their capacity and reach. Diplomatic pressure and advocacy efforts should be exerted to hold repressive governments accountable for human rights abuses and violations of democratic principles.

Furthermore, collaboration and networking among activists, intellectuals, and civil society organizations should be encouraged. By sharing knowledge, experiences, and best practices, they can strengthen their collective impact and learn from each other's successes and challenges. Platforms for dialogue and exchange should be created to facilitate collaboration and coordination, fostering a sense of unity and shared purpose.

Education and awareness initiatives are also vital in nurturing a culture of democratic values and active citizenship. Governments, civil society organizations, and educational institutions should prioritize democratic education, civic literacy, and human rights awareness programs. By equipping individuals with the knowledge and skills necessary for democratic participation, they can foster a society that values democratic principles and actively engages in the democratic process.

The role of activists, intellectuals, and civil society organizations in democratic movements is crucial for promoting social justice, human rights, and political reform. Their tireless efforts, courage, and dedication have led to significant societal transformations and have paved the way for more inclusive, just, and accountable societies. By supporting and protecting these actors, promoting collaboration and networking, and investing in education and awareness initiatives, we can further strengthen their role and contribute to the advancement of democratic values worldwide.

"Democracy, the new Everest for Nepal, conquered by the strength of its people."

Origin, Necessity and Evolution of Political Parties in Nepal and the Major Political Parties of Nepal

The political landscape of Nepal has been shaped by the emergence and evolution of political parties. These parties play a crucial role in the country's democratic process, representing the diverse interests and aspirations of the Nepali people. This chapter delves into the origin, necessity, and evolution of political parties in Nepal, highlighting their significance in the country's political development. Furthermore, we will explore the major political parties that have had a significant impact on Nepal's political landscape.

- ***Origin and Necessity of Political Parties in Nepal:*** The origin of political parties in Nepal can be traced back to the early 1950s when the country underwent a political transformation from an autocratic Rana regime to a constitutional monarchy. The political parties emerged as platforms for various ideologies and groups seeking representation and participation in the democratic process. These parties aimed to advocate for the rights and welfare of the Nepali people, promote social justice, and shape the country's political landscape.
- ***The evolution of political parties in Nepal:*** The evolution of political parties in Nepal has been marked by significant milestones and challenges. Initially, the Nepali Congress (NC), founded in 1947, played a prominent role in the country's political landscape. It led the democratic movement that resulted in the overthrow of the Rana regime, leading to the reinstatement of the monarchy and the establishment of a parliamentary system. However, political instability, internal divisions, and ideological differences led to frequent changes in government and hindered the growth and consolidation of political parties.

The 1990s marked a crucial turning point in Nepal's political history. The pro-democracy movement, popularly known as the Jana Andolan, led to the restoration of multi-party democracy and the promulgation of a new constitution. This period witnessed the emergence of several political parties, including the Communist Party of Nepal (Unified Marxist-Leninist) (CPN-

UML) and various communist factions, which played a significant role in shaping Nepal's political landscape.

Major Political Parties of Nepal:

- ***Nepali Congress (NC):*** The Nepali Congress is one of the oldest political parties in Nepal and has played a pivotal role in the country's democratic movement. It advocates for social democracy, pluralism, and inclusive governance. The NC has alternated in power with other political parties and has contributed significantly to Nepal's political and social reforms.
- ***Communist Party of Nepal (Unified Marxist-Leninist) (CPN-UML):*** The CPN-UML emerged as a major political force in Nepal following the restoration of democracy in the 1990s. It promotes Marxist-Leninist principles and advocates for the rights of the working class. The party has experienced various splits and mergers but remains a prominent force in Nepali politics.
- ***Communist Party of Nepal (Maoist Center):*** The Maoist insurgency in Nepal, which lasted from 1996 to 2006, led to the formation of the Communist Party of Nepal (Maoist Center). Initially, the party pursued an armed struggle against the monarchy and advocated for radical social and political reforms. However, after the signing of the Comprehensive Peace Accord in 2006, the party transitioned into a democratic political force and participated in mainstream politics.
- ***Rastriya Janata Party Nepal (RJPN):*** The Rastriya Janata Party Nepal represents the interests of the Madhesi community and other marginalized groups in Nepal. Formed in 2017 through the merger of several regional parties, the RJPN advocates for federalism, proportional representation, and the rights of marginalized communities. It has emerged as a significant political force in the southern plains of Nepal.
- ***Samajwadi Party Nepal (SPN):*** The Samajwadi Party Nepal is a socialist political party that aims to address socioeconomic inequalities and promote social justice. It was formed in 2017 through the merger of the Socialist Party Nepal and several other socialist-oriented groups. The SPN advocates for progressive policies and has gained support among youth and marginalized communities.

- ***Rastriya Prajatantra Party (RPP):*** The Rastriya Prajatantra Party is a right-wing political party that advocates for Hindu nationalism and constitutional monarchy. It has its roots in the political parties that supported the monarchy during the transition to democracy. The RPP emphasizes the preservation of Nepal's cultural and religious identity.
- ***Janata Samajbadi Party Nepal (JSPN):*** The Janata Samajbadi Party Nepal is a socialist-oriented party formed in 2020 through the merger of the Rastriya Janata Party Nepal and the Samajbadi Party Nepal. The party represents the interests of marginalized communities and aims to address social and economic inequalities through progressive policies.

The Role of Political Parties in Nepal's Political Landscape:

Political parties in Nepal have played a crucial role in shaping the country's political landscape and democratic process. They have been instrumental in mobilizing public opinion, advocating for policy reforms, and representing the interests of various sections of society. Political parties have also been involved in coalition governments, policy formulation, and legislative processes.

However, Nepal's political parties have faced challenges in terms of internal divisions, ideological differences, and allegations of corruption. These issues have at times led to political instability, hindering the country's progress and development. Additionally, the dominance of a few major political parties has raised concerns about inclusivity and representation.

Political parties in Nepal have evolved significantly since the establishment of multi-party democracy in the 1990s. They have played a crucial role in advocating for people's rights, shaping policies, and participating in the democratic process. The Nepali Congress, CPN-UML, Maoist Center, RJP, SPN, RPP, and JSPN are among the major political parties that have left a significant impact on Nepal's political landscape.

"From the palace to the people: Nepal's democracy is a people-centric narrative."

---

4. THE PEOPLE'S MOVEMENT OF 1990

"Democracy is the voice of people, and Nepal's journey from monarchy represents the triumph of that voice"

The People's Movement of 1990 in Nepal: A Turning Point in History

The People's Movement of 1990 stands as a significant milestone in the history of Nepal. This movement, also known as the Jana Andolan, brought about a wave of change and transformed the political landscape of the country. Spanning several months, the movement marked the beginning of a new era, where the people of Nepal demanded democracy, freedom, and social justice. This chapter aims to delve into the key events, causes, and consequences of the People's Movement of 1990 and highlight its long-lasting impact on Nepalese society.

- ***Historical Background:*** To understand the context of the People's Movement of 1990, it is crucial to explore the historical backdrop that led to its emergence. Nepal, a landlocked country in South Asia, had long been governed by the Rana dynasty, followed by the Shah dynasty. Under the Shah monarchy, Nepal remained an absolute monarchy with limited political freedom and widespread social and economic disparities. The political system was characterized by authoritarian rule, censorship, and suppression of dissent.
- ***Causes of the People's Movement:*** Several factors contributed to the eruption of the People's Movement in 1990. Firstly, the prolonged autocratic rule of King Mahendra and his successor, King Birendra, had created a sense of discontent among the Nepalese people. The monarchy's failure to address the socio-economic issues faced by the general population, such as poverty, unemployment, and inequality, fueled public frustration. Additionally, the government's curtailment of civil liberties, including freedom of speech and assembly, further deepened the people's discontent.
- ***Key Events and Progression:*** The People's Movement of 1990 began in earnest with a series of protests and demonstrations across Nepal. The movement gained momentum following the death of King Birendra in June 2001, which led to the ascension of King Gyanendra to the throne. The royal massacre, where King Gyanendra's brother, Birendra, and several members of the royal family were killed, raised suspicions and added fuel to the growing movement for change.

The movement saw the active participation of various political parties, civil society organizations, student groups, and the general public. Protesters took to the streets, demanding an end to the authoritarian rule, the establishment of a multiparty democracy, and the formation of a constitutional assembly. The movement faced violent crackdowns by security forces, leading to casualties and arrests. However, the resilience and determination of the people remained unwavering.

• ***Major Achievements and Consequences:*** The People's Movement of 1990 achieved significant milestones that shaped the course of Nepal's history. The movement compelled King Gyanendra to concede to the demands of the people and reinstate democracy. In April 1990, King Gyanendra announced the restoration of the House of Representatives, dissolved earlier by his predecessor. This move paved the way for the formation of a multiparty government and the drafting of a new constitution.

The movement also witnessed the signing of the 12-point agreement, which brought together seven political parties and the Communist Party of Nepal (Maoist). This agreement laid the foundation for the Comprehensive Peace Agreement of 2006, which ended the decade-long civil war in Nepal and initiated a process of political restructuring.

Moreover, the People's Movement of 1990 marked a turning point in Nepal's international relations. The movement garnered international attention and support, with the international community urging the Nepalese government to respect human rights and democratic principles. Nepal's transition to democracy following the movement led to improved diplomatic relations with various countries and increased foreign aid and investments.

Furthermore, the People's Movement of 1990 had a profound impact on Nepalese society. It instilled a sense of empowerment and political consciousness among the general population. The movement encouraged civic engagement, participation in the political process, and the exercise of fundamental rights and freedoms. The Nepalese people realized the power they held collectively and their ability to bring about change through peaceful means.

The movement also paved the way for the establishment of a more inclusive political system. The 1990 Constitution of Nepal guaranteed fundamental rights, including freedom of expression, the press, and assembly.

It provided a framework for democratic governance, with regular elections, separation of powers, and checks and balances. This shift towards democracy opened up opportunities for marginalized groups, such as women, Dalits, and ethnic minorities, to have a voice in the political process and contribute to decision-making.

However, it is important to acknowledge that while the People's Movement of 1990 marked a significant milestone, Nepal's journey towards a stable and inclusive democracy has been fraught with challenges. The country has faced political instability, frequent changes in government, and struggles with corruption and governance issues. The Maoist insurgency that followed the movement highlighted the deep-rooted socio-economic disparities and grievances that still needed to be addressed.

In recent years, Nepal has witnessed further political transformations, including the adoption of a new constitution in 2015 and the transition from a monarchy to a federal democratic republic. These developments reflect the ongoing efforts to consolidate democratic institutions, ensure the rule of law, and promote social justice.

The People's Movement of 1990 in Nepal was a pivotal moment in the country's history, marking the triumph of the people's aspirations for democracy, freedom, and social justice. The movement brought about significant changes, including the restoration of democracy, the signing of peace agreements, and the beginning of a process of political restructuring. It empowered the Nepalese people, fostering civic consciousness and promoting inclusivity in the political process.

However, challenges persist, and Nepal continues to grapple with the complexities of democratic governance. It is crucial for the country to address socio-economic disparities, strengthen democratic institutions, and ensure the meaningful participation of all sections of society. The People's Movement of 1990 serves as a reminder of the power of collective action and the importance of upholding democratic values in building a just and prosperous nation.

Furthermore, the People's Movement of 1990 had a profound impact on Nepalese society. It instilled a sense of empowerment and political consciousness among the general population. The movement encouraged civic engagement, participation in the political process, and the exercise of fundamental rights and freedoms. The Nepalese people realized the power they held collectively and their ability to bring about change through peaceful means.

The movement also paved the way for the establishment of a more inclusive political system. The 1990 Constitution of Nepal guaranteed fundamental rights, including freedom of expression, the press, and assembly. It provided a framework for democratic governance, with regular elections, separation of powers, and checks and balances. This shift towards democracy opened up opportunities for marginalized groups, such as women, Dalits, and ethnic minorities, to have a voice in the political process and contribute to decision-making.

However, it is important to acknowledge that while the People's Movement of 1990 marked a significant milestone, Nepal's journey towards a stable and inclusive democracy has been fraught with challenges. The country has faced political instability, frequent changes in government, and struggles with corruption and governance issues. The Maoist insurgency that followed the movement highlighted the deep-rooted socio-economic disparities and grievances that still needed to be addressed.

In recent years, Nepal has witnessed further political transformations, including the adoption of a new constitution in 2015 and the transition from a monarchy to a federal democratic republic. These developments reflect the ongoing efforts to consolidate democratic institutions, ensure the rule of law, and promote social justice.

However, Nepal's transition to democracy has not been without challenges. Political parties have often been plagued by internal divisions and struggles for power. Corruption remains a significant issue, hindering the effective functioning of democratic institutions and impeding socio-economic development. There are also ongoing concerns regarding the rights and representation of marginalized groups, including women, Dalits, and ethnic minorities. Despite these challenges, the People's Movement of 1990 laid the foundation for a more inclusive and participatory political system in Nepal.

Looking ahead, it is crucial for Nepal to continue its efforts to strengthen democratic institutions, promote good governance, and address socio-economic disparities. This includes ensuring equal access to education, healthcare, and economic opportunities for all citizens, regardless of their social background. It is also important to foster a culture of political tolerance, respect for human rights, and pluralism to build a strong and resilient democracy.

The People's Movement of 1990 in Nepal was a watershed moment in the country's history. It marked a turning point in the struggle for democracy, freedom, and social justice. The movement empowered the Nepalese people, leading to the restoration of democracy and the establishment of a more inclusive political system. While challenges persist, Nepal continues to make progress in its democratic journey. The lessons learned from the People's Movement of 1990 provide valuable insights for the country's ongoing efforts to build a prosperous, inclusive, and democratic society.

"Nepal's journey mirrors the phoenix, rising from the ashes of the old to embrace the new."

People Movements in 1990: An Analysis of Background and Causes

The year 1990 witnessed significant people movements across the globe, as populations were compelled to migrate due to various internal and external factors. This chapter aims to provide a detailed analysis of the background and causes of these people movements, exploring the forces both externally and internally responsible for shaping the migration patterns during this pivotal year. By examining different regions and contexts, including political, economic, and social factors, this analysis seeks to shed light on the complex dynamics that led to the mass movement of people in 1990.

The year 1990 was marked by a series of transformative events that fundamentally reshaped the geopolitical landscape. The dissolution of the Soviet Union, the end of the Cold War, and the collapse of communist regimes in Eastern Europe had profound implications for the movement of people worldwide. While these historic events certainly played a significant role, it is crucial to delve deeper into the underlying factors that prompted individuals and communities to migrate during this period.

Political Factors:

- ***The Dissolution of the Soviet Union:*** The dissolution of the Soviet Union in 1991 had far-reaching consequences on migration patterns. The newly formed independent states faced immense political and economic challenges, leading to internal conflicts, ethnic tensions, and nationalist movements. This political turmoil triggered large-scale migrations within and across the newly established borders.
- ***Collapse of Communism in Eastern Europe:*** The collapse of communist regimes in Eastern Europe, particularly in countries like East Germany, Poland, and Czechoslovakia, created a wave of political change. The dismantling of the Berlin Wall in 1989 symbolized the end of the Cold War era, inspiring hope for democratic reforms. However, this transition also led to significant population movements, with individuals seeking better political conditions, reunification with families, and improved opportunities.

Economic Factors:

- ***Socioeconomic Disparities:*** Economic factors played a crucial role in people movements during 1990. Many individuals were driven by economic disparities, seeking better employment prospects, higher wages, and improved living conditions. The disparity between Western and Eastern European economies, for instance, motivated individuals from the latter to migrate to the former in search of better opportunities.
- ***Economic Reforms:*** Several countries implemented economic reforms during this period, transitioning from centralized planning to market-oriented systems. These reforms often resulted in economic restructuring, privatization, and the dismantling of state-owned industries. These changes, while creating opportunities in some sectors, also led to unemployment and economic uncertainty. Consequently, people were forced to migrate in search of stability and livelihood.

Social Factors:

- ***Ethnic and Religious Conflicts:*** Ethnic and religious conflicts were prevalent in various parts of the world in 1990. The disintegration of Yugoslavia, for example, resulted in intense inter-ethnic conflicts and wars. Similarly, tensions between different ethnic and religious groups in regions like Africa and the Middle East led to mass displacements as people sought safety and security elsewhere.
- ***Humanitarian Crises:*** Humanitarian crises, including famine, civil wars, and natural disasters, often triggered large-scale migrations. The Ethiopian famine of 1990, for instance, resulted in mass displacement as people sought refuge in neighboring countries. Similarly, civil wars in countries such as Angola, Mozambique, and Sudan forced people to flee their homes in search of safety and survival.

Environmental Factors:

- ***Natural Disasters:*** Environmental factors also played a significant role in people movements during 1990. The occurrence of natural disasters, such as earthquakes, floods, hurricanes, and droughts, often resulted in the displacement of populations. These events rendered homes uninhabitable, destroyed infrastructure, and disrupted livelihoods, forcing individuals and communities to seek refuge in safer regions.

- ***Climate Change Impacts:*** Although the term "climate change" was not widely recognized in 1990, the impacts of environmental degradation and global warming were already evident. Rising sea levels, desertification, and changes in rainfall patterns affected agricultural productivity and livelihoods in many parts of the world. These environmental challenges, combined with socioeconomic factors, contributed to the migration of vulnerable communities, particularly from developing countries.

External Factors:

- ***Globalization and Increased Connectivity:*** The process of globalization, which gained momentum in the late 20th century, facilitated the movement of people across borders. Improved transportation, communication, and accessibility to information enabled individuals to explore opportunities beyond their immediate surroundings. The increasing interconnectedness of the world played a pivotal role in shaping migration patterns in 1990.
- ***Refugee and Asylum Policies:*** The political and legal frameworks surrounding refugee and asylum policies influenced people movements during this period. Changes in policies, such as the implementation of the United Nations Convention relating to the Status of Refugees, impacted the flow of refugees and asylum seekers. Political considerations, humanitarian obligations, and regional dynamics influenced the acceptance or rejection of individuals seeking refuge.

Internal Factors:

- ***Push and Pull Factors:*** Internal factors within countries also contributed to people movements. Push factors, such as political oppression, social unrest, economic hardships, and lack of opportunities, compelled individuals to leave their homes. Simultaneously, pull factors, including political stability, economic prosperity, and social welfare systems, attracted migrants to specific destinations that promised a better life.

- ***Demographic Pressures:*** Demographic pressures, such as population growth, urbanization, and changing family structures, influenced migration patterns. Overcrowding, limited resources, and lack of employment opportunities in rural areas often prompted individuals to migrate to urban centers or other countries in search of a better standard of living. These internal demographic dynamics shaped migration trends in 1990.

The people movements witnessed in 1990 were driven by a complex interplay of various factors. Political changes, economic disparities, social conflicts, environmental challenges, external influences, and internal dynamics all contributed to the mass migration of individuals and communities. Understanding the background and causes of these people movements is crucial for comprehending the consequences and implications they had on both the countries of origin and the receiving nations. By analyzing these forces, policymakers and stakeholders can develop informed strategies to address the challenges and maximize the potential benefits associated with migration in the future.

"The pages of Nepal's history turn, revealing a democratic narrative written by the people."

The 1990 People's Movement: A Paradigm Shift in Democracy

The year 1990 marked a significant turning point in the history of Nepal, as the nation witnessed a remarkable event known as the "People's Movement." Fueled by public discontent and a yearning for democracy, the movement saw widespread protests and demonstrations across the country. This chapter delves into the key events and notable protests that occurred during the 1990 People's Movement, which ultimately led to the restoration of democracy in Nepal.

- ***Prelude to the Movement:*** In the years leading up to 1990, Nepal was under the autocratic rule of King Birendra and the Panchayat system, which had been in place since 1962. The Panchayat system, characterized by its centralized power structure and limited political freedoms, had increasingly become a source of frustration for the Nepalese people. The movement towards democracy gained momentum as political parties, intellectuals, and the general public began demanding political reforms and the restoration of civil liberties.

<u>Protests and Demonstrations: A Groundswell of People's Power</u>

- ***The Martyrs' Memorial Movement:*** On February 18, 1990, the government's decision to suppress a peaceful student demonstration in Kathmandu's Tripureshwor area sparked outrage among the public. The incident led to the tragic death of several protesters, who would later be known as martyrs. This incident served as a catalyst for the burgeoning movement, with citizens taking to the streets in large numbers to express their dissent against the brutal crackdown.
- ***The Nationwide Strike and Curfew:*** Following the Martyrs' Memorial Movement, the movement rapidly gained momentum, leading to a nationwide general strike on April 6, 1990. The strike paralyzed the country, with businesses, transportation, and educational institutions coming to a standstill. The government responded by imposing strict curfews and deploying security forces to suppress the protests, but these measures failed to quell the determination of the people.

- ***The Mass Rally in Kathmandu:*** As the movement intensified, a historic mass rally was organized in Kathmandu on April 8, 1990. Hundreds of thousands of Nepalese citizens from all walks of life gathered in the capital, demanding an end to the Panchayat system and the establishment of democracy. The sheer size and peaceful nature of the rally sent a powerful message to the government and the international community about the overwhelming desire for change among the Nepalese people.
- ***The Royal Proclamation:*** Under mounting pressure from the protests and the international community, King Birendra made a historic proclamation on April 16, 1990. In this proclamation, the King announced the restoration of multi-party democracy, effectively dissolving the Panchayat system. The announcement was met with jubilation and a sense of hope among the Nepalese population, as it marked a significant step towards realizing their aspirations for political freedom and social justice.
- ***Formation of the Interim Government:*** Following the royal proclamation, an interim government was formed with leaders from various political parties. This government, led by Krishna Prasad Bhattarai, played a crucial role in overseeing the transition to democracy and laying the foundation for a more inclusive and participatory political system in Nepal.
- ***Constitutional Reforms and Democratic Consolidation:*** The success of the 1990 People's Movement paved the way for significant constitutional reforms and the establishment of a democratic framework in Nepal. A new constitution was drafted, emphasizing fundamental rights, freedom of speech, and the separation of powers. Political parties flourished, and elections were held, allowing for the formation of a representative government that reflected the will of the people. This marked a crucial step towards democratic consolidation in the country.
- ***Empowerment of Marginalized Groups:*** The 1990 People's Movement also sparked a broader social awakening, with marginalized groups demanding their rights and recognition. The movement encouraged discussions on social justice, equality, and inclusivity, leading to the empowerment of previously marginalized communities, such as women, Dalits, and ethnic minorities. It laid

the foundation for progressive policies and affirmative actions aimed at bridging social gaps and ensuring equal opportunities for all Nepalese citizens.

- ***International Recognition and Inspiration:*** The 1990 People's Movement garnered significant international attention and admiration. The peaceful nature of the protests, coupled with the determination and resilience of the Nepalese people, inspired democratic movements worldwide. Nepal became a symbol of hope and a testament to the power of people's movements in bringing about political change. The success of the movement inspired similar pro-democracy movements in other countries facing autocratic regimes.

Challenges and Lessons Learned

While the 1990 People's Movement achieved remarkable progress in Nepal's democratic journey, it also faced challenges and exposed certain shortcomings. The transition to democracy was not without difficulties, as political parties grappled with ideological differences, power struggles, and governance issues. Additionally, the movement's initial euphoria gave way to the realization that democracy required constant vigilance, active citizen participation, and effective governance to address the diverse needs of the population.

Continued Activism and Struggles

Although the 1990 People's Movement brought about significant political changes, the journey towards a mature and inclusive democracy in Nepal has been an ongoing process. Following the establishment of democratic governance, various social and political issues continued to demand attention and activism.

- ***Madhesi Movement:*** In the early 2000s, the Madhesi community, residing in the southern plains of Nepal, launched a movement demanding equal representation and rights. The Madhesi Movement highlighted the need for addressing regional disparities, ensuring proportional representation, and addressing the grievances of marginalized groups.
- ***Women's Rights Activism:*** Despite the democratic reforms, women in Nepal still faced challenges in terms of gender equality, representation, and access to resources. Women's rights activists and

organizations have continued to advocate for gender equality, empowerment, and the elimination of discriminatory practices.

- ***Maoist Insurgency:*** In the late 1990s and early 2000s, Nepal experienced a violent Maoist insurgency, driven by political and socio-economic grievances. The insurgency, which lasted for a decade, resulted in significant loss of life and property. The conflict eventually ended with the Comprehensive Peace Agreement in 2006, leading to the integration of Maoist combatants into the political mainstream.

The Road to Federalism

One of the significant milestones in Nepal's post-1990 democratic journey was the adoption of a federal system through the promulgation of a new constitution in 2015. The new constitution aimed to address historical grievances, ensure inclusivity, and empower local communities. However, its implementation has faced challenges, including issues related to delineation of federal boundaries and representation.

Recent Protests and Demonstrations

In the years following the adoption of the new constitution, Nepal has witnessed various protests and demonstrations highlighting concerns regarding the constitution's provisions and their impact on marginalized groups. Protests by ethnic communities, such as the Tharu and Limbu, have called for greater representation and the protection of their cultural identities.

A Continuing Journey

The 1990 People's Movement was a landmark event that brought democracy to the forefront in Nepal. It paved the way for constitutional reforms, political pluralism, and the empowerment of marginalized groups. However, the path to a thriving democracy has not been without challenges. Ongoing activism and struggles have highlighted the need for addressing social, political, and economic disparities and ensuring equal opportunities for all citizens.

Nepal's democratic journey is an ongoing process, requiring sustained efforts to address the evolving needs and aspirations of its diverse population. The lessons learned from the 1990 People's Movement continue to guide the nation, reminding its people of the power of collective action and the importance of active citizen participation in shaping a just and inclusive society. As Nepal moves forward, it is essential to build upon the achievements of the past and work towards strengthening democratic institutions, promoting social justice, and securing a prosperous future for all Nepalese.

"In every ballot cast, Nepal redefines its destiny and reimagines its future."

---

5. CHALLENGES & SETBACKS

"Democracy offers Nepal the opportunity to build a society rooted in equality, justice, and freedom"

Political Instability and Factionalism in Nepal: A Deep Dive into the Challenges of Governance

Nepal, a landlocked country nestled between India and China, has a long and complex history marked by political instability and factionalism. Despite its rich cultural heritage and potential for development, Nepal has struggled to achieve sustained political stability, leading to economic setbacks and social unrest. This chapter aims to explore the root causes, consequences, and potential solutions to the issues of political instability and factionalism in Nepal.

- ***Historical Context: A Legacy of Instability:*** Nepal's political landscape has been shaped by a tumultuous history of monarchy, authoritarian rule, civil unrest, and transition to democracy. The abolition of the monarchy in 2008 marked a significant milestone, but the subsequent years witnessed a series of political crises, including frequent changes in government and a lack of consensus among political parties.
- ***Ethnic and Regional Divisions:*** One of the major challenges contributing to political instability in Nepal is the existence of deep-seated ethnic and regional divisions. The country is home to diverse ethnic communities, each with its own aspirations and demands. The failure to address these divisions adequately has led to social tensions and political fragmentation, often exploited by various factions for their own gain.
- ***Political Parties and Factionalism:*** Nepal's political landscape is characterized by a multitude of political parties, each representing different ideologies, interests, and ethnic groups. However, this diversity has also paved the way for intense factionalism within parties, hindering effective governance. Factional disputes over leadership, power-sharing, and policy priorities have frequently led to government instability and paralysis.
- ***Corruption and Governance Challenges:*** Corruption is another pervasive issue that has plagued Nepal's political system, undermining public trust and exacerbating political instability. Nepalese citizens have long struggled with weak governance, ineffective public institutions, and a lack of accountability. The prevalence of corruption stifles economic growth, erodes public services, and perpetuates a culture of impunity.

- ***External Interference and Geopolitical Factors:*** Nepal's geopolitical location between two regional giants, India and China, has also exerted influence on its politics and stability. Both nations have strategic interests in Nepal, leading to external interference in domestic affairs. These external factors often exacerbate internal divisions and complicate efforts to achieve political stability and national unity.
- ***Economic Challenges and Development Impediments:*** Political instability and factionalism have had a profound impact on Nepal's economic development. Frequent changes in government, policy inconsistencies, and a lack of long-term planning have hindered investments and economic growth. The country also faces significant challenges in infrastructure development, poverty alleviation, and job creation, exacerbating social inequality and discontent.
- ***Need for Strong Institutions and Rule of Law:*** Addressing political instability and factionalism in Nepal requires the establishment of strong institutions and the rule of law. Strengthening the judiciary, enhancing the capacity of law enforcement agencies, and ensuring an independent and impartial electoral system are crucial steps toward building a stable political framework.
- ***Inclusive Governance and Power-Sharing:*** Promoting inclusive governance and power-sharing is essential to address the ethnic and regional divisions that fuel factionalism. Encouraging dialogue, fostering consensus-building, and implementing affirmative action policies can help bridge the gaps and ensure meaningful representation of all communities in decision-making processes.
- ***Anti-corruption Measures and Transparency:*** Tackling corruption is vital for restoring trust in Nepal's political system and improving governance. Robust anti-corruption measures, such as strengthening anti-corruption agencies, implementing transparent financial systems, and promoting a culture of accountability, are necessary. Additionally, promoting transparency in public procurement, political financing, and government decision-making processes can help curb corrupt practices and ensure the efficient use of public resources.
- ***Constitutional Reforms and Power Devolution:*** Nepal's current constitution, promulgated in 2015, was a significant step towards establishing a federal democratic republic. However, there remains a need for further constitutional reforms to address the grievances of marginalized communities

and ensure equitable power devolution. A comprehensive review of the constitution, with a focus on accommodating diverse identities and aspirations, is crucial for fostering political stability and social harmony.

- ***Strengthening Civil Society and Media:*** Civil society organizations and independent media play a crucial role in promoting transparency, accountability, and good governance. Empowering these institutions by safeguarding their freedom of expression, ensuring their financial independence, and encouraging their active participation in policy debates can contribute to a more informed and engaged citizenry. This, in turn, can help hold political leaders accountable and reduce the influence of factional interests.
- ***Education and Civic Engagement:*** Investing in education and promoting civic engagement are essential for building a politically aware and active citizenry. By fostering critical thinking, civic values, and democratic principles, education can empower individuals to actively participate in political processes, question authority, and hold elected representatives accountable. Promoting civic education in schools and colleges, as well as encouraging community-based initiatives, can help nurture a culture of democratic participation and reduce the susceptibility to factionalism.
- ***International Support and Cooperation:*** Addressing the challenges of political instability and factionalism in Nepal requires international support and cooperation. The international community, including neighboring countries, can play a constructive role by promoting dialogue, facilitating conflict resolution, and providing technical assistance in areas such as institution-building, governance reforms, and capacity development. International actors should respect Nepal's sovereignty and work in collaboration with national stakeholders to ensure sustainable and locally-driven solutions.

"The Himalayan spirit is indomitable, and Nepal's democracy is its manifestation."

Ethnic and Regional Tensions in Nepal: Understanding the Dynamics and Seeking Unity

Nepal, a country known for its cultural diversity and ethnic richness, has long grappled with ethnic and regional tensions. These tensions, rooted in historical, socio-economic, and political factors, have posed significant challenges to national unity, governance, and social harmony. This chapter aims to delve into the complexities of ethnic and regional tensions in Nepal, exploring their historical context, contributing factors, consequences, and potential avenues for fostering unity and inclusivity.

- ***Historical Background: Diversity and Pluralism:*** Nepal's ethnic and regional tensions stem from its rich tapestry of cultural and linguistic diversity. The country is home to more than 125 ethnic groups, each with its unique customs, traditions, and languages. The legacy of a feudal society and a hierarchical social structure has contributed to the marginalization and exclusion of certain ethnic communities, laying the groundwork for tensions that persist to this day.
- ***Ethnic Identity and Political Mobilization:*** Ethnic identity plays a crucial role in shaping the political landscape of Nepal. Various ethnic communities have sought recognition, representation, and rights, leading to political mobilization along ethnic lines. Ethnic-based political parties and movements have emerged, driven by a desire to redress historical injustices and secure a fair share of political power and resources. This mobilization, while giving voice to marginalized communities, has also intensified ethnic tensions and fragmentation.
- ***Inequality and Marginalization:*** Persistent socio-economic disparities and marginalization have fueled ethnic and regional tensions in Nepal. Historically marginalized groups, such as Dalits (low-caste communities), Janajatis (indigenous peoples), and Madhesis (inhabitants of the southern plains), have faced discrimination, limited access to education, healthcare, and economic opportunities. The failure to address these inequalities has perpetuated a sense of injustice and exclusion, leading to social unrest and demands for greater inclusion.
- ***Language and Cultural Identity:*** Language and cultural identity are intricately linked to ethnic tensions in Nepal. The dominance of Nepali

language and culture, primarily associated with the hill Brahmin-Chhetri communities, has created a sense of marginalization among other ethnic groups. The preservation and promotion of diverse languages, cultures, and traditions are crucial for fostering inclusivity and recognizing the contributions of all ethnic communities.

- ***Federalism and Power Distribution:*** The introduction of federalism in Nepal's governance structure was intended to address regional disparities and empower local communities. However, the implementation of federalism has been fraught with challenges, including conflicts over the delineation of federal boundaries and power distribution. Disputes over resource allocation, representation, and decision-making authority at the federal, provincial, and local levels have exacerbated ethnic tensions and hindered effective governance.
- ***Political Representation and Identity Politics:*** The quest for political representation and identity-based politics has further deepened ethnic and regional tensions in Nepal. While affirmative action measures, such as quotas for marginalized groups, have been introduced, the effectiveness and implementation of these policies remain contentious. Identity-based politics, driven by electoral considerations, have sometimes prioritized short-term gains over long-term inclusive development, exacerbating divisions and hindering collective nation-building efforts.
- ***Media and Communication Challenges:*** The media landscape in Nepal has been marred by biases, sensationalism, and the amplification of divisive narratives. The lack of responsible and inclusive journalism has contributed to the exacerbation of ethnic and regional tensions. Promoting media ethics, encouraging diverse representation in media organizations, and supporting independent journalism can help foster a more inclusive and constructive media environment.
- ***Education and Awareness:*** Education plays a pivotal role in addressing ethnic and regional tensions by promoting understanding, empathy, and respect for diversity. Incorporating inclusive and culturally sensitive curricula in schools and universities can help nurture a sense of national identity while celebrating the unique heritage of different ethnic communities. Additionally, awareness campaigns and civic education initiatives can promote dialogue, dispel stereotypes, and foster a culture of inclusivity and tolerance.
- ***Dialogue, Reconciliation, and Conflict Resolution:*** Meaningful dialogue and reconciliation processes are essential for addressing ethnic and regional

tensions in Nepal. Engaging in open and constructive conversations, involving diverse stakeholders, and creating platforms for dialogue can help bridge divides, foster understanding, and build consensus on shared goals and aspirations. Additionally, promoting community-based conflict resolution mechanisms and utilizing traditional dispute resolution practices can contribute to the healing and reconciliation process.

- ***Strengthening Institutions and Governance:*** Strengthening institutions and governance is crucial for addressing ethnic and regional tensions in Nepal. Ensuring equal access to justice, promoting transparency and accountability, and strengthening local governance structures can help build trust among different ethnic communities. Additionally, empowering local governments to address local development needs and providing them with the necessary resources and capacity can promote inclusive development and reduce regional disparities.
- ***Economic Empowerment and Poverty Alleviation:*** Addressing economic disparities and promoting inclusive economic growth are vital for reducing ethnic and regional tensions. Implementing targeted poverty alleviation programs, promoting entrepreneurship, and improving access to quality education and healthcare in marginalized communities can help uplift disadvantaged groups and foster social and economic integration. Economic empowerment can contribute to a sense of dignity, reduce social inequalities, and create opportunities for all ethnic communities.
- ***National Identity and Unity:*** Fostering a sense of national identity and unity is crucial for overcoming ethnic and regional tensions. Emphasizing shared values, collective history, and a common vision for the future can help transcend ethnic divisions and promote a sense of belonging among all Nepalese citizens. Celebrating national festivals, promoting cultural exchanges, and encouraging cross-ethnic interactions can contribute to a shared identity that transcends ethnic boundaries.

"Nepal's democratic ascent is a testament to the power of a united nation."

Maoist Insurgency and Its Impact on Democracy in Nepal

Nepal, a country nestled in the Himalayas, has a rich history and a complex political landscape. One of the defining chapters in Nepal's recent history is the Maoist insurgency, which lasted for over a decade and profoundly impacted the nation's democratic development. This chapter aims to delve into the origins, progression, and consequences of the Maoist insurgency in Nepal and to analyze its long-term impact on the country's democracy.

- ***Historical Background:*** To understand the Maoist insurgency, it is essential to delve into Nepal's historical background. Nepal was ruled by an absolute monarchy for centuries until the People's Movement of 1951 led to the establishment of a constitutional monarchy. However, political instability, corruption, and socioeconomic inequalities continued to plague the country, leading to growing discontent among the marginalized and oppressed sections of society.
- ***Origins of the Maoist Insurgency:*** The roots of the Maoist insurgency can be traced back to the early 1990s when a group of communist leaders split from the mainstream Communist Party of Nepal (Unified Marxist-Leninist) and formed the Communist Party of Nepal (Maoist). Inspired by Mao Zedong's ideology and the success of the People's War in China, the Maoists believed in armed struggle as the means to establish a communist state in Nepal.
- ***Progression of the Insurgency:*** The Maoist insurgency officially began on February 13, 1996, with a series of targeted attacks on government institutions, security forces, and infrastructure. The insurgency quickly spread across rural areas, gaining support from marginalized communities and exploiting their grievances regarding land redistribution, caste discrimination, and political exclusion.

The conflict escalated into a full-scale civil war, with the Maoists employing guerrilla warfare tactics, including ambushes, bombings, and extortion. The Royal Nepalese Army, supported by international assistance, launched counter-insurgency operations, resulting in a protracted and brutal conflict that lasted until the signing of the Comprehensive Peace Agreement in 2006.

Impact on Democracy:

- ***Erosion of Civil Liberties and Human Rights:*** During the insurgency, both the Maoists and security forces committed grave human rights violations, including extrajudicial killings, disappearances, torture, and arbitrary arrests. The erosion of civil liberties and human rights had a detrimental effect on Nepal's democratic fabric, undermining the principles of justice, equality, and freedom.
- ***Political Instability and Governance Crisis:*** The Maoist insurgency created a state of political instability and governance crisis in Nepal. Frequent changes in government, weak institutions, and a lack of accountability hindered the effective functioning of democracy. The conflict exacerbated divisions among political parties, rendering them unable to find a common ground for governance.
- ***Socioeconomic Impacts:*** The insurgency adversely affected Nepal's economy and development prospects. The violence and disruption caused by the conflict hampered infrastructure projects, tourism, and foreign investments. The rural areas, which were the epicenter of the conflict, suffered the most, with widespread displacement, destruction of livelihoods, and a decline in education and healthcare facilities.
- ***Impact on Marginalized Communities:*** While the Maoist insurgency aimed to address the grievances of marginalized communities, the actual impact on these groups was mixed. While some marginalized communities experienced a sense of empowerment and social mobility during the insurgency, others faced increased violence, displacement, and forced recruitment.
- ***Peace Process and Transitional Period:*** The Maoist insurgency eventually led to a peace process and the signing of the Comprehensive Peace Agreement in 2006. The agreement paved the way for the integration of Maoist combatants into the national army and the drafting of a new constitution. However, the transition period following the peace process was marked by political disagreements, delays in constitution drafting, and sporadic outbreaks of violence.

- ***Constitutional Reforms and Inclusion:*** One of the significant outcomes of the Maoist insurgency was the demand for constitutional reforms and greater inclusion of marginalized communities in the political process. As a result, the Interim Constitution of 2007 and subsequent constitutions incorporated provisions for inclusive representation, proportional representation, and affirmative action. These reforms aimed to address historical inequalities and ensure that marginalized groups had a stake in Nepal's democracy.
- ***Rise of Leftist Politics:*** The Maoist insurgency also had a profound impact on the political landscape of Nepal. The Communist Party of Nepal (Maoist) transformed into a mainstream political party and participated in democratic elections. Over time, the party evolved ideologically and rebranded itself as the Communist Party of Nepal (Unified Marxist-Leninist-Maoist), embracing a more moderate approach. The rise of leftist politics in Nepal can be attributed, in part, to the legacy of the Maoist insurgency.
- ***Post-Conflict Reconciliation and Justice:*** The Maoist insurgency left behind a legacy of grievances, trauma, and a need for reconciliation. The process of addressing human rights violations and ensuring justice for the victims has been a complex and challenging task. Various mechanisms, including truth and reconciliation commissions, have been established to investigate past abuses and promote healing. However, progress in achieving justice and reconciliation has been slow, and many victims continue to seek redress.
- ***Impact on Democracy in the Long Term:*** The Maoist insurgency had a profound and long-term impact on Nepal's democracy. While the conflict exposed the weaknesses and shortcomings of the political system, it also provided an opportunity for introspection and reform. The insurgency highlighted the need for greater inclusivity, social justice, and equitable development. It forced Nepali society and political actors to confront issues such as caste discrimination, gender inequality, and regional disparities.

The democratic journey of Nepal post-insurgency has been characterized by both progress and challenges. The country witnessed the successful conduct of constituent assembly elections, the promulgation of a new constitution in 2015, and peaceful transitions of power through democratic elections. However, political polarization, ethnic tensions, and the slow pace of implementing constitutional provisions remain significant challenges for Nepal's democracy.

The Maoist insurgency in Nepal brought about significant changes, both positive and negative, to the country's democratic landscape. It exposed deep-rooted social and political inequalities, leading to demands for reforms and greater inclusivity. While the conflict caused immense suffering and hindered democratic progress in the short term, it also acted as a catalyst for change and paved the way for important constitutional reforms.

Moving forward, Nepal must continue to address the legacies of the Maoist insurgency, including reconciliation, justice, and socioeconomic development. Strengthening democratic institutions, promoting dialogue and consensus-building among political parties, and ensuring the meaningful participation of all citizens will be crucial for Nepal's democratic consolidation and long-term stability.

"From monarchy's shadow to democracy's light, Nepal emerges stronger than ever."

---

6. THE INTERIM PERIOD & THE CONSTITUENT ASSEMBLY

"Nepal's shift from monarchy to democracy signifies the birth of a nation that values the collective will of its people"

The New Constitution of Nepal: Transitioning from a Hindu State to a Secular Nation

Nepal, a landlocked country situated in the Himalayas, made a historic transition from being a Hindu state to a secular nation with the promulgation of its new constitution. The move aimed to ensure religious freedom, equality, and social harmony among its diverse populace. This chapter delves into the reasons behind Nepal's decision to adopt a secular stance, the impact of this constitutional change, and the challenges and opportunities it presents for the country's future.

Historical Background:

Nepal has a rich cultural and religious heritage deeply rooted in Hinduism. For centuries, the country's monarchs played a central role in preserving and promoting Hindu traditions and rituals. However, Nepal's socio-political landscape underwent a significant transformation in recent decades, driven by demands for inclusivity, secularism, and respect for religious diversity. These factors paved the way for the rewriting of Nepal's constitution.

The Case for Secularism:

- ***Protecting Religious Freedom:*** The transition to a secular state signifies Nepal's commitment to safeguarding the fundamental right of all citizens to practice their chosen religion freely. By eliminating the privileged status of Hinduism, the state acknowledges the importance of protecting the rights and beliefs of religious minorities, including Buddhists, Muslims, Christians, and others.
- ***Fostering Social Harmony:*** Nepal is home to diverse religious and ethnic groups, each with its distinct cultural practices and beliefs. Embracing secularism recognizes the value of this diversity and promotes social cohesion by treating all religions equally. It encourages dialogue, understanding, and mutual respect among different communities, fostering a sense of unity and shared national identity.
- ***Encouraging Modernization and Progress:*** Transitioning to a secular state positions Nepal in line with global trends and aspirations

for progress. It opens doors for international collaborations, trade, and cultural exchanges, enhancing the country's global standing. By embracing secularism, Nepal signals its commitment to modern values, human rights, and democratic principles, attracting investment and fostering economic growth.

Impact of the Secular Constitution:

- ***Legal Framework:*** The new constitution provides a legal framework that upholds the principles of secularism, religious freedom, and equality. It guarantees the rights of individuals to practice, profess, and propagate any religion without discrimination, ensuring that the state remains neutral in matters of faith.
- ***Social Transformation:*** The shift towards secularism has had a profound impact on Nepalese society. It has challenged traditional hierarchies and power structures, encouraging marginalized groups to assert their rights and demand equal treatment. This transformative process has the potential to reshape social norms, eradicate religious discrimination, and promote gender equality.
- ***Interfaith Dialogue and Understanding:*** The adoption of secularism offers an opportunity for interfaith dialogue and understanding, fostering harmony and cooperation among different religious communities. It encourages open discussions, mutual learning, and the celebration of shared values, leading to a more inclusive and tolerant society.

Challenges and Opportunities:

- ***Cultural Resistance*:** The transition from a Hindu state to a secular nation may face resistance from conservative factions or those deeply attached to traditional religious practices. It is crucial to address these concerns sensitively, ensuring that the rights and sentiments of all citizens are respected while promoting progressive ideals of secularism.
- ***Implementation and Enforcement:*** The successful implementation and enforcement of the secular constitution depend on effective governance, impartial judicial systems, transparent policies, and a commitment to upholding the rule of law. Nepal must invest in building institutional capacities, educating its citizens about their

rights, and training public officials to ensure the smooth implementation of the secular provisions.

- ***Bridging Divides and Promoting Inclusivity:*** While the secular constitution aims to promote religious harmony, it is essential to address historical divisions and inequalities. Nepal must work towards bridging socio-economic gaps, empowering marginalized communities, and promoting inclusivity. This requires affirmative action, education, and economic opportunities for disadvantaged groups, fostering a sense of belonging and equal participation in the nation's progress.
- ***International Engagement:*** The transition to a secular state provides Nepal with an opportunity to enhance its diplomatic relationships and engage with the global community. By aligning itself with international norms of religious freedom, Nepal can foster partnerships, attract foreign investment, and promote cultural exchanges. This engagement can contribute to the country's development, economic growth, and overall well-being.

The adoption of a secular constitution in Nepal marks a significant milestone in the country's journey towards inclusivity, religious freedom, and social harmony. This constitutional change reflects Nepal's commitment to modernize, respect diversity, and uphold fundamental rights. However, the successful implementation of secularism requires addressing challenges, including cultural resistance, effective governance, and bridging socio-economic divides. By embracing the opportunities presented by this transition, Nepal can build a more inclusive, tolerant, and prosperous society for all its citizens.

"As the curtain falls on monarchy, Nepal's democracy takes center stage."

The Interim Constitution and the Formation of Constituent Assembly: A Momentous Step Towards Democracy

The Interim Constitution and the formation of a Constituent Assembly mark a pivotal period in the political history of a nation. It signifies a decisive step towards establishing a democratic framework that reflects the aspirations and values of its people. This chapter delves into the significance, context, and process involved in the creation of an Interim Constitution and the subsequent formation of a Constituent Assembly, exploring its transformative impact on governance and the path to democratic consolidation.

The Need for an Interim Constitution:

- ***Historical Context:*** Discuss the historical context leading to the need for an Interim Constitution, such as political transitions, conflicts, or constitutional crises.
- ***Transitional Governance:*** Highlight the necessity of an Interim Constitution to provide a legal framework during the transition period, ensuring continuity, stability, and the protection of citizens' rights.
- ***Inclusive Representation:*** Emphasize the importance of inclusivity in the Interim Constitution, accommodating diverse political ideologies, ethnicities, and marginalized groups, fostering national unity.

Key Features of the Interim Constitution:

- ***Basic Principles:*** Discuss the fundamental principles enshrined in the Interim Constitution, such as sovereignty, separation of powers, human rights, and the rule of law.
- ***Transitional Provisions:*** Outline specific provisions addressing transitional justice, electoral processes, power-sharing arrangements, and the establishment of a Constituent Assembly.

- ***Safeguards and Checks:*** Highlight mechanisms within the Interim Constitution to safeguard against abuse of power, ensure accountability, and protect individual and collective rights.

Formation of the Constituent Assembly:

- ***Purpose and Mandate:*** Explain the purpose and mandate of the Constituent Assembly, which includes drafting a permanent constitution, shaping the political trajectory, and representing the will of the people.
- ***Electoral Process:*** Discuss the methods employed to elect members of the Constituent Assembly, such as direct elections, proportional representation, or other mechanisms, ensuring broad-based participation and legitimacy.
- ***Political Representation:*** Analyze the composition of the Constituent Assembly, including the participation of political parties, civil society organizations, women, and minority groups, fostering inclusivity and representation.

Challenges and Opportunities:

- ***Political Challenges:*** Explore the political challenges faced during the formation of the Constituent Assembly, such as ideological differences, power struggles, and negotiating competing interests.
- ***Constitutional Deliberations:*** Highlight the complex process of drafting a permanent constitution, including debates, consultations, and compromises among assembly members, ensuring a balance between conflicting views.
- ***Public Engagement:*** Discuss the role of public participation, consultations, and civic education in the deliberation process, fostering public ownership and legitimacy of the constitution.

Impact and Legacy:

- ***Democratic Consolidation:*** Examine the transformative impact of the Interim Constitution and the Constituent Assembly in strengthening democratic institutions, promoting civic engagement, and fostering a culture of constitutionalism.

- ***Rule of Law and Human Rights:*** Assess the provisions within the permanent constitution that protect human rights, ensure the rule of law, and establish a framework for democratic governance.
- ***Lessons Learned:*** Reflect on the lessons learned from the process of creating an Interim Constitution and a Constituent Assembly, providing insights for future constitutional reforms and democratic transitions.

The Interim Constitution and the formation of a Constituent Assembly represent a crucial chapter in a nation's journey towards democracy. It signifies a collective effort to establish a legal and political framework that reflects the aspirations and values of the people. Through the Interim Constitution, transitional governance is ensured, providing stability and protecting citizens' rights during a period of political transition.

The Interim Constitution incorporates key principles such as sovereignty, separation of powers, human rights, and the rule of law. These principles lay the foundation for democratic governance and serve as a guide for the drafting of a permanent constitution. Additionally, the Interim Constitution includes transitional provisions that address critical issues such as transitional justice, power-sharing arrangements, and the establishment of a Constituent Assembly.

The formation of the Constituent Assembly is a significant milestone in the process of constitutional development. It is tasked with the responsibility of drafting a permanent constitution that reflects the will of the people. The assembly is typically composed of elected representatives, ensuring political representation and inclusivity. The electoral process used to select assembly members should be designed to promote broad-based participation and legitimacy.

However, the formation of a Constituent Assembly is not without challenges. Political differences, power struggles, and competing interests can hinder the process and prolong deliberations. It requires negotiation, compromise, and the ability to balance diverse views to achieve consensus on key constitutional provisions. Public engagement, through consultations and civic education, plays a crucial role in fostering public ownership and legitimacy of the constitution.

The impact of the Interim Constitution and the Constituent Assembly extends beyond the drafting of a permanent constitution. It contributes to the consolidation of democracy by strengthening democratic institutions, promoting civic engagement, and establishing the rule of law. The provisions within the permanent constitution safeguard human rights, ensure accountability, and provide a framework for democratic governance.

Lessons learned from the process of creating an Interim Constitution and a Constituent Assembly can inform future constitutional reforms and democratic transitions. It highlights the importance of inclusivity, public participation, and consensus-building in the constitutional drafting process. It also underscores the significance of transitional provisions in ensuring stability and continuity during political transitions.

The Interim Constitution and the formation of a Constituent Assembly represent a watershed moment in a nation's pursuit of democracy. It signifies the commitment to establish a legal and political framework that upholds democratic principles, protects citizens' rights, and fosters national unity. The process of drafting a permanent constitution through the Constituent Assembly paves the way for democratic consolidation, rule of law, and sustainable governance.

"In the heart of the Himalayas, democracy beats as the pulse of Nepal."

Comprehensive Peace Agreement (CPA): A Landmark Accord for Lasting Peace

The Comprehensive Peace Agreement (CPA) stands as a pivotal milestone in the history of conflict resolution and peace-building efforts. This chapter delves into the details of the CPA, its key provisions, and its impact on the affected region.

- ***Background and Context:*** To understand the significance of the CPA, it is crucial to grasp the context in which it was negotiated. Here, we provide an overview of the conflict, the parties involved, and the circumstances leading to the agreement.
- ***Negotiations and Mediation:*** The second section explores the intricacies of the negotiations and the key actors involved in mediating the peace process. It highlights the challenges faced, the breakthroughs achieved, and the compromises made by the conflicting parties in order to reach a common ground.
- ***Key Provisions:*** This section delves into the core provisions of the CPA. It dissects the agreement, outlining specific points such as ceasefire arrangements, demilitarization processes, power-sharing mechanisms, political reforms, and the establishment of transitional justice mechanisms. It also discusses the timeline for implementing these provisions.
- ***Challenges and Implementation:*** While the signing of the CPA marked a significant achievement, its successful implementation was not without its obstacles. This section explores the challenges faced during the implementation phase, including issues related to disarmament, reintegration of combatants, economic recovery, and the establishment of democratic institutions. It also sheds light on the role of international actors in supporting the implementation process.
- ***Socio-economic Impacts:*** The CPA's impact extended beyond political arrangements. This section explores the socio-economic consequences of the agreement, such as the provision of humanitarian aid, infrastructure development, and programs aimed at poverty alleviation and social inclusion. It highlights the positive changes brought about by the CPA and the challenges that remain.

- ***Reconciliation and Healing:*** Addressing the wounds of conflict and fostering reconciliation are crucial elements of any comprehensive peace agreement. This section examines the efforts made through the CPA to promote truth and reconciliation commissions, community dialogues, and other initiatives aimed at healing the societal divisions caused by the conflict.
- ***International Community's Role:*** The international community played a significant role in supporting the negotiations, implementation, and post-conflict efforts related to the CPA. This section explores the involvement of regional and global actors, their contributions, and the lessons learned from their engagement.
- ***Legacy and Future Prospects:*** The final section reflects on the legacy of the CPA and its long-term implications for peace and stability in the region. It also discusses the challenges that remain and the steps that need to be taken to ensure the sustainability of the peace achieved through the agreement.

The Comprehensive Peace Agreement (CPA) represents a significant achievement in conflict resolution and post-conflict reconstruction. Its provisions, implementation challenges, and socio-economic impacts have shaped the affected region in profound ways. While acknowledging the progress made, it is important to recognize that sustained efforts are necessary to consolidate peace and address the underlying causes of the conflict. The CPA serves as a reminder that durable peace is possible through dialogue, compromise, and genuine commitment to a shared vision of a better future.

- ***Lessons Learned:*** Reflecting on the Comprehensive Peace Agreement (CPA), it is essential to draw lessons from its negotiation and implementation processes. This section examines the key lessons learned from the CPA experience, including the importance of inclusive dialogue, the need for trust-building measures, the significance of addressing root causes of conflict, and the role of international support in sustaining peace.
- ***Regional and Global Implications:*** The impact of the CPA extends beyond the immediate conflict-affected region. This section explores the regional and global implications of the agreement, such as its influence on neighboring countries, the potential for regional cooperation and integration, and the lessons it offers to other ongoing conflicts worldwide. It also highlights the importance of sharing best practices and promoting synergy among peacebuilding endeavors.

• ***Monitoring and Evaluation:*** Monitoring and evaluating the implementation of the CPA is crucial to ensure accountability and address any shortcomings. This section discusses the mechanisms put in place to monitor the progress of the agreement and assess its impact. It also emphasizes the importance of ongoing evaluation to identify areas that require adjustments or additional support.

• ***Sustainable Peace and Beyond:*** While the CPA marked a significant step towards peace, sustaining and building upon the achievements of the agreement is equally vital. This section explores the measures necessary to consolidate peace in the long term, including promoting good governance, fostering inclusive political processes, investing in socio-economic development, and addressing any remaining grievances or tensions.

• ***Case Studies and Success Stories:*** To illustrate the tangible outcomes of the CPA, this section presents specific case studies and success stories resulting from the implementation of the agreement. These examples highlight positive changes in areas such as security, governance, human rights, reconciliation, and socio-economic development. They serve as inspiring examples of what can be achieved through committed peacebuilding efforts.

• ***Challenges Ahead:*** Despite the progress made, challenges and obstacles persist on the path towards lasting peace. This section examines the remaining challenges, such as the reintegration of ex-combatants, the resolution of land and resource disputes, the healing of societal divisions, and the prevention of future conflicts. It emphasizes the need for continued engagement and support from all stakeholders to overcome these challenges.

"Nepal's transition from monarchy to democracy is the people reclaiming their narrative."

Nepal's Interim Period and the Constituent Assembly: A Journey towards Democratic Transformation

Nepal, a landlocked nation in South Asia, has witnessed significant political and constitutional transformations in recent decades. The country's interim period and the establishment of a Constituent Assembly marked a crucial phase in Nepal's journey towards democratic governance. This chapter delves into the intricacies of Nepal's interim period, the formation of the Constituent Assembly, and the subsequent impact on the country's political landscape. By exploring the challenges, achievements, and lessons learned during this transformative period, we gain a deeper understanding of Nepal's democratic aspirations.

Historical Background:

To comprehend the significance of Nepal's interim period and the Constituent Assembly, it is essential to understand the historical context. Nepal remained under the monarchy for centuries, with limited democratic processes. However, the pro-democracy movement of 1951 marked the beginning of a struggle to establish a democratic system. Subsequently, Nepal experienced several political changes, including the transition from an absolute to a constitutional monarchy in 1990.

The Interim Period:

- ***The People's Movement of 2006:*** The people's movement of 2006 was a turning point in Nepal's political trajectory. Mass protests against the autocratic rule of King Gyanendra led to a comprehensive peace agreement between the government and the Maoist rebels. The agreement paved the way for an interim period aimed at transitioning Nepal into a democratic republic.
- ***Comprehensive Peace Agreement (CPA):*** The CPA signed between the Seven-Party Alliance and the Communist Party of Nepal (Maoist) in November 2006 established the framework for the interim period. It focused on several key aspects, including the integration of Maoist

combatants into the security forces, interim governance, and the formation of a Constituent Assembly.

- ***Interim Constitution of Nepal:*** To govern the country during the interim period, an Interim Constitution was promulgated in January 2007. It aimed to ensure the smooth functioning of the state, protect human rights, and create an inclusive political environment. The interim constitution also outlined the process for the formation of a Constituent Assembly to draft a new constitution.

The Constituent Assembly:

- ***Election and Composition:*** In April 2008, Nepal held its first Constituent Assembly elections. The election saw significant participation from various political parties and resulted in the formation of a Constituent Assembly comprising 601 members. The assembly represented diverse ethnic, geographic, and political groups, reflecting Nepal's commitment to inclusivity.
- ***Drafting of the Constitution:*** One of the primary responsibilities of the Constituent Assembly was to draft a new constitution for Nepal. The drafting process involved extensive deliberations, consultations, and negotiations among the assembly members. It aimed to address the diverse aspirations of Nepali citizens, including federalism, secularism, and the protection of fundamental rights.
- ***Challenges and Achievements:*** The Constituent Assembly faced numerous challenges during the drafting process, including disagreements over federal boundaries, ethnic representation, and the role of the judiciary. However, it also achieved significant milestones, such as the declaration of Nepal as a federal democratic republic and the inclusion of provisions to protect the rights of marginalized groups.

Impact and Lessons Learned:

- ***Transition to Federalism:*** The establishment of federalism was a landmark achievement of the Constituent Assembly. Nepal transitioned from a unitary system to a federal structure, aiming to address regional disparities, promote local governance, and empower marginalized communities. The federal structure aimed to ensure greater participation and representation at the grassroots level, fostering a sense of inclusivity and strengthening the democratic fabric of the nation.

- ***Protection of Fundamental Rights:*** The new constitution enshrined fundamental rights and liberties, ensuring the protection of individual freedoms, equality, and social justice. It recognized the rights of women, minorities, indigenous communities, and other marginalized groups, promoting their empowerment and inclusion in the political and social spheres.
- ***Political Stability and Governance:*** The Constituent Assembly played a crucial role in establishing political stability in Nepal. The formation of a democratically elected government and the adoption of a new constitution provided a framework for governance and decision-making. The assembly's deliberations and consensus-building efforts contributed to building a sense of trust among political stakeholders and fostering a culture of dialogue and cooperation.
- ***Inclusivity and Social Cohesion:*** The Constituent Assembly's inclusive composition and its commitment to addressing the aspirations of diverse ethnic, linguistic, and religious communities played a significant role in promoting social cohesion. By recognizing the rights and identities of different groups, the constitution aimed to bridge societal divisions and promote a harmonious and inclusive society.
- ***Lessons Learned:*** The interim period and the Constituent Assembly process in Nepal offer valuable lessons for nations undergoing political transitions and constitution-making processes. Some key lessons include the importance of inclusivity, consensus-building, and accommodating diverse aspirations within a democratic framework. The experience of Nepal highlights the need for open dialogue, compromise, and a long-term vision to overcome challenges and ensure the legitimacy and durability of democratic institutions.

Nepal's interim period and the establishment of a Constituent Assembly marked a significant milestone in the country's democratic transformation. Through extensive consultations, negotiations, and compromises, Nepal successfully transitioned from a monarchy to a federal democratic republic. The Constituent Assembly's efforts in drafting and adopting a new constitution reflected the aspirations of the Nepali people for a more inclusive, equitable, and democratic society. The lessons learned from Nepal's experience can serve as a valuable guide for other nations navigating similar political transitions and constitution-making processes. As Nepal continues its journey towards democratic consolidation, the interim period and the Constituent Assembly will remain pivotal chapters in the nation's history.

"Democracy in Nepal is the Everest of human rights, standing tall and proud."

The Peace Process in Nepal: A Journey Toward Stability and Reconciliation

Nepal, a beautiful Himalayan nation nestled between India and China, has had a tumultuous history marked by conflicts, political unrest, and a decade-long civil war. The peace process in Nepal, which began in 2006, has been a significant milestone in the country's efforts to achieve stability, social harmony, and democratic governance. This chapter delves into the key aspects of Nepal's peace process, highlighting its challenges, achievements, and the way forward.

- ***Background and Causes of Conflict:*** Nepal's civil war took place between 1996 and 2006, resulting from long-standing socio-political grievances and demands for greater representation by marginalized groups. The Communist Party of Nepal (Maoist) led a rebellion against the monarchy and the government, seeking to establish a more inclusive society. The conflict claimed thousands of lives and left lasting scars on the nation's social fabric.
- ***Comprehensive Peace Agreement (CPA):*** The Comprehensive Peace Agreement, signed in November 2006, marked a crucial step toward ending the armed conflict. The CPA established a framework for peace negotiations, including the integration of Maoist combatants into the security forces, drafting a new constitution, and addressing issues of transitional justice.
- ***Disarmament, Demobilization, and Reintegration (DDR):*** One of the primary challenges of the peace process was the integration of Maoist combatants into the security forces. The United Nations Mission in Nepal (UNMIN) played a crucial role in managing the DDR process, which involved the registration, disarmament, demobilization, and rehabilitation of Maoist combatants. This step aimed to transform the Maoist movement into a peaceful political force.
- ***Transitional Justice and Reconciliation:*** The peace process in Nepal also necessitated addressing the legacy of human rights abuses and ensuring justice for the victims. The establishment of the Truth and Reconciliation Commission (TRC) and the Commission of Investigation on Enforced Disappeared Persons (CIEDP) aimed to investigate and provide redress for human rights violations during the conflict. However, the implementation of

transitional justice mechanisms has faced challenges, including political interference and limited resources.

- ***Constitution-Making Process:*** The peace process included the drafting and promulgation of a new constitution, which was a significant milestone for Nepal's democratic transition. After a lengthy and contentious process, the new constitution was adopted in September 2015. It institutionalized federalism, secularism, and inclusive representation, addressing some of the key demands raised during the conflict.
- ***Political Transition and Power-Sharing:*** The peace process also involved a significant shift in Nepal's political landscape. The Maoists, who were once deemed an insurgent group, transformed into a mainstream political party. The process of power-sharing and political transition faced its own set of challenges, including the formation of coalition governments and the need for broader consensus among political stakeholders.
- ***Socio-Economic Reforms and Development:*** Building a sustainable peace required addressing the root causes of the conflict, including socio-economic disparities. Efforts were made to implement inclusive policies, promote social justice, and enhance development in marginalized regions. However, the pace of socio-economic reforms has been slow, and the equitable distribution of resources remains a challenge.
- ***Role of International Community:*** The international community, particularly the United Nations and neighboring countries, played a critical role in facilitating Nepal's peace process. The United Nations Mission in Nepal (UNMIN) provided technical expertise, monitoring, and support throughout the peace process. International actors also supported Nepal's political dialogue, mediation efforts, and capacity-building initiatives to strengthen democratic institutions and ensure a smooth transition.
- ***Challenges and Setbacks:*** Despite significant progress, Nepal's peace process has faced several challenges and setbacks. The lingering issues of transitional justice, including the prosecution of perpetrators and reparations for victims, have been a source of frustration and disappointment. Political instability, frequent changes in government, and disagreements among political parties have hindered the effective implementation of peace agreements and reforms.
- ***The Way Forward:*** To consolidate peace and foster reconciliation in Nepal, several key steps need to be taken. First, the government must prioritize the implementation of transitional justice mechanisms, ensuring

that victims' rights to truth, justice, and reparations are upheld. It is essential to build a society that acknowledges past atrocities and works toward healing and reconciliation.

Second, Nepal's political leaders must demonstrate a commitment to inclusive governance and address the socio-economic disparities that fueled the conflict. Investing in education, healthcare, infrastructure, and job creation will contribute to long-term stability and sustainable development.

Third, fostering dialogue and trust-building among diverse communities and stakeholders is crucial. Encouraging open and inclusive discussions on contentious issues, such as federalism, identity, and resource allocation, will help address grievances and build consensus.

Fourth, the international community should continue to support Nepal's peace process by providing technical assistance, capacity-building, and diplomatic engagement. Sharing best practices and lessons learned from other post-conflict societies can contribute to Nepal's efforts toward peacebuilding and reconciliation.

Nepal's peace process has been a complex and challenging journey, marked by both achievements and setbacks. While significant strides have been made in ending the armed conflict, the process of reconciliation, justice, and socio-economic transformation remains ongoing. It is vital for all stakeholders to remain committed to the principles of inclusivity, accountability, and dialogue. By addressing the root causes of the conflict, Nepal can pave the way for a more peaceful, prosperous, and harmonious future for its people.

"The metamorphosis of Nepal reflects the resilience of a nation on its path to democracy."

---

7. WRITING THE NEW CONSTITUTION

"In embracing democracy, Nepal embraces the principle that every citizen's voice matters"

Deliberations, Debates, and Challenges in the Nepalese Constitution

The Nepalese Constitution, adopted in 2015, marked a significant milestone in the country's democratic journey. However, its implementation has been accompanied by a series of deliberations, debates, and challenges. This chapter explores the key issues and controversies surrounding the Nepalese Constitution, shedding light on the complexities of its development and the ongoing efforts to address various concerns.

- ***Historical Context and Constitution-Making Process:*** The Nepalese Constitution emerged as a response to the political transition that followed the end of the decade-long civil war in 2006. The Constitution Assembly, comprising elected representatives, was entrusted with the task of drafting the constitution. The process involved extensive deliberations and negotiations, aiming to address the diverse interests and aspirations of the Nepalese people.
- ***Federalism and Identity Politics:*** One of the most contentious aspects of the Nepalese Constitution is its federal structure. The country transitioned from a unitary system to a federal one, dividing it into seven provinces. This move aimed to address regional imbalances and empower marginalized communities. However, debates have arisen regarding the boundaries and names of these provinces, often driven by identity politics and regional aspirations.
- ***Inclusion and Representation:*** The Nepalese Constitution emphasizes inclusivity and aims to ensure representation for historically marginalized groups, including women, Dalits, indigenous communities, Madhesis, and other ethnic minorities. However, there have been concerns regarding the implementation of these provisions, with some arguing that they have not translated into adequate representation and meaningful participation.
- ***Language and Cultural Rights:*** The Nepalese Constitution recognizes Nepali as the official language, while also granting rights to preserve and promote other languages and cultures. However, debates have emerged over the dominance of Nepali and the protection of linguistic and cultural diversity. There have been calls to strengthen provisions safeguarding linguistic rights and promoting multiculturalism.

- ***Judicial Independence and Constitutional Interpretation:*** Ensuring the independence of the judiciary is vital for the effective functioning of any constitution. The Nepalese Constitution established a separate judicial body and outlined provisions to safeguard judicial independence. However, questions have been raised regarding the appointment process, the accountability of judges, and the interpretation of constitutional provisions, necessitating ongoing discussions and reforms.
- ***Transitional Justice and Human Rights:*** The Nepalese Constitution acknowledges the need for transitional justice mechanisms to address human rights violations committed during the civil war. However, the implementation of these mechanisms has faced significant challenges, including a lack of political will, delays, and limited accountability. The quest for justice, truth, and reconciliation remains a critical issue in Nepal's constitutional landscape.
- ***Political Stability and Governance:*** The transition from a monarchy to a republic system brought new challenges to Nepal's political stability and governance. The Constitution introduced a parliamentary system with a mix of proportional representation and first-past-the-post electoral systems. However, political fragmentation, frequent changes in government, and a lack of effective governance have presented obstacles to stability and hindered the realization of constitutional goals.
- ***Constitutional Amendments and Democratic Discourse:*** The Nepalese Constitution includes a provision for its amendment, recognizing the evolving needs and aspirations of the people. However, the process of amending the Constitution has become a subject of intense debate and controversy. Differing political ideologies, party interests, and identity-based demands have led to challenges in forging consensus and achieving meaningful reforms.

"The monarchy's eclipse marks the dawn of Nepal's democratic era."

Key Provisions and principles of the new constitution of Nepal

- ***Preamble:*** The preamble of the constitution declares Nepal as a sovereign, independent, inclusive, democratic, and federal democratic republic. It emphasizes the commitment to socialism-oriented people's democracy, inclusive development, and respect for fundamental rights and freedoms.
- ***Basic Structure:*** The constitution establishes a federal system of governance, dividing Nepal into seven provinces. It defines the powers and responsibilities of the federal, provincial, and local governments. The three-tier structure ensures decentralization of power and effective service delivery.
- ***Fundamental Rights:*** The constitution guarantees a comprehensive set of fundamental rights and freedoms to all citizens. These include the right to equality, freedom of expression, religion, and assembly, as well as the right to education, health, and a clean environment. The constitution also prohibits discrimination based on gender, caste, ethnicity, religion, or any other ground.
- ***Citizenship:*** The constitution outlines the provisions for acquiring and losing Nepali citizenship. It distinguishes between citizenship by descent, birth, naturalization, and marriage. The new constitution allows citizenship to be passed through either the father or the mother, ensuring gender equality in citizenship rights.
- ***Social Justice and Inclusion:*** The constitution emphasizes the principles of social justice and inclusion to address historical marginalization and discrimination. It envisions a society based on proportional representation, affirmative action, and the elimination of social, economic, and gender disparities. The constitution reserves seats for women, Dalits, indigenous groups, Madhesis, Tharus, and other marginalized communities in various state organs.
- ***Separation of Powers:*** The constitution upholds the principle of separation of powers among the executive, legislative, and judicial branches of the government. It establishes a bicameral federal parliament consisting of the House of Representatives and the National Assembly. The executive power is vested in the President, while the Prime Minister is the head of government.

- ***Judiciary and Rule of Law:*** The constitution ensures an independent and impartial judiciary as a cornerstone of the rule of law. It establishes the Supreme Court as the apex judicial body, with the power of judicial review. The constitution guarantees the right to a fair trial, due process, and access to justice. It also establishes a Judicial Council responsible for the appointment, promotion, and disciplinary actions of judges.
- ***Electoral System:*** The constitution provides for a mixed electoral system, combining the first-past-the-post (FPTP) and proportional representation (PR) systems. It allows citizens to directly elect representatives through FPTP in constituencies and through PR based on party lists. This system aims to ensure representation of diverse voices and political parties in the parliament.
- ***Amendment Process:*** The constitution outlines the procedures for amending its provisions. It requires a two-thirds majority in parliament or a national referendum for amendments related to substantive provisions, federal structures, or fundamental rights. This provision ensures that constitutional amendments are subject to careful deliberation and broad consensus.
- ***Secularism:*** The new constitution declares Nepal as a secular country, ensuring religious freedom and the protection of the rights of individuals from all religious backgrounds. It prohibits any form of discrimination or imposition of religious beliefs.
- ***Transitional Justice:*** The constitution includes provisions for transitional justice to address the legacy of the armed conflict that took place in Nepal from 1996 to 2006. It establishes two transitional justice mechanisms: the Truth and Reconciliation Commission (TRC) and the Commission on the Investigation of Enforced Disappeared Persons (CIEDP). These bodies are entrusted with investigating and addressing human rights violations committed during the conflict, providing reparations to victims, and promoting reconciliation.
- ***Language and Cultural Rights:*** The constitution recognizes Nepal as a multi-lingual and multicultural country. It guarantees the right of all communities to preserve, promote, and develop their languages, cultures, and traditions. It also enshrines the right of every citizen to receive education in their mother tongue.
- ***Natural Resources and Environment:*** The constitution recognizes the importance of sustainable development and environmental conservation. It mandates the protection of Nepal's natural resources, including forests, water

bodies, and biodiversity. The constitution also ensures the right of every citizen to live in a clean and healthy environment.

- ***Emergency Provisions:*** The constitution provides for emergency provisions in situations of war, armed rebellion, or natural disasters. It outlines the conditions and procedures for declaring a state of emergency, allowing the government to take exceptional measures to safeguard national security and public order.
- ***Local Self-Governance:*** The constitution emphasizes the importance of local self-governance and devolution of power to the grassroots level. It envisions a strong and autonomous local government system with elected representatives. The constitution outlines the functions, powers, and responsibilities of local governments in service delivery and development planning.
- ***Constitutional Bodies:*** The constitution establishes various constitutional bodies to ensure checks and balances, transparency, and accountability in the governance system. These bodies include the Election Commission, National Human Rights Commission, Commission for the Investigation of Abuse of Authority, and others. They play a crucial role in safeguarding democratic processes and protecting citizens' rights.
- ***Gender Equality:*** The constitution recognizes the principle of gender equality and prohibits discrimination based on gender. It ensures the representation of women in all state mechanisms, including the provision of reserved seats in parliament and other decision-making bodies. The constitution also prohibits gender-based violence and provides for legal remedies and support for victims.
- ***Federalism and State Restructuring:*** The constitution envisions a federal structure for Nepal, dividing the country into seven provinces. It outlines the powers and responsibilities of federal, provincial, and local governments, promoting decentralization and devolution of authority. The process of state restructuring aims to address historical disparities, ensure equitable resource distribution, and empower local communities.
- ***Economic Policies:*** The constitution outlines the principles of Nepal's economic policies, emphasizing the promotion of a mixed economy, sustainable development, and social justice. It seeks to address poverty, unemployment, and regional disparities through equitable economic growth, investment, and resource mobilization.

• ***National Security and Defense:*** The constitution defines the roles and responsibilities of the security forces, including the Nepal Army, Nepal Police, and Armed Police Force. It ensures civilian control over the military and emphasizes the protection of national security, territorial integrity, and sovereignty.

• ***Right to Information:*** The constitution guarantees the right to information, enabling citizens to access public information held by state authorities. This provision promotes transparency, accountability, and citizen participation in governance processes.

• ***Intellectual Property Rights:*** The constitution recognizes the importance of intellectual property rights and encourages creativity and innovation. It provides for the protection of intellectual property, including copyrights, patents, and trademarks.

• ***Education and Health:*** The constitution emphasizes the right to education and healthcare. It mandates free and compulsory education up to the secondary level and ensures access to quality healthcare services. The constitution also encourages the development of scientific research and technology.

• ***Media and Freedom of Expression:*** The constitution upholds freedom of expression, including the freedom of the press. It recognizes the media's role as a watchdog and ensures the protection of journalists' rights. The constitution prohibits censorship and promotes an open and pluralistic media environment.

• ***Disaster Management:*** Given Nepal's vulnerability to natural disasters, the constitution includes provisions for disaster management and risk reduction. It emphasizes the proactive approach of the state in disaster preparedness, response, and recovery, with a focus on protecting vulnerable communities.

• ***Right to Property:*** The constitution guarantees the right to private property. It ensures that no person shall be deprived of their property except by law and with just compensation. The provision aims to protect property rights while allowing for the acquisition of land for public purposes.

• ***Indigenous Peoples and Ethnic Communities:*** The constitution recognizes and respects the rights of indigenous peoples, ethnic communities, and marginalized groups. It ensures their participation in decision-making processes, protection of their cultural heritage, and access to social and economic opportunities. The constitution also establishes the National Inclusion Commission to address the concerns of marginalized communities.

- ***Constitutional Amendments:*** The constitution outlines the process for amending its provisions. It requires a two-thirds majority in parliament for most amendments. However, some fundamental aspects, such as federalism, secularism, and republican order, can only be amended through a national referendum, ensuring the protection of key constitutional principles.
- ***Federal Police and Provincial Assemblies:*** The constitution establishes a federal police force responsible for maintaining law and order at the federal level. It also provides for the establishment of provincial assemblies and governments, giving provinces significant decision-making powers and autonomy.
- ***Transitional Provisions:*** The constitution includes transitional provisions to manage the transition from the previous governance structure to the federal system. It addresses issues such as the integration and rehabilitation of former Maoist combatants, the restructuring of civil service, and the formation of constitutional bodies.
- ***Right to Social Justice:*** The constitution recognizes the right to social justice and equality. It aims to address historical discrimination, inequalities, and social exclusion by promoting affirmative action and inclusive policies.
- ***Non-Discrimination:*** The constitution prohibits discrimination on various grounds, including gender, caste, ethnicity, religion, language, disability, and sexual orientation. It ensures equal protection and opportunities for all citizens.
- ***Right to Privacy:*** The constitution guarantees the right to privacy and protects individuals' personal information from unauthorized use or disclosure. It emphasizes the importance of privacy in personal and family life, communication, and data protection.
- ***Right to Water and Sanitation:*** The constitution recognizes the right to access clean drinking water and sanitation facilities as a fundamental right. It obligates the state to ensure the availability and accessibility of safe drinking water and sanitation services for all citizens.
- ***Right to Work and Labor Rights:*** The constitution ensures the right to work and fair labor practices. It prohibits forced labor, child labor, and discrimination in employment. The constitution also enshrines the right to form and join trade unions and collective bargaining.

- ***Local Languages and Scripts:*** The constitution acknowledges the linguistic diversity of Nepal and recognizes the rights of different language-speaking communities. It allows the use of local languages in government offices, courts, and educational institutions, promoting cultural diversity and linguistic rights.
- ***Right to Social Security:*** The constitution guarantees the right to social security, including access to social insurance, pensions, and welfare programs. It aims to provide a safety net for individuals and families in times of need and vulnerability.
- ***Environmental Protection:*** The constitution emphasizes environmental protection and sustainable development. It mandates the conservation of natural resources, biodiversity, and ecosystems. It also encourages the promotion of clean and renewable energy sources.
- ***Right to Constitutional Remedies:*** The constitution ensures the right to constitutional remedies, allowing individuals to seek legal remedies and protection in case of violations of their fundamental rights. It empowers the courts to issue writs and orders to safeguard constitutional rights.
- ***International Human Rights Commitments:*** The constitution acknowledges Nepal's international human rights commitments and obligations. It recognizes the universal principles of human rights and encourages cooperation with international bodies and organizations to promote and protect human rights.

It's important to note that the new constitution of Nepal is a comprehensive legal document with numerous provisions covering various aspects of governance, rights, and principles. The provisions listed here provide a general overview, but a thorough understanding of the constitution would require a detailed study of the text, its interpretations, and its implementation through laws and regulations.

"Nepal's democratic journey is an ode to freedom, sung by a chorus of its citizens."

---

8. CONSOLIDATION OF DEMOCRACY

"The monarchy's dissolution in Nepal reminds us that power ultimately rests in the hands of the people"

Post-Constitution Challenges in Nepal: A Comprehensive Analysis

This chapter examines the post-constitution challenges faced by Nepal since the promulgation of its new constitution in 2015. Nepal's journey towards a federal democratic republic was a significant milestone, but it was accompanied by numerous political, social, and economic challenges. This chapter provides an in-depth analysis of the major challenges that have emerged in the aftermath of the constitution's implementation and explores potential solutions to address them.

Nepal, a landlocked country nestled in the Himalayas, underwent a historic transformation with the promulgation of its new constitution on September 20, 2015. The constitution marked a crucial step in Nepal's transition from a monarchy to a federal democratic republic. However, despite these achievements, the country has faced various challenges in the post-constitution period. This chapter aims to shed light on these challenges and offer insights into potential pathways for Nepal's progress.

Political Challenges:

- ***Ethnic and Regional Disparities:*** The federal structure introduced by the constitution aimed to address historical inequalities. However, it has also led to new divisions based on ethnicity and region, resulting in political tensions and demands for more autonomy.
- ***Political Instability:*** Frequent changes in government and the lack of political consensus have hindered the effective implementation of the constitution, undermining stability and governance.

Social Challenges:

- ***Inclusion and Marginalization:*** Despite the constitutional provisions for inclusivity, marginalized communities, such as Dalits, women, and indigenous groups, continue to face discrimination and exclusion, hindering their social progress.
- ***Gender Equality:*** While the constitution made significant strides in ensuring gender equality, the gap between constitutional provisions

and their implementation remains significant, particularly in terms of women's political representation and access to justice.

Economic Challenges:

- ***Poverty and Unemployment:*** Nepal faces pervasive poverty and high unemployment rates, particularly among the youth. The constitution's emphasis on inclusive economic growth has yet to yield significant improvements, posing a challenge to the country's development.
- ***Infrastructure Development:*** Inadequate infrastructure, including roads, electricity, and telecommunications, has impeded economic growth and hindered regional integration.

Governance Challenges:

- ***Corruption:*** Corruption remains a significant challenge in Nepal, hampering effective governance and hindering foreign investment. The constitution's provisions for transparency and accountability need to be reinforced to tackle this issue effectively.
- ***Rule of Law:*** Ensuring the supremacy of the constitution and strengthening the rule of law are critical for establishing an effective and just governance system. However, challenges persist in terms of judicial independence and enforcement of legal provisions.

Security Challenges:

- ***Inclusive Security:*** Nepal's security sector faces challenges in ensuring inclusivity and addressing the needs and aspirations of diverse communities, particularly in conflict-affected regions.
- ***Cross-border Security:*** Nepal shares borders with two regional powers, India and China. Striking a delicate balance in maintaining friendly relations with both countries while safeguarding national interests poses a significant challenge.

The post-constitution period in Nepal has been marked by various challenges that require proactive and sustainable solutions. Addressing these challenges necessitates political will, inclusive governance, and effective implementation of constitutional provisions. By promoting dialogue, inclusivity, and economic growth, Nepal can overcome these hurdles and embark on a path of stability, development and prosperity. The following recommendations can serve as a roadmap for Nepal to overcome the post-constitution challenges:

- ***Enhancing Political Consensus:*** Political stability is crucial for effective governance. Political parties should prioritize national interests over partisan agendas and work towards consensus-building on key issues. Regular dialogues, negotiations, and inclusive decision-making processes can help bridge the political divide and ensure the smooth implementation of the constitution.
- ***Addressing Ethnic and Regional Disparities:*** The government should actively work towards addressing the grievances of marginalized groups and ensuring equal representation and opportunities. Measures such as affirmative action, targeted policies, and inclusive development programs can help alleviate ethnic and regional disparities, promoting social harmony and national unity.
- ***Strengthening Institutions and Rule of Law:*** The constitution provides a framework for transparent, accountable, and impartial governance. It is crucial to strengthen institutions such as the judiciary, anti-corruption bodies, and law enforcement agencies to ensure the rule of law. Promoting judicial independence, enhancing capacity-building, and implementing effective mechanisms to combat corruption are essential steps in this regard.
- ***Promoting Inclusive Economic Growth:*** Nepal needs to prioritize economic development and job creation, particularly in rural areas and for the youth. Investing in infrastructure development, promoting entrepreneurship, attracting foreign investment, and diversifying the economy can help alleviate poverty and unemployment, fostering inclusive growth.
- ***Empowering Marginalized Communities:*** The government should intensify efforts to empower marginalized communities, including Dalits, women, and indigenous groups. Ensuring access to quality education, healthcare, and social protection programs can help uplift these communities and bridge the social gaps created by historical discrimination.
- ***Strengthening Cross-border Relations:*** Nepal's strategic location between India and China presents both opportunities and challenges. The government should pursue a balanced foreign policy that safeguards national interests while fostering cooperation and

mutually beneficial relationships with both neighboring countries. Engaging in regional forums and initiatives can further enhance Nepal's position and leverage regional cooperation to address common challenges.

- ***Promoting Good Governance and Accountability:*** Transparency, accountability, and the fight against corruption are fundamental pillars of good governance. Implementing effective anti-corruption measures, promoting transparency in public administration, and strengthening oversight mechanisms can help build trust between the government and citizens, fostering a culture of accountability.

Nepal's post-constitution period has been marked by various challenges, ranging from political divisions to social disparities and economic obstacles. However, by addressing these challenges through inclusive governance, economic reforms, and social empowerment, Nepal can unlock its potential and pave the way for a prosperous future. It is essential for all stakeholders, including the government, political parties, civil society, and citizens, to work collectively towards overcoming these challenges and realizing the aspirations set forth in the constitution. With determination, resilience, and concerted efforts, Nepal can navigate the post-constitution landscape and emerge as a stable, inclusive, and prosperous nation.

"In the dance of democracy, Nepal finds its rhythm and moves towards a brighter future."

Strengthening of Democratic Institutions in Nepal: Challenges and Prospects

This chapter explores the process of strengthening democratic institutions in Nepal. It examines the challenges faced by the country in consolidating its democratic framework and highlights the importance of robust institutions for sustainable democratic governance. The chapter analyzes key areas of focus, including political parties, the judiciary, the legislature, and civil society, and provides recommendations for enhancing democratic processes and ensuring the long-term stability of Nepal's democratic institutions.

Nepal's transition from a monarchy to a federal democratic republic marked a significant milestone in its history. The establishment of democratic institutions was a vital step towards ensuring people's participation, protecting human rights, and promoting good governance. However, consolidating democratic institutions and practices has been an ongoing process in Nepal. This chapter delves into the challenges faced by Nepal in strengthening its democratic institutions and explores potential avenues for progress and development.

<u>Political Parties:</u>

- ***Internal Democracy:*** Political parties are the backbone of any democratic system. Strengthening internal democracy within political parties is crucial for their effective functioning. Encouraging transparent candidate selection processes, promoting intra-party democracy, and enhancing accountability mechanisms can help build stronger and more representative political parties.
- ***Political Culture:*** Nurturing a culture of dialogue, consensus-building, and respect for democratic values is essential. Political parties should prioritize national interests over partisan agendas and foster a culture of accountability, inclusivity, and constructive engagement to strengthen democratic practices.

Judiciary:

- ***Judicial Independence:*** Upholding the independence of the judiciary is vital for the rule of law and the protection of citizens' rights. Ensuring appointments based on merit, safeguarding judicial autonomy from political interference, and promoting transparency in judicial processes are critical for strengthening the judiciary's role as a guardian of democracy.
- ***Access to Justice:*** Enhancing access to justice for all citizens, particularly marginalized groups, is essential. Measures such as legal aid programs, court reforms, and promoting alternative dispute resolution mechanisms can help bridge the justice gap and ensure equal protection under the law.

Legislature:

- ***Legislative Oversight:*** Strengthening the role of the legislature in providing effective oversight of the executive branch is crucial. Robust parliamentary committees, transparent budgetary processes, and mechanisms for holding the government accountable are essential for ensuring checks and balances within the democratic system.
- ***Representation and Inclusivity:*** The legislature should strive for diverse representation, including women, ethnic minorities, and marginalized communities. Implementing affirmative action measures, promoting inclusive electoral systems, and encouraging meaningful participation of underrepresented groups can foster a more inclusive and representative democracy.

Civil Society:

- ***Civic Engagement:*** Civil society plays a vital role in promoting democratic values, advocating for citizen rights, and holding the government accountable. Strengthening civil society organizations, protecting their independence, and encouraging active citizen engagement can contribute to a vibrant democratic culture.
- ***Transparency and Accountability:*** Civil society can act as a watchdog, promoting transparency, and demanding accountability from both the government and other institutions. Strengthening mechanisms for citizen participation, such as access to information

laws and platforms for public consultation, can enhance transparency and accountability.

Media Freedom:

- ***Press Freedom:*** A free and independent media is crucial for a thriving democracy. Strengthening media freedom, protecting journalists' rights, and promoting ethical journalism can foster an informed citizenry and contribute to greater accountability in democratic governance. Efforts should be made to ensure media pluralism, safeguard journalists' safety, and promote media literacy among citizens.
- ***Regulation and Self-regulation:*** Balancing media freedom with responsible journalism requires a robust regulatory framework. Encouraging self-regulation within the media industry, establishing media councils or ombudsman offices, and promoting ethical reporting standards can help maintain media credibility and integrity.

Electoral Reforms:

- ***Transparent and Inclusive Elections:*** Strengthening electoral processes and institutions is essential for ensuring free and fair elections. Measures such as voter education, enhancing the independence of election management bodies, and addressing issues of electoral fraud and malpractice can bolster confidence in the electoral system.
- ***Campaign Finance Regulations:*** Regulating campaign financing is crucial for preventing undue influence and corruption in the electoral process. Implementing transparent and accountable mechanisms for election campaign financing can contribute to a level playing field and enhance the integrity of democratic elections.

Public Administration and Bureaucracy:

- ***Merit-based Appointments:*** Strengthening public administration requires merit-based recruitment and promotion processes. Depoliticizing the civil service, ensuring professionalism, and providing training and capacity-building opportunities for civil servants can enhance the efficiency and effectiveness of public institutions.

- ***Administrative Reforms:*** Streamlining administrative procedures, promoting transparency, and reducing bureaucratic red tape are essential for efficient service delivery. Embracing e-governance initiatives, citizen-centric approaches, and performance-based evaluations can contribute to better public administration and improved governance.

Strengthening democratic institutions in Nepal is an ongoing process that requires concerted efforts and commitment from all stakeholders. Political parties, the judiciary, the legislature, civil society, and the media play crucial roles in consolidating democratic practices and ensuring the long-term stability of the country's democratic framework. By addressing challenges such as internal party democracy, judicial independence, legislative oversight, and citizen engagement, Nepal can foster a vibrant and inclusive democracy. Additionally, electoral reforms, media freedom, and efficient public administration are key areas that require attention and reform. With a comprehensive approach that emphasizes transparency, accountability, and the active participation of citizens, Nepal can build a strong foundation for sustainable democratic governance that upholds the rights and aspirations of its people.

"The monarchy crumbles, but Nepal's democracy stands tall, unyielding."

Electoral Processes and Political Parties in Nepal: A Comprehensive Analysis

This chapter provides an in-depth analysis of the electoral processes and political parties in Nepal. It explores the historical context of electoral systems in the country, the evolution of political parties, their ideologies, and their impact on governance. Additionally, the chapter discusses the challenges faced by Nepal's electoral processes and suggests potential reforms to strengthen democracy in the nation.

The introduction sets the context and significance of examining electoral processes and political parties in Nepal. It outlines the objectives of the chapter, which include analyzing the historical perspective of electoral systems, understanding the evolution of political parties, assessing the challenges faced by Nepal's electoral processes, and suggesting reforms to strengthen democracy.

- ***Historical Perspective of Electoral Processes in Nepal:*** This section explores the historical context of electoral systems in Nepal, starting from the pre-democratic era to the introduction of multiparty democracy. It discusses the constitutional developments and reforms that have shaped the electoral landscape in the country.
- ***Electoral Systems in Nepal:*** Here, we delve into the major electoral reforms undertaken in Nepal and explain the different electoral systems used in the country. The focus is on the proportional representation system, the first-past-the-post system, and the mixed electoral system, highlighting their advantages and disadvantages.
- ***Political Parties in Nepal: Evolution and Ideologies:*** This section provides an overview of the evolution of political parties in Nepal, starting from the early parties to the major ones that exist today. It discusses the ideological spectrum of political parties, their structures, and internal dynamics.
- ***Challenges in Nepal's Electoral Processes:*** The chapter examines the challenges faced by Nepal's electoral processes, including issues related to voter registration, electoral violence, corruption, ethnic and regional disparities, and gender representation. Each challenge is discussed in detail, highlighting its impact on the electoral system and democracy in Nepal.

- ***Role of Political Parties in Governance:*** This section explores the crucial role played by political parties in governance. It discusses party competition, coalition politics, party funding, campaign finance, party discipline, and internal democracy. Special emphasis is placed on the relationship between political parties and policy formulation.
- ***Reforms for Strengthening Democracy in Nepal:*** To address the challenges identified earlier, this section suggests a range of reforms aimed at strengthening democracy in Nepal. It includes recommendations for enhancing electoral transparency, strengthening the Election Commission, addressing identity and representation issues, promoting women's political participation, and encouraging grassroots democracy.
- ***Case Studies: Recent Elections in Nepal:*** This section analyzes recent elections held in Nepal, focusing on the election results, voter turnout, and participation. It also explores the role of election observation and monitoring in ensuring free and fair elections.
- ***Comparative Analysis: International Electoral Systems:*** Drawing on the experiences of neighboring countries and international examples, this section provides a comparative analysis of different electoral systems. It highlights the strengths and weaknesses of these systems and draws lessons that can be applied to Nepal's electoral processes.

The final section summarizes the key findings of the chapter and offers insights into the future prospects of Nepal's electoral processes. It reiterates the importance of addressing the identified challenges and implementing necessary reforms to foster a robust democratic system in the country.

By providing a comprehensive analysis of electoral processes and political parties in Nepal, this chapter aims to contribute to a better understanding of the country's democratic journey. It emphasizes the significance of continuous reforms and effective governance in ensuring a fair and inclusive electoral system that upholds the principles of democracy.

"As the old guard steps down, Nepal's democracy rises, unfurling like a flag in the wind."

The Contribution of All Prime Ministers: From Mr. K.P. Bhattarai to the Present Prime Minister of Nepal

Nepal, a landlocked country nestled in the Himalayas, has witnessed significant political transformations since its transition from an absolute monarchy to a democratic republic. Throughout its history, Nepal has been led by several Prime Ministers who have played crucial roles in shaping the nation's political, socio-economic, and cultural landscape. This chapter aims to explore the contributions made by each Prime Minister, from Mr. K.P. Bhattarai, the first Prime Minister of Nepal, to the present Prime Minister, in the development and progress of the country.

- ***Mr. K.P. Bhattarai:*** Mr. K.P. Bhattarai served as the first Prime Minister of Nepal after the overthrow of the Rana regime in 1951. He played a pivotal role in establishing democracy and transforming Nepal into a constitutional monarchy. Bhattarai's government implemented various reforms, including the abolition of untouchability, the promotion of women's rights, and the establishment of educational institutions. His tenure laid the foundation for democratic governance in Nepal.
- ***Mr. Tanka Prasad Acharya:*** Mr. Tanka Prasad Acharya served as the Prime Minister of Nepal from 1956 to 1957. His government focused on strengthening Nepal's diplomatic relations with other countries and implementing socio-economic reforms. Acharya's tenure witnessed the establishment of Nepal's first five-year development plan, which aimed to accelerate economic growth and reduce poverty.
- ***Mr. Bishweshwar Prasad Koirala:*** Mr. Bishweshwar Prasad Koirala, a prominent political figure, served as Nepal's Prime Minister multiple times, with his first term beginning in 1959. Koirala played a crucial role in promulgating Nepal's first democratic constitution in 1959. He also emphasized economic development, education, and land reforms. Koirala's contributions to Nepal's political development and nation-building are widely acknowledged.
- ***Mr. Surya Bahadur Thapa:*** Mr. Surya Bahadur Thapa served as Prime Minister of Nepal on five different occasions, starting from 1963 to 1999. Thapa's leadership focused on maintaining political stability and national

security. He introduced economic policies that aimed to foster industrialization and reduce poverty. Thapa's contributions to Nepal's foreign policy and strengthening regional cooperation were notable during his tenure.

- ***Mr. Girija Prasad Koirala:*** Mr. Girija Prasad Koirala, a prominent figure in Nepalese politics, served as the Prime Minister of Nepal multiple times. His leadership played a significant role in Nepal's transition from an absolute monarchy to a constitutional republic in 2008. Koirala's government implemented various socio-economic reforms, including the abolition of the monarchy, the establishment of a federal democratic republic, and the promotion of inclusive governance.
- ***Mr. Pushpa Kamal Dahal "Prachanda":*** Mr. Pushpa Kamal Dahal, also known as Prachanda, served as the Prime Minister of Nepal from 2008 to 2009 and again from 2016 to 2017. As the leader of the Communist Party of Nepal (Maoist), Prachanda played a significant role in the peace process that followed the ten-year-long Maoist insurgency. His government focused on post-conflict reconstruction, integration of former Maoist combatants into the security forces, and the drafting of a new constitution. Prachanda's leadership contributed to the strengthening of Nepal's democratic institutions and the promotion of social inclusion.
- ***Mr. Madhav Kumar Nepal:*** Mr. Madhav Kumar Nepal served as the Prime Minister of Nepal from 2009 to 2011. During his tenure, Nepal faced political instability and challenges in the drafting of a new constitution. Nepal's government worked towards promoting good governance, economic development, and social justice. Although his term was marked by political controversies, Nepal's contributions to Nepal's democratic transition cannot be overlooked.
- ***Mr. Jhala Nath Khanal:*** Mr. Jhala Nath Khanal served as the Prime Minister of Nepal from 2011 to 2011. His tenure focused on the formation of a national consensus government and the successful completion of the peace process. Khanal's government took steps to address the issues of marginalized communities and promote regional cooperation. However, his term was short-lived, and he faced challenges in managing the political dynamics of the country.
- ***Mr. Baburam Bhattarai:*** Mr. Baburam Bhattarai served as the Prime Minister of Nepal from 2011 to 2013. Bhattarai, a former Maoist leader, played a crucial role in the peace process and the drafting of Nepal's new constitution. His government focused on economic reforms, infrastructure development, and the integration of former Maoist combatants into society.

Bhattarai's tenure was marked by efforts to bridge the political divide and promote inclusive governance.

- ***Mr. Sushil Koirala:*** Mr. Sushil Koirala served as the Prime Minister of Nepal from 2014 to 2015. His government's primary focus was on the post-earthquake reconstruction efforts following the devastating earthquakes that hit Nepal in 2015. Koirala's administration worked towards political stability, economic growth, and the drafting of a new constitution. His leadership contributed to the rebuilding and recovery of the nation in the aftermath of the natural disaster.
- ***Mr. K.P. Sharma Oli:*** Mr. K.P. Sharma Oli has served as the Prime Minister of Nepal on two separate occasions, first from 2015 to 2016 and again from 2018 to 2021. Oli's government prioritized infrastructure development, economic growth, and foreign relations. His administration played a crucial role in the successful promulgation of Nepal's new constitution in 2015. Oli's tenure also witnessed advancements in regional connectivity, particularly through initiatives like the Belt and Road Initiative.

"The monarchy's fall echoes the rise of a new era for Nepal — the era of democracy."

---

9. INCLUSION & SOCIAL TRANSFORMATION

"The transition from monarchy to democracy heralds a new dawn of citizens participation and accountability"

Marginalized Groups and Their Inclusion in the Political Sphere: Empowering Democracy

In democratic societies, the political sphere should be a space where all individuals, regardless of their background, have an equal opportunity to participate and contribute to decision-making processes. However, historically, certain groups have been systematically marginalized, facing various forms of discrimination and exclusion from the political arena. In recent years, there has been a growing recognition of the importance of including marginalized groups in the political sphere to ensure a more representative and inclusive democracy. This chapter explores the significance of including marginalized groups in politics and the challenges they face, while highlighting the potential benefits of their participation.

Defining Marginalized Groups

Marginalized groups encompass a diverse range of individuals who have been historically disadvantaged, discriminated against, or excluded from mainstream society due to various factors such as race, ethnicity, gender, socioeconomic status, religion, sexual orientation, disability, or political affiliation. These groups often face systemic barriers that hinder their political participation and representation.

The Importance of Political Inclusion

- ***Enhancing Democracy:*** Including marginalized groups in the political sphere is crucial for the health and vitality of a democratic society. Democracy thrives on diversity and the representation of different perspectives. By ensuring the participation of marginalized groups, societies can benefit from a broader range of viewpoints and experiences, leading to more informed and inclusive policy decisions.
- ***Addressing Inequality and Social Justice:*** Political inclusion provides marginalized groups with a platform to address the structural inequalities and social injustices they face. By participating in the political process, these groups can advocate for policies that address their specific needs and promote social equity. Inclusive

political systems contribute to the dismantling of systemic barriers and the creation of a more just and equal society.

Challenges Faced by Marginalized Groups in Political Participation

- ***Structural Barriers:*** Marginalized groups often encounter structural barriers that limit their access to political participation. These barriers may include discriminatory laws, voter suppression tactics, limited resources for political campaigns, and exclusionary political party structures. Overcoming these barriers requires concerted efforts to create inclusive political systems that actively address and dismantle discriminatory practices.
- ***Lack of Representation:*** Marginalized groups are frequently underrepresented in political institutions. This underrepresentation perpetuates a cycle of marginalization, as policies and decisions made in the absence of diverse voices may fail to address the needs and concerns of these groups. Increasing representation through quotas, affirmative action policies, and targeted support can help overcome this challenge and ensure diverse perspectives are heard and considered.

Strategies for Inclusive Political Participation

- ***Education and Awareness:*** Promoting political education and awareness within marginalized communities is crucial for fostering political engagement. By providing resources, information, and training on civic rights, responsibilities, and political processes, individuals from marginalized groups can develop the confidence and knowledge necessary to participate actively in politics.
- ***Building Coalitions and Alliances:*** Forming alliances and coalitions with like-minded organizations and individuals can amplify the voices of marginalized groups. By working together, these groups can advocate for their shared interests, pool resources, and strengthen their collective impact on political decision-making.
- ***Empowering Grassroots Movements:*** Supporting grassroots movements is instrumental in creating political change and increasing the visibility of marginalized groups. These movements often serve as catalysts for social and political transformation, mobilizing marginalized communities, raising awareness, and

putting pressure on policymakers to address their concerns. Providing financial and organizational support to grassroots initiatives can help empower marginalized groups and amplify their voices in the political sphere.

- ***Policy Reforms and Affirmative Action:*** Implementing policy reforms that promote the inclusion of marginalized groups is vital. Affirmative action measures, such as quotas or reserved seats, can help increase representation and ensure that marginalized communities have a fair chance to participate in political processes. These policies should be accompanied by comprehensive support systems to address any disadvantages faced by marginalized individuals.

Benefits of Inclusive Political Participation

- ***Diverse Perspectives and Innovative Solutions:*** When marginalized groups are included in the political sphere, a broader range of perspectives and experiences are represented. This diversity of thought leads to more innovative and effective policy solutions. By bringing their unique insights to the table, marginalized communities can contribute to the development of inclusive policies that benefit society as a whole.
- ***Strengthening Trust and Legitimacy:*** Inclusive political participation helps build trust and legitimacy in the democratic process. When marginalized groups see themselves represented and their concerns addressed, they are more likely to have faith in the political system and actively participate in civic life. This, in turn, strengthens the overall legitimacy of democratic institutions.
- ***Empowerment and Social Change:*** Political inclusion empowers marginalized individuals and communities, giving them a sense of agency and ownership over their lives. When marginalized groups see themselves as active participants in the political process, they are more likely to engage in other forms of social and civic activism, leading to broader social change and the dismantling of systemic oppression.

Case Studies of Successful Inclusion Efforts

- ***Women's Political Empowerment:*** Efforts to increase women's political representation have gained significant momentum in recent years. Countries such as Rwanda and Bolivia have implemented quotas that have resulted in a significant increase in women's representation in their national legislatures. These initiatives have not only improved gender equality but have also contributed to the development of gender-responsive policies.
- ***Indigenous Rights Movements:*** Indigenous communities around the world have fought for their rights and political inclusion. In countries like Canada and New Zealand, indigenous groups have successfully advocated for increased representation and the recognition of indigenous rights. These efforts have led to the implementation of policies that address historical injustices and promote indigenous self-determination.

The inclusion of marginalized groups in the political sphere is not only a matter of justice and equality but also a fundamental requirement for a thriving democracy. By breaking down barriers, increasing representation, and fostering inclusive political systems, societies can harness the immense potential of diverse perspectives and experiences. Efforts to empower marginalized communities and ensure their active participation in politics are essential for creating a more inclusive and equitable society. Through these collective endeavors, we can build a political landscape that truly represents the interests and aspirations of all individuals, regardless of their background or social standing.

"Nepal's democratic journey is a bridge connecting its past to a future of freedom."

Empowering Dalit Rights, Ethnic Autonomy, and Federalism in Nepal

Nepal, a diverse nation nestled in the heart of the Himalayas, has long grappled with issues of social inequality, ethnic discrimination, and power centralization. Over the years, the country has made significant strides towards addressing these concerns through the promotion of Dalit rights, ethnic autonomy, and the implementation of federalism. This chapter aims to explore these three interconnected themes, highlighting their importance, challenges faced, and the potential for transformative change in Nepal's societal fabric.

Dalit Rights:

- ***Historical context:*** The plight of Dalits in Nepal and their struggle for social, economic, and political equality.
- ***Legal framework and policy initiatives:*** Legislative measures and constitutional provisions aimed at protecting and promoting Dalit rights.
- ***Challenges and setbacks:*** Deep-rooted social prejudices, discrimination, and structural barriers hindering the effective implementation of Dalit rights.
- ***Empowerment initiatives:*** Grassroots movements, civil society organizations, and government programs working towards Dalit upliftment.
- ***The way forward:*** Strategies for enhancing Dalit rights, including education, economic empowerment, and affirmative action policies.

Ethnic Autonomy:

- ***Ethnic diversity in Nepal:*** A mosaic of ethnic communities and the significance of preserving their unique cultural identities.
- ***Historical marginalization:*** The socio-political exclusion of ethnic groups and their struggle for recognition, representation, and autonomy.

- ***Devolution of power:*** The concept of ethnic autonomy within the framework of federalism and its potential for fostering inclusivity and participatory governance.
- ***Ethnic federalism in practice:*** An overview of Nepal's efforts to implement ethnic autonomy through the restructuring of administrative divisions.
- ***Challenges and prospects:*** Addressing concerns related to ethnic tensions, resource distribution, and balancing autonomy with national unity.

<u>Federalism in Nepal:</u>

- ***Context and rationale:*** The transition from a unitary to a federal system in Nepal to address regional disparities and decentralize power.
- ***Federal structure:*** The division of power between the federal, provincial, and local levels of government and its impact on governance and service delivery.
- ***Constitutional framework:*** The constitutional provisions and legal mechanisms promoting federalism, including intergovernmental relations and revenue-sharing mechanisms.
- ***Challenges and implementation issues:*** Administrative capacity building, fiscal decentralization, and ensuring equal representation and participation.
- ***Future prospects:*** The potential benefits of federalism in promoting equitable development, local empowerment, and strengthening democratic institutions.

<u>Intersectionality: Overlapping Challenges and Synergies:</u>

- ***Understanding intersectionality:*** The interconnected nature of Dalit rights, ethnic autonomy, and federalism, and how they intersect with other social issues such as gender inequality, poverty, and access to education and healthcare.
- ***Amplifying marginalized voices:*** Recognizing the multiple layers of discrimination faced by individuals who belong to marginalized communities and the need for inclusive policies that address their unique challenges.

- ***Collaborative approaches:*** Exploring the potential for collaboration and synergy between movements advocating for Dalit rights, ethnic autonomy, and federalism, to create a stronger collective voice against social injustice and discrimination.
- ***Inclusive policymaking:*** The importance of involving representatives from marginalized communities in the decision-making process to ensure that policies are inclusive and address the specific needs of these communities.
- ***Promoting social cohesion:*** Fostering dialogue and understanding between different ethnic and social groups to build bridges and promote social cohesion within the framework of federalism and ethnic autonomy.

International Perspectives and Best Practices:

- ***Comparative analysis:*** Examining international experiences of countries that have successfully implemented measures to promote Dalit rights, ethnic autonomy, and federalism, and drawing lessons from their successes and challenges.
- ***Global frameworks:*** Analyzing international conventions, declarations, and guidelines that emphasize the importance of protecting minority rights and promoting inclusive governance.
- **International support:** Highlighting the role of international organizations, NGOs, and donor agencies in supporting Nepal's efforts to promote social justice, human rights, and inclusive development.
- **Learning from neighboring countries:** Understanding the experiences of countries in the region, such as India, Bhutan, and Sri Lanka, in addressing similar challenges and implementing policies to ensure the rights and autonomy of marginalized communities.
- **Building regional networks:** Exploring opportunities for cross-border collaboration, knowledge-sharing, and cooperation to address common challenges and promote the rights of marginalized communities across South Asia.

Call to Action:

- **Advocacy and awareness:** Emphasizing the need for continued advocacy and awareness campaigns to challenge social norms, prejudices, and discriminatory practices that perpetuate inequality and marginalization.

- **Strengthening institutional mechanisms:** Calling for the establishment of robust institutional frameworks to monitor and enforce Dalit rights, ethnic autonomy, and federalism, and to ensure accountability and transparency in their implementation.
- **Education and empowerment:** Promoting inclusive education and capacity-building programs that empower marginalized communities to be active participants in decision-making processes and contribute to the nation's development.
- **Collaboration and dialogue:** Encouraging dialogue and collaboration between government institutions, civil society organizations, and marginalized communities to foster understanding, trust, and joint action towards social justice and empowerment.
- **International support:** Urging the international community to continue supporting Nepal's efforts through technical assistance, capacity building, and financial resources to strengthen Dalit rights, ethnic autonomy, and federalism.

Nepal stands at a critical juncture in its quest for social justice, inclusion, and equitable development. The promotion of Dalit rights, ethnic autonomy, and federalism is integral to this transformative journey. By recognizing the intersecting challenges faced by marginalized communities, advocating for their rights, and implementing inclusive policies, Nepal can pave the way for a more equal and just society. It is imperative for all stakeholders, including government institutions, civil society organizations, international partners, and individuals, to unite their efforts and work collaboratively towards creating a society where every individual, regardless of their caste, ethnicity, or background, can enjoy equal rights, opportunities, and dignity.

To achieve this vision, it is crucial to address the deep-rooted social prejudices and discrimination that hinder the realization of Dalit rights, ethnic autonomy, and effective federalism. This requires comprehensive strategies that encompass legal reforms, awareness campaigns, and social mobilization efforts. It is essential to empower marginalized communities through education, skill development programs, and economic opportunities, enabling them to participate actively in decision-making processes and shape their own destinies.

Furthermore, fostering an environment of dialogue, understanding, and cooperation among different ethnic and social groups is essential for building a cohesive and inclusive society. By promoting cultural diversity, recognizing the value of each community's heritage, and encouraging intergroup interactions, Nepal can strengthen its social fabric and foster a sense of shared identity within the framework of federalism and ethnic autonomy.

International experiences and best practices offer valuable insights and lessons for Nepal's journey towards social justice. By studying successful models from around the world and learning from the experiences of neighboring countries, Nepal can adapt and implement effective strategies tailored to its unique context. Engaging in regional collaborations and networks can also provide opportunities for knowledge exchange, mutual support, and collective action to address common challenges faced by marginalized communities across South Asia.

Ultimately, the transformation of Nepal into an inclusive, equitable, and just society requires sustained commitment, collaboration, and a long-term vision. It demands the active involvement and participation of all stakeholders, including government agencies, civil society organizations, marginalized communities themselves, and the international community. By working together, Nepal can overcome the challenges, realize the full potential of Dalit rights, ethnic autonomy, and federalism, and build a prosperous and harmonious nation that celebrates diversity and ensures equality for all.

"From the throne to the ballot, Nepal's journey is a paradigm shift towards people's power."

---

10. ECONOMIC DEVELOPMENT & DEMOCRACY

"Democracy in Nepal empowers individuals to shape their own destinities and actively participate in the nation's progress"

Economic Challenges and Opportunities in Nepal: A Comprehensive Analysis

Nepal, a landlocked country nestled in the lap of the Himalayas, has long been grappling with numerous economic challenges while also presenting promising opportunities for growth and development. With a rich cultural heritage and abundant natural resources, Nepal has the potential to transform its economy and improve the living standards of its people. However, several key hurdles must be addressed to unlock its true economic potential. This chapter aims to delve into the economic challenges and opportunities that Nepal faces and provide an in-depth analysis of the way forward.

- ***Political Instability and Governance:*** One of the most significant economic challenges in Nepal is the persistent political instability and governance issues. Frequent changes in government and political unrest have created an uncertain environment for businesses and investors. Weak governance, corruption, and bureaucratic inefficiencies hinder the ease of doing business and discourage foreign direct investment (FDI). Addressing these issues through effective governance reforms is crucial to foster stability and attract economic opportunities.
- ***Infrastructure Development:*** Nepal's underdeveloped infrastructure is another major obstacle to economic growth. Insufficient road networks, inadequate power supply, and limited access to modern transportation systems hinder trade and connectivity within the country. Investments in infrastructure projects, such as road and railway networks, hydropower plants, and urban development initiatives, can unlock tremendous economic potential, boost tourism, and facilitate trade both domestically and internationally.
- ***Agricultural Sector Modernization:*** Agriculture forms the backbone of Nepal's economy, employing a significant portion of the population. However, the sector faces numerous challenges, including low productivity, outdated farming practices, and a heavy reliance on traditional subsistence farming. Modernizing the agricultural sector through the adoption of advanced farming techniques, providing access to credit and technology, and

improving irrigation systems can enhance productivity, increase rural incomes, and reduce poverty.

- ***Diversification and Industrialization:*** Nepal's heavy reliance on a few key sectors, such as agriculture and tourism, leaves its economy vulnerable to external shocks. Diversification and industrialization are essential to achieve sustainable economic growth. Encouraging the growth of manufacturing industries, promoting entrepreneurship and innovation, and attracting investment in sectors such as information technology, renewable energy, and manufacturing can create employment opportunities, reduce dependency on imports, and boost exports.
- ***Human Capital Development:*** Investing in human capital is critical for Nepal's economic progress. Despite having a young and vibrant workforce, the country struggles with high levels of unemployment and underemployment. Enhancing the quality of education, improving vocational and technical training programs, and fostering entrepreneurship can equip Nepali youth with the skills needed for the job market. Additionally, promoting gender equality and social inclusion will unlock the untapped potential of marginalized groups, contributing to overall economic development.
- ***Sustainable Tourism:*** Nepal's breathtaking landscapes, rich cultural heritage, and diverse wildlife make it a prime destination for tourism. However, the sector faces challenges such as inadequate infrastructure, limited promotion, and environmental concerns. By enhancing infrastructure, implementing sustainable tourism practices, and increasing marketing efforts, Nepal can attract a higher number of tourists, create employment opportunities, and generate foreign exchange earnings, thereby contributing to economic growth.
- ***Harnessing Renewable Energy:*** Nepal is blessed with abundant renewable energy resources, including hydropower, solar, and wind. However, the country still relies heavily on imported fossil fuels for its energy needs. Harnessing its renewable energy potential through the development of hydropower projects, incentivizing the use of solar and wind energy, and promoting energy efficiency measures can reduce dependency on fossil fuels, enhance energy security, and open up opportunities for clean energy exports.
- ***Trade and Regional Integration:*** Nepal's geographical location between two economic powerhouses, India and China, offers immense opportunities for trade and regional integration. However, the country faces challenges

related to trade barriers, inadequate trade infrastructure, and complex customs procedures. Strengthening trade ties with neighboring countries, improving cross-border connectivity, and simplifying trade procedures can enhance Nepal's access to regional markets, promote export-oriented industries, and stimulate economic growth.

- ***Financial Inclusion and Access to Credit:*** Access to finance remains a significant challenge for entrepreneurs, especially in rural areas. Limited access to credit hampers business growth and stifles entrepreneurial potential. Expanding financial inclusion through the establishment of microfinance institutions, promoting digital banking services, and implementing supportive policies to encourage lending to small and medium-sized enterprises (SMEs) can spur economic activity, create jobs, and uplift marginalized communities.
- ***Disaster Resilience and Climate Change Adaptation:*** Nepal is highly vulnerable to natural disasters, including earthquakes, floods, and landslides. These events not only result in loss of lives and infrastructure but also cause severe economic setbacks. Strengthening disaster preparedness and response mechanisms, investing in resilient infrastructure, and promoting climate change adaptation measures are crucial for safeguarding lives, protecting assets, and ensuring sustainable economic development in the face of climate-related risks.

Nepal stands at a critical juncture in its economic journey, facing numerous challenges while also harboring significant opportunities. Addressing the issues of political instability, infrastructure development, agricultural sector modernization, diversification, human capital development, sustainable tourism, renewable energy, trade facilitation, financial inclusion, and disaster resilience is essential to unlock Nepal's true economic potential.

"The crown is retired, and Nepal dons the cap of democracy, worn proudly by its people."

Role and Contribution of India in the Development of Nepal

India and Nepal share a unique and multifaceted relationship, characterized by historical, cultural, and geographical ties. Over the years, India has played a significant role in the development of Nepal across various fields. This chapter aims to explore and highlight India's contributions to Nepal's development in key areas, encompassing economic cooperation, infrastructure development, education and healthcare, cultural exchanges, and security cooperation.

- ***Economic Cooperation:*** India has been a major economic partner of Nepal, providing substantial support for its development. Both countries have signed several bilateral agreements, including trade and investment promotion, double taxation avoidance, and transportation. India's economic assistance has contributed to the growth of Nepal's infrastructure, agriculture, energy, and tourism sectors. Financial aid, grants, and concessional loans from India have facilitated the implementation of various development projects, such as roads, bridges, hydropower plants, and irrigation schemes.
- ***Infrastructure Development:*** India has played a significant role in the development of Nepal's infrastructure. Cross-border connectivity projects, such as the construction of highways, bridges, and railways, have enhanced trade and people-to-people connectivity between the two countries. Projects like the Mahakali Bridge, the Integrated Check Posts, and the Raxaul-Kathmandu railway have strengthened Nepal's transportation network and facilitated bilateral trade. India's technical expertise and financial support have been instrumental in the construction and upgradation of critical infrastructure in Nepal.
- ***Education and Healthcare:*** India has actively contributed to the development of education and healthcare sectors in Nepal. Scholarships and educational exchange programs have allowed Nepalese students to pursue higher education in Indian universities, fostering academic and cultural ties. India has also supported the establishment of educational institutions, including schools, colleges, and vocational training centers, in different regions of Nepal. In the healthcare sector, India has provided medical

assistance, technical expertise, and training to Nepalese healthcare professionals, contributing to improved healthcare facilities and services.

- ***Cultural Exchanges:*** Cultural exchanges between India and Nepal have been an integral part of their bilateral relationship. The shared cultural heritage and religious ties have facilitated the exchange of art, music, dance, and literature. Festivals like Dashain, Tihar, and Holi are celebrated with great enthusiasm in both countries. India has supported the preservation and restoration of historical and cultural sites in Nepal, including the Pashupatinath Temple and Lumbini, the birthplace of Lord Buddha. These cultural exchanges have fostered mutual understanding and strengthened the people-to-people bonds between India and Nepal.
- ***Security Cooperation:*** India has been actively involved in enhancing Nepal's security capabilities through various means. The two countries have collaborated on border security, intelligence sharing, and counterterrorism efforts. India has provided training and equipment to the Nepalese security forces, contributing to the maintenance of peace and stability in the region. Cooperation in disaster management, search and rescue operations, and humanitarian assistance has been crucial in addressing natural calamities and emergencies in Nepal.

India's role and contribution to the development of Nepal across various fields have been substantial and far-reaching. Through economic cooperation, infrastructure development, education and healthcare initiatives, cultural exchanges, and security cooperation, India has played a vital role in supporting Nepal's progress and growth. The enduring friendship between the two countries continues to strengthen the bonds between their peoples, fostering regional cooperation and shared prosperity

- ***Tourism and Heritage Conservation:*** India's contribution to Nepal's tourism sector has been significant. The open border between the two countries has facilitated the movement of tourists, allowing Indian tourists to explore Nepal's natural beauty, cultural heritage, and adventure tourism opportunities. India has actively promoted Nepal as a tourist destination and supported the development of tourism infrastructure, including hotels, resorts, and trekking routes. Additionally, India has collaborated with Nepal in the preservation and conservation of heritage sites, recognizing their importance in attracting tourists and promoting cultural exchange.

- ***Energy Cooperation:*** Energy cooperation between India and Nepal has been a crucial aspect of their bilateral relationship. India has supported Nepal in harnessing its hydropower potential, which plays a vital role in addressing Nepal's energy needs and promoting economic growth. Joint projects such as the Upper Karnali and Arun-III hydropower plants have been undertaken with Indian investment and technical assistance. These projects contribute to Nepal's energy security and have the potential to generate revenue through cross-border electricity trade.
- ***Cross-Border Trade and Transit:*** India has facilitated cross-border trade and transit for Nepal, serving as a vital gateway for its imports and exports. Through various agreements and protocols, India has provided transit facilities to Nepal, ensuring smooth movement of goods and enhancing its trade connectivity with the rest of the world. India's ports, including Kolkata and Visakhapatnam, have been crucial transit points for Nepal's trade, reducing landlocked challenges and promoting economic integration.
- ***Humanitarian Assistance and Disaster Relief:*** India has been at the forefront of providing humanitarian assistance and disaster relief to Nepal during times of crisis. Following major earthquakes and natural disasters, India has extended immediate support in terms of rescue operations, medical aid, and relief supplies. The close geographical proximity and historical ties have enabled India to respond swiftly, providing much-needed assistance to Nepal in times of need.
- ***Future Prospects and Challenges:*** While India's contributions to Nepal's development have been significant, there are also challenges that need to be addressed. Ensuring equitable development across regions, enhancing connectivity and infrastructure in remote areas, and addressing trade imbalances are areas that require attention. Strengthening people-to-people ties, promoting cultural exchanges, and expanding educational opportunities can further deepen the relationship between the two countries.

"In every vote cast, Nepal writes its democratic destiny with ink that echoes freedom."

Foreign Aid and Investment in Nepal: Boosting Economic Development

Nepal, a landlocked country nestled in the Himalayas, has been actively seeking foreign aid and investment to accelerate its economic growth and development. Over the years, international assistance and foreign investments have played a crucial role in various sectors, including infrastructure, education, healthcare, and agriculture. This chapter explores the significance and impact of foreign aid and investment in Nepal, highlighting the benefits it brings to the nation.

- ***Foreign Aid and Development Projects:*** Foreign aid has been a key contributor to Nepal's development projects. Bilateral and multilateral aid from countries, organizations, and development agencies has helped finance critical infrastructure projects such as road networks, hydroelectric power plants, and telecommunications. These initiatives have improved connectivity within Nepal and enhanced its ability to attract foreign investment.
- ***Strengthening Healthcare and Education:*** Foreign aid has played a significant role in strengthening Nepal's healthcare and education systems. Donor countries have supported the construction and renovation of hospitals, clinics, and schools, while also providing medical equipment and educational materials. These initiatives have enhanced access to quality healthcare services and improved educational opportunities for Nepali citizens.
- ***Agricultural Development:*** Agriculture forms the backbone of Nepal's economy, and foreign aid has been instrumental in promoting agricultural development. Assistance from international organizations and countries has helped introduce modern farming techniques, irrigation systems, and high-yield crop varieties. These initiatives have increased agricultural productivity, improved food security, and boosted rural incomes.
- ***Employment Opportunities:*** Foreign investment in Nepal has created employment opportunities for the local population. Foreign companies, particularly in sectors such as tourism, manufacturing, and information technology, have set up operations in Nepal, thus generating jobs and stimulating economic growth. This has helped reduce unemployment rates and alleviate poverty in various regions.

- ***Infrastructure Development:*** Foreign investment has played a vital role in infrastructure development in Nepal. Investors from countries such as China, India, and Japan have contributed to the construction of highways, airports, and hydropower projects. These infrastructure developments have not only improved transportation and energy availability but have also attracted more foreign investment by creating a favorable business environment.
- ***Technology Transfer and Knowledge Exchange:*** Foreign aid and investment have facilitated technology transfer and knowledge exchange in Nepal. International collaborations and partnerships have allowed for the transfer of expertise, best practices, and advanced technologies. This exchange has helped Nepal develop its human capital, improve research capabilities, and enhance innovation across various sectors.

Foreign aid and investment have been crucial in Nepal's journey towards economic development. These contributions have helped strengthen infrastructure, healthcare, education, and agriculture, while also creating employment opportunities and fostering technological advancements. By continuing to attract foreign aid and investment, Nepal can further accelerate its progress and improve the quality of life for its citizens, ultimately achieving sustainable development goals.

Financial Aid and Funding by UN Agencies in Nepal's Development: Catalyzing Progress in an Underdeveloped Country

Nepal, a landlocked country nestled in the Himalayas, has long grappled with the challenges of underdevelopment. In its pursuit of progress, the United Nations (UN) and its specialized agencies have played a vital role in providing financial aid and funding to support Nepal's development efforts. This chapter explores the various UN agencies that have contributed to Nepal's development, highlighting their programs, initiatives, and financial assistance, which have been instrumental in catalyzing positive change in the country.

- ***United Nations Development Programme (UNDP):*** The UNDP has been actively engaged in Nepal for several decades, working closely with the government and other stakeholders to address key development challenges. The agency has provided substantial financial aid to support Nepal's efforts in poverty reduction, sustainable livelihoods, governance, and disaster risk reduction. Through its programs, the UNDP has helped strengthen institutions, promote inclusive growth, and enhance capacities at the national and local levels.
- ***United Nations Children's Fund (UNICEF):*** UNICEF has been a steadfast partner in Nepal's development, with a primary focus on improving the well-being of children and women. The agency has allocated substantial funding for initiatives related to education, health, nutrition, child protection, and water and sanitation. UNICEF's support has led to significant advancements in child rights, access to quality education, and the reduction of child mortality rates in Nepal.
- ***World Food Programme (WFP):*** As a country that faces food security challenges, Nepal has received considerable assistance from the WFP. The agency has provided financial aid and technical expertise to enhance food production, storage, and distribution systems. WFP's initiatives have contributed to improving food security, addressing malnutrition, and building resilience among vulnerable communities, particularly in remote and marginalized areas.
- ***United Nations Population Fund (UNFPA):*** UNFPA has been actively involved in Nepal's development agenda, focusing on reproductive health,

gender equality, and population dynamics. The agency has supported programs aimed at improving maternal health, promoting family planning, preventing gender-based violence, and empowering women and girls. UNFPA's financial aid has helped strengthen healthcare services and promote gender-responsive policies and legislation.

- ***United Nations Human Settlements Programme (UN-Habitat):*** Given Nepal's rapid urbanization, UN-Habitat has played a pivotal role in supporting sustainable urban development and improving living conditions in cities and towns. The agency has provided funding for housing projects, urban planning, and the development of basic infrastructure. UN-Habitat's assistance has contributed to building resilient and inclusive cities, enhancing access to affordable housing, and promoting sustainable urban practices.
- ***United Nations Educational, Scientific and Cultural Organization (UNESCO):*** UNESCO has been actively involved in Nepal's education sector, focusing on improving access to quality education, preserving cultural heritage, and promoting media literacy. The agency has allocated financial aid for initiatives such as teacher training, curriculum development, and the restoration of cultural sites. UNESCO's support has helped strengthen education systems, preserve Nepal's rich cultural heritage, and promote cultural diversity.
- ***United Nations Industrial Development Organization (UNIDO):*** UNIDO has been instrumental in supporting Nepal's industrial development and economic growth. The agency has provided financial aid and technical assistance to enhance productivity, promote sustainable industrial practices, and foster entrepreneurship. UNIDO's initiatives have contributed to job creation and economic diversification, particularly in sectors such as manufacturing, renewable energy, and agribusiness.
- ***United Nations Environmental Programme (UNEP):*** As a country with rich biodiversity and environmental challenges, Nepal has received significant support from UNEP. The agency has allocated financial aid for conservation projects, climate change mitigation and adaptation, and the promotion of sustainable natural resource management. UNEP's assistance has contributed to the preservation of Nepal's unique ecosystems, the promotion of renewable energy, and the adoption of environmentally friendly practices.
- ***International Labour Organization (ILO):*** The ILO has been actively engaged in Nepal, focusing on promoting decent work, labor rights, and social protection. The agency has provided financial aid and technical expertise to improve working conditions, enhance skills development, and

combat child labor and forced labor. ILO's support has led to the creation of employment opportunities, the strengthening of labor regulations, and the promotion of social dialogue in Nepal.

- ***World Health Organization (WHO):*** WHO has been a key partner in Nepal's healthcare sector, particularly in the areas of disease prevention, healthcare delivery, and emergency response. The agency has allocated financial aid for initiatives related to immunization, disease control, healthcare infrastructure development, and capacity building. WHO's support has contributed to improving healthcare services, reducing disease burdens, and strengthening epidemic preparedness in Nepal.

The United Nations and its specialized agencies have played a crucial role in supporting Nepal's development as an underdeveloped country. Through their financial aid and funding, these agencies have helped address key challenges in areas such as poverty reduction, education, healthcare, food security, gender equality, and environmental conservation. The support provided by the UN agencies has not only catalyzed positive change but also contributed to building resilience, promoting sustainable practices, and empowering vulnerable communities in Nepal. Continued collaboration between Nepal and the UN agencies will be essential in achieving the country's sustainable development goals and advancing the well-being of its people.

"Democracy in Nepal is not just a system but a spirit, breathing life into the nation."

Contribution of India in the Development of Nepal: Democracy and Post-Democracy

India and Nepal share a unique and multifaceted relationship, characterized by historical, cultural, and geographical ties. Over the years, India has played a significant role in the development of Nepal, particularly in the fields of democracy and post-democracy. This chapter aims to explore the contributions of India in shaping Nepal's democratic journey and its subsequent development in the post-democratic era.

- ***Historical Context:*** India and Nepal's relationship dates back centuries, marked by cultural exchanges, trade, and diplomatic ties. India's influence in Nepal can be traced to historical factors, including the close proximity of the two nations and socio-cultural similarities. The Treaty of Peace and Friendship signed in 1950 laid the foundation for a close and cooperative relationship between India and Nepal.
- ***Democracy in Nepal:*** India has been instrumental in supporting and promoting democracy in Nepal. During Nepal's transition from monarchy to a democratic system in the early 1950s, India provided diplomatic support and played a crucial role in facilitating the process. India's own experience as the world's largest democracy has been a source of inspiration for Nepal, fostering a democratic ethos and values.
- ***Assistance in Democratic Institutions:*** India has extended support to Nepal in strengthening its democratic institutions. This includes providing technical assistance, capacity building, and sharing best practices in governance, electoral processes, and parliamentary procedures. Indian experts and institutions have collaborated with their Nepalese counterparts to enhance the functioning and efficiency of democratic institutions.
- ***Peace Process and Conflict Management:*** Nepal witnessed a decade-long armed conflict between the government and Maoist insurgents, which ended in 2006 with the Comprehensive Peace Agreement (CPA). India played a crucial role in facilitating the peace process, acting as a mediator and providing diplomatic support. The Indian government helped initiate dialogue between the conflicting parties, leading to the successful conclusion of the peace agreement.

- ***Economic Cooperation and Development:*** India has been a key partner in Nepal's economic development. Bilateral trade, investment, and economic cooperation between the two nations have flourished over the years. India has provided financial assistance and development grants to support infrastructure projects, energy cooperation, and socio-economic development initiatives in Nepal. These investments have contributed to Nepal's economic growth and development.
- ***Connectivity and Infrastructure Development:*** India has played a vital role in enhancing connectivity and infrastructure development in Nepal. Projects such as the construction of roads, bridges, and transmission lines have improved transportation networks, facilitated trade, and boosted economic activities. The development of cross-border connectivity has not only strengthened bilateral ties but also contributed to Nepal's overall development.
- ***Educational and Cultural Exchanges:*** India has been a significant source of educational opportunities for Nepalese students. Many Nepalese students pursue higher education in India, benefiting from scholarships and educational exchange programs. Additionally, cultural exchanges between the two countries have fostered mutual understanding, cultural enrichment, and people-to-people ties.
- ***Post-Democracy Assistance:*** Following the promulgation of Nepal's new constitution in 2015, India has continued to support Nepal in its post-democracy phase. This includes assistance in constitutional implementation, federalism, and governance reforms. India has shared its own experiences and lessons learned from its federal structure, assisting Nepal in addressing challenges related to devolution of power and governance.
- ***Disaster Management and Humanitarian Assistance:*** Nepal is prone to natural disasters, including earthquakes, floods, and landslides. India has been at the forefront of providing disaster management and humanitarian assistance to Nepal. During times of crisis, such as the devastating earthquakes in 2015, India promptly mobilized resources, including relief materials, medical aid, and search-and-rescue teams. India's assistance has been critical in mitigating the impact of disasters and supporting Nepal in its recovery and rebuilding efforts.
- ***Cross-Border Cooperation:*** India and Nepal have actively engaged in cross-border cooperation on various fronts. This includes cooperation in areas such as trade facilitation, transit routes, energy sharing, tourism promotion,

and cultural exchanges. These collaborative efforts have not only strengthened bilateral ties but have also contributed to Nepal's socio-economic development, job creation, and revenue generation.

- ***Challenges and the Way Forward:*** While India's contributions to Nepal's development have been substantial, challenges and areas for improvement exist. Some key challenges include addressing border issues, managing trade imbalances, ensuring equitable distribution of benefits from development projects, and enhancing coordination in policy implementation. It is crucial for both nations to continue engaging in open dialogue and collaborative efforts to address these challenges and further strengthen their partnership.

In the future, India and Nepal can work together to enhance people-to-people ties, promote tourism, and foster cultural exchanges. Strengthening trade and investment cooperation, particularly in sectors such as agriculture, manufacturing, and services, can contribute to Nepal's economic growth and job creation. Collaboration in areas of renewable energy, water resource management, and climate change adaptation can also be prioritized to address common challenges.

India's contributions to Nepal's development, particularly in the realms of democracy and post-democracy, have been significant. From supporting Nepal's democratic transition to providing assistance in governance, infrastructure, education, and disaster management, India has played a crucial role in shaping Nepal's development trajectory. The partnership between India and Nepal continues to evolve, with a focus on addressing challenges, promoting sustainable development, and fostering mutual cooperation. By further strengthening their collaboration, India and Nepal can create a prosperous and inclusive future for their people and deepen the bonds of friendship between the two nations.

Major Projects and Schemes Implemented in Nepal by India

India and Nepal share a long-standing relationship marked by mutual cooperation and collaboration in various sectors. Over the years, India has implemented several major projects and schemes in Nepal, contributing to the country's socio-economic development. This chapter aims to provide an overview of some of the key projects and schemes implemented by India in Nepal, highlighting their objectives, impact, and significance.

Pancheshwar Multipurpose Project:

The Pancheshwar Multipurpose Project is a joint venture between India and Nepal aimed at harnessing the potential of the Mahakali River. The project entails the construction of a large dam, generating hydroelectric power and facilitating irrigation. It has the potential to contribute significantly to Nepal's energy needs and enhance irrigation facilities, thereby promoting agricultural productivity and rural development.

Integrated Check Posts (ICPs):

India has established Integrated Check Posts at various border points with Nepal to facilitate trade and transit activities. These ICPs, such as the Raxaul-Birgunj and Jogbani-Biratnagar ICPs, provide modern infrastructure and streamlined processes for customs clearance, thereby promoting bilateral trade and enhancing cross-border economic activities.

Postal Highway Project:

The Postal Highway Project, also known as the Hulaki Rajmarg, is a significant infrastructure project implemented by India in Nepal. The project aims to upgrade and expand the road network, connecting various regions of Nepal. The improved connectivity enhances trade, transportation, and accessibility, promoting economic growth and improving the livelihoods of people living in remote areas.

Arun-III Hydropower Project:

The Arun-III Hydropower Project is a flagship project in Nepal's energy sector, developed with Indian investment and expertise. With a capacity of 900 MW, the project is expected to contribute significantly to Nepal's energy generation, addressing the country's power deficit and promoting industrial growth. It also provides opportunities for revenue generation and employment creation.

Raxaul-Amlekhgunj Petroleum Pipeline:

The Raxaul-Amlekhgunj Petroleum Pipeline is a landmark project that has enhanced the efficiency and reliability of petroleum supply in Nepal. The pipeline, stretching from Raxaul in India to Amlekhgunj in Nepal, eliminates the reliance on tankers and ensures a continuous and cost-effective supply of petroleum products. This project has had a positive impact on Nepal's energy security and reduced transportation costs.

Cross-Border Transmission Lines:

India has supported the development of cross-border transmission lines to facilitate the exchange of electricity between the two countries. Projects such as the Dhalkebar-Muzaffarpur and Butwal-Gorakhpur transmission lines have strengthened the power connectivity, allowing for the import and export of electricity. This cooperation has played a crucial role in addressing Nepal's energy demand and diversifying its energy sources.

Mahakali Bridge:

The Mahakali Bridge, also known as the Banbasa Bridge, is a vital infrastructure project linking India and Nepal. The bridge, spanning the Mahakali River, enhances connectivity and trade between the two nations. It serves as a strategic trade route, facilitating the movement of goods, people, and services, and promoting economic integration.

Scholarship Schemes:

India has been providing scholarships to Nepalese students at various levels of education. Schemes such as the Indian Technical and Economic Cooperation (ITEC) and the General Cultural Scholarship

Scheme (GCSS) offer opportunities for Nepalese students to pursue higher education in India. These scholarships cover a wide range of disciplines, including engineering, medicine, agriculture, and social sciences, enabling students to gain knowledge and skills that contribute to Nepal's human resource development.

Health and Medical Assistance:

India has extended support to Nepal in the field of healthcare, including medical assistance and capacity building. Indian medical teams have been deployed in Nepal during emergencies and natural disasters to provide immediate medical relief. Additionally, India has facilitated the training of Nepalese medical professionals in Indian hospitals and institutions, strengthening Nepal's healthcare system.

Border Infrastructure Development:

India has undertaken projects to develop border infrastructure, including roads, bridges, and customs facilities. This infrastructure development improves connectivity and facilitates trade and transit activities between India and Nepal. Upgrades to border crossing points such as the

Biratnagar-Belahiya and Nepalganj Road Network have enhanced efficiency and ease of movement across the border.

Cultural Preservation and Restoration:

India has supported the preservation and restoration of cultural heritage sites in Nepal. Projects such as the restoration of earthquake-damaged temples and monuments in Kathmandu's Durbar Square have been undertaken with Indian assistance. These initiatives contribute to the preservation of Nepal's rich cultural heritage and promote tourism, which is vital for economic growth.

Agriculture and Rural Development:

India has implemented various projects in the agriculture sector to enhance agricultural productivity and rural development in Nepal. Initiatives include the provision of agricultural machinery, training programs for farmers, and support for agro-processing units. These projects aim to improve farm productivity, income generation, and food security in rural areas.

Vocational Training and Skill Development:

India has collaborated with Nepal in the field of vocational training and skill development. Skill development programs, such as the Skill India initiative, have been extended to Nepalese youth, equipping them with industry-relevant skills. These programs enhance employment prospects and contribute to Nepal's efforts in reducing unemployment and promoting economic growth.

Disaster Management and Relief Assistance:

India has been at the forefront of providing disaster management and relief assistance to Nepal during times of crises. This includes immediate relief aid, medical support, search-and-rescue teams, and reconstruction assistance in the aftermath of natural disasters, such as earthquakes and floods. India's assistance has played a crucial role in alleviating human suffering and supporting Nepal's recovery efforts.

The projects and schemes implemented by India in Nepal cover a wide range of sectors, including infrastructure development, energy, education, healthcare, agriculture, and disaster management. These initiatives have contributed significantly to Nepal's socio-economic development, addressing key challenges and fostering bilateral cooperation. The collaboration between India and Nepal in various fields underscores the close ties and shared aspirations between the two nations. Continued efforts and strengthened partnerships will further enhance the development trajectory of Nepal, promoting prosperity and well-being for its people.

"Nepal's democratic tapestry is woven with threads of sacrifice, hope, and determination."

---

11. INTERNATIONAL PERSPECTIVES & RELATIONS

"Nepal's embrace of democracy showcases the nation's commitment to progress, inclusivity, and well – being of its citizens"

Regional Dynamics and Cooperation in Nepal: A Comprehensive Overview

Nepal, nestled in the lap of the Himalayas, has long been a significant player in regional dynamics and cooperation in South Asia. As a landlocked country situated between two regional giants, India and China, Nepal's geopolitical positioning has shaped its foreign policy and regional engagements. This chapter aims to provide a comprehensive overview of the regional dynamics and cooperation in Nepal, highlighting key aspects such as bilateral relations, economic cooperation, regional organizations, and challenges faced by the country.

<u>Bilateral Relations:</u>

- **Nepal-India Relations:** Nepal shares a unique and complex relationship with its southern neighbor, India. Historically, the two countries have enjoyed close cultural, social, and economic ties. However, bilateral relations have faced occasional challenges, including border disputes, trade imbalances, and political issues. The 2015 Nepal earthquake strained relations, but subsequent efforts have been made to strengthen cooperation in various areas such as trade, infrastructure development, and people-to-people contacts.
- **Nepal-China Relations:** Nepal's northern neighbor, China, has emerged as a significant player in Nepal's regional dynamics. In recent years, Nepal has pursued a policy of enhancing ties with China, primarily through infrastructure projects and economic cooperation. The Belt and Road Initiative (BRI) has been instrumental in fostering connectivity and trade between the two countries. However, concerns have been raised regarding the potential implications of growing Chinese influence in Nepal, leading to a delicate balancing act between India and China.

<u>Economic Cooperation:</u>

- **Trade Relations:** Nepal's economy heavily relies on trade with its neighbors. India has been Nepal's largest trading partner, accounting for a significant share of its imports and exports. Efforts have been made to address trade imbalances and promote a more equitable trading relationship. Additionally, Nepal has sought to diversify its trade by exploring opportunities with other regional partners, including China and countries in Southeast Asia.

- **Cross-Border Infrastructure:** Enhancing cross-border connectivity and infrastructure development has been a key focus of regional cooperation in Nepal. Projects such as the Nepal-India cross-border railway, road networks, and energy cooperation have aimed to foster economic integration and facilitate trade. Similarly, Nepal's participation in the BRI has led to significant investments in infrastructure development, including the construction of roads, bridges, and hydropower projects.

Regional Organizations:

- **South Asian Association for Regional Cooperation (SAARC):** Nepal is an active member of SAARC, a regional organization comprising eight South Asian nations. SAARC aims to promote regional cooperation in various areas, including trade, investment, and cultural exchanges. However, the organization has faced challenges due to political tensions between member states, particularly India and Pakistan. Despite these challenges, SAARC continues to play a vital role in promoting regional dialogue and cooperation.
- **Bay of Bengal Initiative for Multi-Sectoral Technical and Economic Cooperation (BIMSTEC):** Nepal is also a member of BIMSTEC, a regional organization comprising seven countries from South Asia and Southeast Asia. BIMSTEC focuses on enhancing cooperation in sectors such as trade, energy, tourism, and technology. The organization provides an alternative platform for Nepal to engage with regional partners beyond the confines of SAARC, promoting greater regional integration and economic cooperation.

Challenges and Future Prospects:

- **Political Instability:** Nepal has experienced political instability in recent years, with frequent changes in government and a volatile political landscape. This instability has at times hindered the country's ability to effectively engage with regional partners and pursue long-term cooperative initiatives. Strengthening political stability and ensuring a conducive environment for sustained regional cooperation remain crucial challenges.

- **Geopolitical Balancing Act:** Nepal's unique geographical location places it in a delicate position between two regional powers, India and China. Balancing relations with these two countries while safeguarding its national interests is a complex task. Nepal must navigate carefully to leverage the benefits of cooperation with both neighbors without compromising its sovereignty or becoming overly dependent on any single country.
- **Infrastructure Development and Connectivity:** While Nepal has made significant strides in infrastructure development, there is still a need for greater investment and connectivity projects. Improving road networks, transport links, and energy infrastructure will enhance regional connectivity, facilitate trade, and attract foreign direct investment. Collaborative efforts with regional partners can play a pivotal role in addressing these infrastructure gaps.
- **Socio-Economic Development:** Nepal faces numerous socio-economic challenges, including poverty, inequality, and lack of access to basic services. Regional cooperation can contribute to addressing these issues by promoting inclusive economic growth, sharing best practices, and fostering knowledge exchange. Efforts should be made to prioritize sectors such as agriculture, tourism, and sustainable development, which can generate employment opportunities and improve the living standards of the population.
- **Climate Change and Natural Disasters:** Nepal is highly vulnerable to the impacts of climate change, including glacial melt, erratic monsoons, and increased frequency of natural disasters. Regional cooperation is crucial in tackling these challenges, as climate change knows no borders. Collaborative initiatives on disaster management, water resource management, and climate adaptation can help Nepal and its regional partners build resilience and mitigate the adverse effects of climate change.

"From autocracy to democracy, Nepal's metamorphosis is a story of liberation."

Influence of International Actors on Nepalese Democratic Transition

Nepal, a landlocked country in South Asia, embarked on a challenging journey towards democratic transition after the abolition of the monarchy in 2008. The transition from a decade-long armed conflict to a democratic system posed numerous hurdles and complexities. During this period, international actors played a significant role in supporting and influencing Nepal's democratic transition. This chapter aims to explore the influence exerted by international actors on Nepal's democratic transition, examining the diverse contributions, challenges, and implications they brought to the process.

- ***Role of the United Nations:*** The United Nations (UN) has been a pivotal international actor in Nepal's democratic transition. It played a crucial role in monitoring the peace process, facilitating negotiations between conflicting parties, and coordinating international assistance. The UN Mission in Nepal (UNMIN) successfully supervised the management of arms and armies, ensuring the peaceful integration of Maoist combatants into the national army.
- ***Assistance from Bilateral Partners:*** Various countries provided substantial financial, technical, and diplomatic support to Nepal's democratic transition. Countries such as the United States, India, and the United Kingdom played instrumental roles in assisting Nepal in establishing democratic institutions, building capacity, and promoting political stability. Bilateral partnerships contributed to strengthening rule of law, human rights, and governance in Nepal.
- ***Economic Assistance and Development Agencies:*** International financial institutions, including the International Monetary Fund (IMF) and the World Bank, extended financial aid and technical expertise to Nepal during its democratic transition. This assistance aimed to stabilize the economy, promote sustainable development, and alleviate poverty. However, challenges such as corruption and mismanagement hindered the effective utilization of aid.
- ***Mediation and Support from Regional Actors:*** Regional actors, particularly India and China, have played significant roles in Nepal's democratic transition. India, being Nepal's immediate neighbor, has

historically exerted substantial influence over Nepalese politics. It has facilitated negotiations among political parties, supported the peace process, and played a crucial role in Nepal's constitutional drafting process. Similarly, China has increased its engagement in Nepal, primarily through economic investments and development projects.

- ***Civil Society and Non-Governmental Organizations (NGOs):*** International non-governmental organizations (INGOs) and civil socicty groups have been actively involved in Nepal's democratic transition. These organizations played a crucial role in advocating for human rights, gender equality, and social justice. They have contributed to raising awareness, promoting civic education, and fostering democratic values among the Nepalese population.
- ***Challenges and Criticisms:*** While international actors have made significant contributions to Nepal's democratic transition, their involvement has not been without challenges and criticisms. Some argue that external actors' interventions have led to interference in Nepal's internal affairs, compromising its sovereignty. Additionally, concerns have been raised regarding the effectiveness and sustainability of aid programs, as well as the potential for foreign actors to influence domestic politics.
- ***Implications and Lessons Learned:*** The influence of international actors on Nepal's democratic transition has had several implications and lessons for both Nepal and the international community. Firstly, it highlights the significance of external support in post-conflict countries, particularly in building democratic institutions, promoting peace, and ensuring stability. The experience of Nepal can serve as a valuable case study for other countries undergoing similar transitions.

Secondly, the involvement of international actors has shed light on the complexities of managing external assistance. It has underscored the importance of effective coordination, transparency, and accountability in aid programs. Lessons can be drawn regarding the need for robust mechanisms to ensure the efficient and equitable utilization of resources.

- ***Future Challenges and Recommendations:*** As Nepal continues its democratic journey, it faces several challenges that require ongoing attention. One challenge is the need to consolidate democratic institutions and ensure their effectiveness and inclusivity. Strengthening the rule of law, promoting good governance, and addressing corruption are critical areas that demand sustained efforts.

Moreover, Nepal must navigate its relationship with international actors, striking a balance between external assistance and safeguarding its sovereignty. Engaging in strategic partnerships based on mutual respect and shared objectives can enhance Nepal's democratic transition.

Additionally, building the capacity of domestic institutions and civil society organizations is vital for sustaining democratic practices and addressing socio-economic disparities. Encouraging citizen participation, fostering civic education, and promoting a culture of dialogue and tolerance are essential for nurturing a vibrant democracy.

The influence of international actors on Nepal's democratic transition has been multifaceted, encompassing diplomatic, financial, and technical support. The United Nations, bilateral partners, regional powers, and civil society organizations have played pivotal roles in shaping Nepal's democratic trajectory. While their involvement has yielded positive outcomes, challenges and criticisms persist. The experience of Nepal provides valuable lessons for other countries undergoing democratic transitions, emphasizing the importance of effective coordination, sovereignty protection, and sustainable development. Moving forward, Nepal must navigate the complexities of external assistance while focusing on consolidating democratic institutions, fostering citizen engagement, and addressing socio-economic disparities to ensure a robust and inclusive democracy for its people.

"The people's voice echoes through the mountains, heralding Nepal's democratic awakening."

Nepal's Relationship with Neighboring Countries and Global Powers: A Comprehensive Analysis

Nepal, a landlocked country situated in the heart of the Himalayas, has a unique geopolitical position that has shaped its relationships with neighboring countries and global powers. This chapter aims to provide a comprehensive analysis of Nepal's relationships with its neighboring countries, India and China, and its engagement with global powers such as the United States, the European Union, and other nations. By examining historical, political, economic, and cultural factors, we can gain a deeper understanding of Nepal's foreign policy choices and the implications of these relationships for Nepal's domestic development and regional stability.

Nepal-India Relations

- ***Political Relations:*** Nepal's relationship with India is multifaceted, characterized by historical, cultural, and people-to-people ties. The 1950 Treaty of Peace and Friendship laid the foundation for bilateral relations, emphasizing close cooperation and mutual respect. However, challenges have emerged periodically, such as border disputes, the impact of Indian policies on Nepal, and the perception of Indian influence in domestic affairs.
- ***Economic Relations:*** Economically, India is Nepal's largest trading partner and a significant source of investment and development assistance. Trade agreements, transit facilities, and the open border between Nepal and India promote economic integration. However, issues like trade imbalances, non-tariff barriers, and the need for infrastructure development remain areas of concern.
- ***Security and Defense Cooperation:*** Nepal and India share a close security relationship, focusing on counterterrorism, border security, and intelligence sharing. The 1950 Treaty of Peace and Friendship guarantees mutual security interests. However, some incidents along the border have strained the relationship, highlighting the need for effective border management and coordination.
- ***Cultural and People-to-People Exchanges:*** Nepal and India have deep cultural ties, strengthened by shared religious traditions, pilgrimage sites, and cultural exchanges. People-to-people contacts,

tourism, and educational exchanges further enhance the relationship. However, cultural differences and occasional misunderstandings require sustained efforts to foster mutual understanding and respect.

Nepal-China Relations

- ***Historical Overview:*** Nepal and China have a long history of cultural and economic exchanges, rooted in the ancient Silk Road. The 1955 Treaty of Peace and Friendship between Nepal and China laid the foundation for bilateral relations. Over the years, Nepal and China have developed a cordial relationship based on mutual respect and non-interference in each other's internal affairs.
- ***Political Relations:*** Nepal's relationship with China has gained prominence in recent years, driven by increased diplomatic engagements and high-level visits. Both countries have expressed a commitment to enhancing political dialogue, promoting cooperation in various fields, and maintaining regional stability. However, challenges such as Tibet-related issues and concerns over sovereignty need careful management.
- ***Economic Relations:*** China has emerged as a significant economic partner for Nepal, providing foreign direct investment, development assistance, and market access. The Belt and Road Initiative (BRI) has opened avenues for infrastructure development and connectivity projects in Nepal. However, ensuring transparency, addressing debt sustainability concerns, and maximizing the benefits of economic cooperation remain crucial.
- ***Infrastructure and Connectivity Projects:*** China's involvement in infrastructure development in Nepal, including the construction of roads, bridges, and hydropower projects, has the potential to transform Nepal's connectivity and trade routes. Projects like the China-Nepal Railway and the Trans-Himalayan Multi-Dimensional Connectivity Network could have far-reaching implications for regional connectivity and economic integration.
- ***Geopolitical Implications:*** China's growing influence in Nepal has geopolitical implications for the region. It has led to a reconfiguration of power dynamics, with Nepal seeking to balance its relationships with both India and China. Nepal's strategic location has made it an

important factor in the larger geopolitical competition between India and China, necessitating a delicate foreign policy approach.

<u>Nepal's Relationship with Other Neighboring Countries</u>

- ***Nepal-Bhutan Relations:*** Nepal and Bhutan enjoy friendly and cooperative relations, characterized by cultural affinities, people-to-people exchanges, and shared developmental challenges. Both countries have worked together on issues such as hydropower cooperation, trade facilitation, and regional connectivity.
- ***Nepal-Bangladesh Relations:*** Nepal and Bangladesh have maintained cordial relations, focusing on trade, transit, and energy cooperation. The development of regional connectivity projects, such as the Bangladesh-Nepal-India-Bhutan (BBIN) Initiative, has the potential to enhance economic integration and people-to-people exchanges.
- ***Nepal-Pakistan Relations:*** Nepal and Pakistan maintain diplomatic relations, but the bilateral engagement remains relatively limited. Efforts to enhance economic cooperation, trade, and tourism between the two countries have been initiated, although there is room for further exploration of potential areas of collaboration.

<u>Nepal's Engagement with Global Powers</u>

- ***United States:*** The United States has been a significant development partner for Nepal, providing economic assistance, supporting democratic processes, and promoting governance and human rights. The U.S. has also played a role in Nepal's peace process and post-earthquake reconstruction efforts.
- ***European Union:*** The European Union (EU) has been actively engaged in Nepal, providing development assistance, supporting governance reforms, and promoting human rights and social inclusion. The EU's focus on sustainable development, trade preferences, and good governance aligns with Nepal's priorities.
- ***Japan:*** Japan is an important development partner for Nepal, providing financial assistance, infrastructure development support, and technical cooperation. Japan's contributions in sectors such as transportation, energy, and disaster management have been instrumental in Nepal's development efforts.

- ***Russia:*** Nepal and Russia maintain diplomatic relations, with cooperation in areas such as trade, tourism, and education. Russia has provided technical assistance and scholarships to Nepali students. However, the overall depth of engagement between the two countries remains limited.
- ***Other Countries:*** Nepal has engaged with other countries, such as Australia, Canada, South Korea, and Gulf countries, on various fronts, including trade, investment, labor migration, and development cooperation. These engagements contribute to Nepal's economic diversification and global outreach.

Implications for Nepal's Domestic Development

- ***Economic Cooperation and Development Aid:*** Nepal's relationships with neighboring countries and global powers play a crucial role in its economic development. Economic cooperation, development aid, and foreign direct investment from these partners contribute to infrastructure development, poverty reduction, and economic growth in Nepal. However, it is essential for Nepal to ensure that these engagements are aligned with its national development priorities and promote sustainable and inclusive economic development.
- ***Infrastructure and Connectivity Projects:*** Infrastructure development and connectivity projects supported by neighboring countries and global powers have the potential to transform Nepal's physical infrastructure and enhance its connectivity within the region. Improved transportation networks, energy infrastructure, and digital connectivity can facilitate trade, tourism, and economic integration. However, careful planning, transparency, and effective governance are necessary to maximize the benefits and minimize potential risks associated with such projects.
- ***Trade and Investment Opportunities:*** Nepal's relationships with neighboring countries and global powers open up trade and investment opportunities. Access to larger markets, preferential trade agreements, and foreign direct investment can stimulate economic growth, create employment opportunities, and diversify Nepal's export base. Strengthening trade facilitation mechanisms, addressing non-tariff barriers, and enhancing the competitiveness of Nepali industries are critical to fully harnessing these opportunities.

- ***Humanitarian and Development Assistance:*** Foreign aid and humanitarian assistance provided by neighboring countries and global powers have played a significant role in Nepal's post-disaster recovery and reconstruction efforts. Assistance in areas such as education, healthcare, agriculture, and rural development contributes to improving the livelihoods and well-being of the Nepali population. Aligning aid with national development priorities, ensuring transparency and accountability, and building local capacity are essential for effective utilization of assistance.

Regional Implications and Challenges

- ***Nepal's Role in Regional Organizations:*** Nepal's relationships with neighboring countries and global powers intersect in regional organizations such as the South Asian Association for Regional Cooperation (SAARC) and the Bay of Bengal Initiative for Multi-Sectoral Technical and Economic Cooperation (BIMSTEC). Active participation in these forums allows Nepal to address regional issues, promote cooperation, and advance its national interests. However, regional dynamics, diverging interests among member states, and geopolitical rivalries pose challenges to regional integration efforts.
- ***Cross-Border Security Issues:*** Nepal shares porous borders with India and China, making it vulnerable to cross-border security challenges such as illegal border crossings, smuggling, and transnational crimes. Strengthening border management, intelligence sharing, and cooperation in combating cross-border security threats are crucial for maintaining peace and stability in the region.
- ***Water Resource Management:*** Nepal is rich in water resources, and several transboundary rivers flow through its territory, impacting downstream countries. Water resource management, including hydropower development, flood management, and water-sharing agreements, requires cooperation and dialogue with neighboring countries. Balancing national interests, environmental considerations, and the needs of downstream communities is essential for sustainable water resource management.
- ***Geopolitical Considerations:*** Nepal's unique geopolitical location between India and China makes it an arena for geopolitical competition and influence. Carefully navigating the interests of these

regional powers, maintaining neutrality, and safeguarding national sovereignty are crucial for Nepal's foreign policy. Nepal's approach of maintaining friendly relations with all countries and pursuing an independent foreign policy is key to ensuring regional stability and promoting its national interests.

"Nepal's journey from monarchy to democracy is a celebration of unity in diversity."

Nepal as a Hub for International Agencies: A Strategic Choice

Nepal, a landlocked country nestled in the heart of the Himalayas, has emerged as a strategic hub for several international agencies, including the United Nations (UN). This chapter aims to explore the reasons behind Nepal's status as a favored location for the establishment of various international offices. With a rich cultural heritage, breathtaking landscapes, and a unique geopolitical position, Nepal offers numerous advantages that make it an ideal destination for these organizations. This chapter delves into the key factors that have contributed to Nepal's appeal as a host country for international agencies.

- ***Geopolitical Significance:*** Nepal's geographical location holds immense strategic significance. Situated between two global powers, India and China, Nepal serves as a bridge between South Asia and East Asia. This unique positioning allows international agencies to establish a presence in Nepal to facilitate political, economic, and cultural exchanges between these regions. Nepal's stability and neutrality have also played a crucial role in attracting international organizations seeking to foster collaboration and cooperation among neighboring countries.
- ***Peace and Stability:*** Nepal's successful transition from a decade-long civil war to a democratic republic has bolstered its reputation as a peaceful and stable nation. The Comprehensive Peace Agreement in 2006 and subsequent political developments have created an environment conducive to the functioning of international agencies. Nepal's commitment to maintaining peace and stability has been instrumental in earning the trust of these organizations, ensuring the safety of their personnel, and allowing them to carry out their mandates effectively.
- ***Humanitarian and Development Needs:*** Nepal's socio-economic landscape presents a myriad of challenges, making it an ideal location for international agencies focusing on humanitarian assistance and development initiatives. The country is prone to natural disasters such as earthquakes, floods, and landslides, which require swift and coordinated responses. Furthermore, Nepal faces numerous socio-economic issues, including poverty, gender inequality, and inadequate infrastructure. By establishing

offices in Nepal, international agencies can directly address these pressing needs, providing vital aid and contributing to Nepal's sustainable development.

- ***Cultural and Biodiversity Richness:*** Nepal's diverse cultural heritage and stunning biodiversity serve as a magnet for international agencies involved in cultural preservation and environmental conservation. The country is home to numerous UNESCO World Heritage sites, including the Kathmandu Valley, Lumbini (the birthplace of Lord Buddha), and Sagarmatha National Park. Nepal's commitment to preserving its unique cultural and natural assets aligns with the objectives of many international organizations, fostering collaboration in areas such as heritage conservation, tourism, and sustainable development.
- ***Mountaineering and Adventure Tourism:*** Nepal's reputation as the gateway to the Himalayas, home to the world's highest peak, Mount Everest, has made it a popular destination for mountaineering and adventure tourism. International agencies involved in adventure sports, mountain research, and environmental studies find Nepal to be an ideal base for their operations. The abundance of trekking trails, climbing routes, and research opportunities in the Himalayas has attracted organizations seeking to explore and study this unique ecosystem.
- ***Collaboration and Partnerships:*** Nepal's commitment to international cooperation and partnerships has played a crucial role in attracting international agencies. The government of Nepal actively encourages collaboration with various organizations and provides support for their operations. This collaborative approach has resulted in the establishment of joint initiatives, knowledge-sharing platforms, and capacity-building programs, benefiting both Nepal and the international agencies operating within its borders. The willingness of the Nepalese government to work hand in hand with international agencies has fostered a positive and conducive environment for their presence in the country.
- ***Regional Connectivity:*** Nepal's efforts to strengthen regional connectivity have further enhanced its appeal as a hub for international agencies. The country is part of various regional organizations such as the South Asian Association for Regional Cooperation (SAARC) and the Bay of Bengal Initiative for Multi-Sectoral Technical and Economic Cooperation (BIMSTEC). These platforms provide opportunities for collaboration, dialogue, and the exchange of ideas among member countries. By

establishing offices in Nepal, international agencies can take advantage of this regional connectivity and engage in regional-level initiatives and partnerships.

- ***Skilled Human Resources:*** Nepal boasts a highly skilled and educated workforce, making it an attractive destination for international agencies seeking qualified personnel. The country has a strong tradition of education, with numerous universities and educational institutions producing a pool of talented individuals in various fields. Nepalese professionals have made significant contributions to the work of international agencies, bringing their expertise and knowledge to global development efforts. The availability of skilled human resources has been a driving factor in the establishment of offices and operations in Nepal.
- ***Local Support and Hospitality:*** The warmth, hospitality, and support extended by the Nepalese people have been instrumental in attracting and retaining international agencies. The friendly nature of the locals and their willingness to collaborate and engage with international personnel create an inclusive and welcoming environment. The sense of community and cooperation in Nepal fosters strong relationships between international agencies and the local population, ensuring the smooth functioning of operations and the achievement of common goals.

Nepal's emergence as a hub for international agencies is the result of a combination of factors. Its strategic geopolitical location, peace and stability, humanitarian and development needs, cultural richness, adventure tourism opportunities, collaborative mindset, regional connectivity, skilled human resources, and local support all contribute to its appeal. Nepal's commitment to international cooperation, coupled with its unique offerings, makes it an ideal host country for international agencies seeking to address a wide range of global challenges. As Nepal continues to evolve and grow, the presence of international agencies will play a vital role in supporting the country's development and fostering global partnerships for a better future.

"Democracy in Nepal is a collective dream realized, a triumph against the odds."

Nepal's Strategic Dilemma: The Geopolitical Dance between India and China

Nepal, nestled in the heart of the Himalayas, finds itself in a unique position as a buffer state between two regional giants, India and China. This geographical location has placed Nepal at the center of a complex geopolitical dance, where both India and China vie for influence and strategic benefits. This chapter delves into the intricate dynamics that shape Nepal's foreign policy choices and attempts to answer the question of which country Nepal would choose if given the opportunity.

- ***Historical Background:*** To understand Nepal's current foreign policy predicament, it is crucial to examine the historical context. Nepal has maintained a delicate balancing act between India and China for centuries. It shares deep cultural, religious, and historical ties with India, while also cherishing its sovereignty and independence. Similarly, Nepal shares a long border with China and has sought to leverage its relationship with the rising Asian power.
- ***India's Influence:*** India, as Nepal's immediate neighbor and historical ally, holds significant influence over the landlocked nation. The two countries share a porous border, people-to-people ties, and cultural affinities. India has been Nepal's largest trading partner and a major source of investment and development aid. Additionally, the open border between Nepal and India allows for the free movement of people, creating social and economic interdependencies.
- ***China's Outreach:*** In recent years, China's influence in Nepal has grown significantly. China has emerged as Nepal's second-largest trading partner and a crucial source of investment, particularly in infrastructure development. Chinese initiatives, such as the Belt and Road Initiative (BRI), have presented Nepal with opportunities for economic growth and connectivity.

China's outreach to Nepal is not solely limited to economic endeavors. It has also engaged in cultural diplomacy, promoting exchanges and scholarships. Furthermore, China has positioned itself as a counterbalance to India's influence in Nepal, offering an alternative partner for the landlocked country.

• ***Nepal's Strategic Considerations:*** Nepal's foreign policy choices are shaped by a range of factors, including historical ties, economic considerations, geostrategic concerns, and domestic politics. While Nepal has maintained friendly relations with both India and China, it faces the challenge of balancing their competing interests.

• ***Economic Factors:*** Nepal, as a developing nation, seeks economic opportunities and investment to foster its development. Both India and China offer unique advantages in this regard. India's proximity and established trade routes present opportunities for cross-border trade, while China's investments can contribute to Nepal's infrastructure development. Nepal must carefully weigh these economic considerations when formulating its foreign policy.

• ***Geopolitical Considerations:*** Nepal's geopolitical location between India and China provides it with the potential to serve as a bridge between the two powers. Nepal's leaders have strived to position the country as a neutral player, benefiting from the economic and diplomatic advantages offered by both India and China. However, Nepal must navigate this delicate balance to avoid being entangled in the geopolitical rivalries between the two giants.

• ***Domestic Politics:*** Nepal's foreign policy choices are also influenced by domestic politics. Political parties in Nepal often differ in their approach to India and China. Some advocate a closer relationship with India, emphasizing the historical, cultural, and economic ties, while others lean towards strengthening ties with China, focusing on the potential economic benefits and the desire for an alternative partner. The domestic political landscape plays a significant role in shaping Nepal's foreign policy decisions.

• ***Nepal's Independent Foreign Policy:*** Despite the pressures and influences from India and China, Nepal has maintained a policy of non-alignment and an emphasis on its sovereignty and independence. Nepal has sought to engage with both countries while safeguarding its national interests. This approach allows Nepal to avoid being overly dependent on a single power and gives it room for maneuverability in the complex regional dynamics.

• ***Nepal's Strategic Choices:*** Given the intricate dynamics at play, it is challenging to predict definitively which country Nepal would choose if given a chance. Nepal's foreign policy decisions are based on a range of factors, including economic opportunities, geopolitical considerations, domestic politics, and the desire for maintaining an independent foreign policy.

However, Nepal's historical ties, open border, and economic interdependencies with India make it a crucial partner for the country. India's engagement with Nepal spans various sectors, including trade, investment, development aid, and people-to-people ties. The cultural affinities and historical connections further strengthen the bond between the two nations.

On the other hand, China's growing influence in Nepal cannot be disregarded. China's economic initiatives, such as the BRI, have the potential to transform Nepal's infrastructure and connectivity. China's investments in Nepal, though relatively recent, have been substantial and have the potential to shape Nepal's economic landscape.

Nepal finds itself in a challenging position as a buffer state between India and China. Both countries seek to woo Nepal for their strategic benefits, leading to a complex geopolitical dance. Nepal's foreign policy choices are a delicate balancing act, influenced by historical ties, economic considerations, geopolitical dynamics, and domestic politics.

While it is difficult to predict definitively which country Nepal would choose if given the opportunity, Nepal's commitment to maintaining an independent foreign policy and its historical ties with India make India a crucial partner. However, China's growing influence and economic initiatives cannot be ignored, and Nepal has sought to leverage its relationship with China as well.

Ultimately, Nepal's strategic choices will depend on its ability to navigate the competing interests of India and China while safeguarding its national interests, maintaining sovereignty, and fostering economic development. Nepal's unique position as a buffer state offers opportunities for engagement with both regional powers, and it is in Nepal's best interest to carefully balance its relationships with India and China to maximize benefits and mitigate risks.

"In the dance of democracy, Nepal's every step is a leap towards progress and inclusivity."

Nepal-India Friendship Treaty of 1950: An Analysis of Violations and Strained Relations

The Nepal-India Friendship Treaty of 1950 has long been regarded as a significant milestone in the bilateral relations between Nepal and India. However, strains in this historic friendship emerged in the late 1980s when Nepal's decision to import weapons and equipment from China violated the clauses of the treaty. This chapter aims to delve into the violations that occurred, analyze the repercussions on both countries' diplomatic ties, and explore the subsequent implications for the region.

- ***Historical Background of Nepal-India Friendship Treaty:*** The Nepal-India Friendship Treaty, signed on July 31, 1950, facilitated a unique relationship between the two nations. The treaty aimed to foster economic cooperation, maintain peace and security, and solidify the existing cultural and historical ties. It also granted India a special status in Nepal's foreign affairs and defense matters.
- ***The Violations and Import of Weapons from China:*** In the late 1980s, Nepal's decision to import weapons and equipment from China marked a departure from the provisions outlined in the 1950 treaty. The Nepalese government, facing internal challenges and seeking to diversify its sources of arms, turned to China as an alternative supplier. This move was seen as a violation of the treaty's clause, which required Nepal to consult with India before entering into any military agreement with a third party.
- ***Strained Relations and Implications for Nepal:*** Nepal's decision to import arms from China strained its relations with India. The Indian government interpreted this action as a breach of trust and a departure from the spirit of the friendship treaty. As a consequence, India expressed concerns over Nepal's growing proximity to China and its potential impact on regional security dynamics.
- ***India's Response and Diplomatic Challenges:*** India's response to Nepal's violation of the friendship treaty was multifaceted. It involved diplomatic efforts to engage with Nepal, express concerns, and seek clarification on the decision to import arms from China. The strained relations posed significant challenges for both countries, as they had to navigate a delicate balance

between safeguarding their national interests and maintaining the strategic importance of the bilateral relationship.

- ***China's Role and Influence:*** China's growing influence in Nepal during this period cannot be overlooked. Beijing's provision of military assistance to Kathmandu was seen as an opportunity for China to expand its presence in the region and counterbalance India. This raised concerns in India about encroachment into its traditional sphere of influence.
- ***The Way Forward and Restoring Trust:*** To address the strained relations, both Nepal and India undertook diplomatic initiatives to rebuild trust. High-level visits, dialogue forums, and confidence-building measures were implemented to ensure the restoration of the bilateral relationship. The focus shifted towards strengthening economic ties, promoting people-to-people exchanges, and enhancing cooperation in various sectors.
- ***Lessons Learned and Future Prospects:*** The violation of the Nepal-India Friendship Treaty in the late 1980s served as a wake-up call for both countries. It highlighted the need for open communication, mutual respect for sovereignty, and a commitment to upholding the spirit of the treaty. The incident also emphasized the importance of maintaining a delicate balance between regional alliances and safeguarding national interests.

The violation of the Nepal-India Friendship Treaty in the late 1980s, when Nepal imported weapons and equipment from China, strained the bilateral relations between the two nations. This incident underscored the complexities and challenges of maintaining strong diplomatic ties in a region characterized by geopolitical dynamics.

Moving forward, it is crucial for Nepal and India to learn from this episode and take proactive steps to strengthen their friendship and cooperation. Both countries need to engage in open and transparent dialogue, address concerns, and ensure that the provisions of the friendship treaty are upheld. Additionally, efforts should be made to diversify and deepen the bilateral relationship beyond just defense and security matters.

Economic cooperation, trade, tourism, and cultural exchanges can play a significant role in fostering mutual understanding and trust. Enhancing connectivity through infrastructure development projects can further facilitate people-to-people interactions and strengthen economic interdependence.

Moreover, both Nepal and India should maintain a delicate balance in their foreign policies, taking into account the interests and concerns of each other. While Nepal has the right to pursue its own independent foreign policy, it is essential to ensure that it does not compromise the strategic ties and mutual trust built over the years.

Regional stability and cooperation should remain a priority for both countries. Engaging in multilateral forums and initiatives can provide a platform for addressing common challenges, such as climate change, transnational crime, and disaster management. By working together, Nepal and India can contribute to the overall development and prosperity of the region.

The violation of the Nepal-India Friendship Treaty in the late 1980s, when Nepal imported weapons and equipment from China, strained the bilateral relations between the two nations. However, both countries have since made efforts to restore trust and rebuild their friendship. It is imperative that lessons are learned from this incident, and proactive measures are taken to strengthen the bilateral relationship, promote economic cooperation, and ensure regional stability. By doing so, Nepal and India can pave the way for a more prosperous and harmonious future.

"From royal edicts to the people's verdicts, Nepal's democracy redefines governance."

The Thai Airlines Crash of 1992: A Tale of Tragedy, Frustration, and Strained International Relations

Aviation disasters have always been marked by profound tragedy, loss, and the pressing need for swift recovery efforts. In 1992, Nepal found itself grappling with one such disaster, as Thai Airways Flight 311 crashed in the mountains near Kathmandu, resulting in the loss of over 100 lives. The incident not only revealed the challenges of conducting search and rescue operations in treacherous terrain but also led to a diplomatic deadlock between Nepal and India. This chapter delves into the details surrounding the crash, the prolonged wreckage search operations, the requisition of Indian assistance, the subsequent denial of Indian aid, and the strained relations that ensued.

The Thai Airways Flight 311 Disaster

- ***Overview of Thai Airways Flight 311:*** Thai Airways Flight 311, a Boeing 737-400 aircraft, was scheduled to fly from Bangkok, Thailand, to Kathmandu, Nepal, on July 31, 1992. The flight was carrying 99 passengers and 14 crew members. The passengers included tourists, business travelers, and a number of Nepalese nationals returning home.
- ***Route and Circumstances of the Crash:*** Tragically, Flight 311 veered off course during its approach to Kathmandu's Tribhuvan International Airport. The aircraft crashed into the mountains, approximately 25 kilometers south of Kathmandu. The exact cause of the crash was later determined to be a combination of adverse weather conditions, pilot error, and miscommunication between the flight crew and air traffic control.
- ***Fatalities and Immediate Response:*** The crash of Thai Airways Flight 311 resulted in the loss of all 113 people on board. The immediate response to the disaster was hampered by the remote and rugged terrain, making access to the crash site challenging. Nepalese authorities quickly mobilized search and rescue teams but faced significant difficulties due to the treacherous conditions.

- ***Challenges Faced in Wreckage Search Operations:*** The wreckage search operations were marred by numerous challenges. The crash site was located at an altitude of around 2,900 meters, with steep slopes and dense forests, making it extremely challenging for ground teams to reach the area. The rugged terrain also posed risks to the safety of search and rescue personnel. Additionally, adverse weather conditions, including heavy rain and fog, further complicated the operations.

The Quest for Assistance

- ***Nepal's Plea for International Aid:*** Recognizing the challenges they faced, Nepalese authorities urgently sought international assistance in their search and recovery efforts. Given the severity of the crash and the need for specialized equipment and expertise, Nepal reached out to neighboring India for support.
- ***Indian Assistance Offer: The Arrival of MI 17 Helicopters:*** Responding to Nepal's request, the Indian government swiftly offered assistance and dispatched two MI 17 helicopters to aid in the search operations. The MI 17 helicopters, known for their capability to operate in challenging terrain, were well-suited for the task at hand.
- ***Importance of Indian Aid in Search Operations:*** The arrival of the Indian helicopters brought a glimmer of hope to the search and rescue teams. The MI 17 helicopters were equipped with advanced search and surveillance equipment, enabling them to cover vast areas and locate debris more effectively. Their assistance was seen as crucial in expediting the recovery of the victims and the investigation into the crash.
- ***Nepalese Royal Air Force's Objections:*** However, despite the urgency and the clear benefits of Indian assistance, the Nepalese Royal Air Force objected to the use of the Indian helicopters in the search operations. Citing concerns over sovereignty and security, the Nepalese authorities insisted that only their own military helicopters should be deployed in the mission.

The Denial of Indian Assistance

- ***Reasons Cited by the Nepalese Royal Air Force:*** The Nepalese Royal Air Force's objection to the use of Indian MI 17 helicopters was primarily rooted in concerns over national sovereignty. The decision was based on the belief that the involvement of foreign military aircraft in search operations would set a precedent that could compromise Nepal's sovereignty
- ***Diplomatic Implications and Strained Relations:*** The denial of Indian assistance in the aftermath of the Thai Airways crash had significant diplomatic implications. India, feeling frustrated and disappointed by Nepal's decision, lodged a strong protest against the Nepalese authorities. The incident strained the relations between the two countries, which had previously maintained a relatively amicable bilateral relationship.
- ***India's Strong Protest:*** A Reaction to Nepal's Decision: India's reaction to Nepal's denial of assistance was marked by a strong protest. The Indian government expressed its deep concern and disappointment, emphasizing the humanitarian aspect of the situation and the need for swift action to recover the victims and provide closure to their families. The protest reflected India's belief that the denial of assistance was not only an unnecessary hindrance to the search operations but also a failure to prioritize the well-being of the affected families.
- ***Public and International Response to the Denial:*** Nepal's decision to deny Indian assistance and the subsequent diplomatic tensions attracted significant public and international attention. The families of the victims, as well as the general public, expressed their frustration and anguish over the prolonged search operations and the lack of cooperation between Nepal and India. The international community, too, closely followed the developments and called for a resolution that would prioritize the recovery efforts and the well-being of the affected families.

The Prolonged Wreckage Search Operations

- ***Challenges Faced by Nepalese Authorities:*** In the absence of the Indian helicopters, the Nepalese authorities faced numerous challenges in conducting the wreckage search operations. The difficult terrain, adverse weather conditions, and limited resources posed significant hurdles in their efforts to locate and recover the victims. Ground teams had to navigate treacherous slopes, dense forests, and unpredictable weather, which significantly slowed down the search and recovery process.

- ***Alternative Search and Recovery Measures:*** Despite the absence of the Indian helicopters, the Nepalese authorities persevered in their search operations. They employed additional ground teams, including local rescue personnel and volunteers, to comb through the rugged terrain manually. The use of sniffer dogs, specialized search equipment, and coordination with international experts also played a crucial role in the search efforts.
- ***Impact on Families and the Nation:*** The prolonged search operations had a profound impact on the families of the victims and the nation as a whole. The families experienced prolonged uncertainty and anguish as they awaited news about their loved ones. The delay in recovering the victims' remains and providing closure added to their emotional distress. The nation, too, felt the weight of the tragedy as it grappled with the challenges of recovering from such a devastating incident.
- ***Closure and Lessons Learned:*** After several weeks of exhaustive search operations, the wreckage of Thai Airways Flight 311 was finally located, and the remains of the victims were recovered. The process of identification and repatriation brought a sense of closure to the families, though it could never fully heal the wounds caused by the tragedy. The incident served as a sobering reminder of the importance of efficient disaster response mechanisms, coordination between nations, and the need for improved protocols and resources to handle such situations in the future.

The Aftermath and Reconciliation

- ***Subsequent Investigations and Findings:*** Following the recovery of the wreckage, comprehensive investigations were conducted to determine the cause of the crash and identify any lapses or shortcomings. The findings helped shed light on the factors that led to the tragedy and provided valuable insights to prevent similar incidents in the future. The investigation report highlighted the role of adverse weather conditions, pilot error, and miscommunication as contributing factors to the crash of Thai Airways Flight 311.

- ***Efforts to Strengthen Cooperation and Communication:*** In the aftermath of the Thai Airways crash and the strained relations between Nepal and India, both countries recognized the need to strengthen cooperation and communication in disaster response and aviation safety. Bilateral discussions took place to address the issues that had arisen and to establish protocols and mechanisms for future collaborations in emergency situations.
- ***Long-term Impact on Nepal-India Relations:*** While the denial of Indian assistance in the Thai Airways crash initially strained relations between Nepal and India, the incident also served as a turning point for both countries. Recognizing the importance of cooperation and mutual support in times of crisis, Nepal and India worked towards rebuilding trust and strengthening their bilateral ties. The incident prompted a reevaluation of protocols and procedures for cross-border assistance in emergency situations, leading to more effective collaboration in the years that followed.
- ***Lessons Learned and Improved Disaster Response Mechanisms:*** The Thai Airways crash in Nepal in 1992 highlighted the importance of robust disaster response mechanisms and coordination between nations. The incident served as a catalyst for both Nepal and India to reassess their preparedness for aviation disasters and to improve their disaster response capabilities. Lessons learned from the crash led to the implementation of enhanced training programs, the establishment of dedicated search and rescue teams, and the development of protocols for international cooperation during emergencies.

"Nepal's democracy is a phoenix, rising with the strength and resilience of its people."

The Historic Reopening of Bhairwa Checkpoint: A Milestone in Indo-Nepal Relations

In a significant move aimed at strengthening bilateral ties and promoting regional cooperation, India and Nepal made history as they decided to end the long-standing blockade and formally reopen the Bhairwa checkpoint. This momentous event, which took place under the able guidance of influential figures such as Shri Mulayam Singh, the then Chief Minister of Uttar Pradesh, and Shri KP Bhattarai, the Prime Minister of Nepal, marked a turning point in the relationship between the two nations. This chapter delves into the details of this extraordinary event, discussing its significance, the key individuals involved, and the broader implications for Indo-Nepal relations.

- ***Background of the Bhairwa Checkpoint:*** The Bhairwa checkpoint, located on the India-Nepal border, holds immense strategic and economic importance for both nations. Historically, it has served as a vital trade and transit route, facilitating cross-border movement of goods, people, and cultural exchanges. However, over the years, the checkpoint became a contentious issue, with occasional closures leading to diplomatic strains and hindrance to bilateral trade.
- ***The Decision to End the Blockade:*** Amidst escalating tensions, the governments of India and Nepal took a momentous decision to end the blockade and reopen the Bhairwa checkpoint. This decision was driven by a shared vision of fostering regional cooperation, enhancing economic ties, and promoting people-to-people connectivity. It reflected the commitment of both nations to address long-standing grievances and pave the way for a more amicable relationship.
- ***The Role of Shri Mulayam Singh and Shri KP Bhattarai:*** The formal reopening of the Bhairwa checkpoint was a moment of great significance, and it was graced by the presence of two eminent leaders – Shri Mulayam Singh and Shri KP Bhattarai. Shri Mulayam Singh, the Chief Minister of Uttar Pradesh, played a pivotal role in advocating for the reopening of the checkpoint and ensuring a smooth transition. Shri KP Bhattarai, the Prime Minister of Nepal, lent his support and actively engaged in the negotiations, showcasing his commitment to strengthening bilateral ties.

• ***The Organizational Efforts:*** A successful event of this magnitude requires meticulous planning and execution. Col Arvind Sharma, the military attaché, and Lt Gen SK Sinha, the Indian Ambassador, played instrumental roles in organizing the reopening ceremony of the Bhairwa checkpoint. Their experience, expertise, and diplomatic acumen ensured that the event was conducted seamlessly, fostering an atmosphere of goodwill and camaraderie.

• ***Significance for Indo-Nepal Relations:*** The reopening of the Bhairwa checkpoint holds immense significance for Indo-Nepal relations. It signifies a renewed commitment by both nations to prioritize dialogue, cooperation, and mutual understanding. The event serves as a stepping stone towards resolving long-standing border disputes, promoting trade and investment, and facilitating the movement of people between the two countries. Furthermore, it paves the way for a more comprehensive engagement on regional issues, fostering stability and prosperity in the South Asian region.

• ***Economic Implications:*** The reopening of the Bhairwa checkpoint has far-reaching economic implications for India and Nepal. It revives the potential for cross-border trade, creating new avenues for economic growth and development. The increased movement of goods, services, and investments will leverage the geographical proximity and cultural ties between the two nations, facilitating greater economic integration and cooperation. It opens up opportunities for joint ventures, cross-border investments, and the expansion of trade networks, benefiting industries such as agriculture, manufacturing, tourism, and services. The renewed trade flows will contribute to job creation, poverty reduction, and enhanced living standards for the people of both countries.

• ***Cultural Exchange and People-to-People Connectivity:*** The reopening of the Bhairwa checkpoint not only facilitates economic transactions but also promotes cultural exchange and people-to-people connectivity. It allows for the free movement of individuals, fostering closer ties between communities residing along the border. Cultural exchanges, such as festivals, art exhibitions, and educational programs, can flourish, leading to a deeper understanding and appreciation of each other's heritage. Increased tourism between the two nations will also promote cultural immersion, boosting the local economies and promoting cross-cultural understanding.

• ***Security and Border Management:*** The reopening of the Bhairwa checkpoint also holds implications for security and border management. With the checkpoint functioning effectively, there will be enhanced opportunities for collaboration between the security forces of India and Nepal. Closer coordination and information sharing can contribute to the prevention of illicit activities, smuggling, and unauthorized border crossings. Joint efforts in maintaining border security will create a safer environment for both nations and foster greater trust and cooperation between their respective law enforcement agencies.

- ***Challenges and the Way Forward:*** While the reopening of the Bhairwa checkpoint marks a significant milestone, there are challenges that need to be addressed for sustained cooperation and smooth functioning. Issues such as infrastructure development, customs procedures, and harmonization of regulations require attention to ensure seamless cross-border trade. Bilateral dialogues and joint working groups can play a crucial role in resolving these challenges and fostering an environment conducive to long-term cooperation.

In terms of broader Indo-Nepal relations, the reopening of the Bhairwa checkpoint sets a positive precedent for resolving other outstanding issues between the two countries. It serves as a reminder of the shared history, culture, and aspirations that bind India and Nepal together. It is an opportunity to build upon the existing goodwill and forge a stronger partnership based on mutual trust, respect, and cooperation.

The formal reopening of the Bhairwa checkpoint by Shri Mulayam Singh and Shri KP Bhattarai marked a historic milestone in Indo-Nepal relations. The event, organized under the guidance of Col Arvind Sharma and Lt Gen SK Sinha, showcased the commitment of both nations to overcome challenges and work towards a shared vision of regional cooperation, economic integration, and cultural exchange. The reopening of the checkpoint holds immense promise for enhancing trade, people-to-people connectivity, and security cooperation. It serves as a foundation for building a stronger, more prosperous Indo-Nepal relationship, benefiting the people of both nations and contributing to regional stability and development.

"As the monarchy recedes, Nepal's democracy emerges as the guiding star in the night sky."

---

12. REFLECTIONS & FUTURE PROSPECTS

"Democracy in Nepal provides a platform for diverse voices to be heard, fostering a more vibrant and dynamic"

Challenges and Prospects for the Future: Nepal's Path Forward

Nepal, a landlocked country nestled in the Himalayas, has made significant progress in various aspects of development. However, it continues to face numerous challenges that hinder its journey towards sustainable growth. This chapter explores the challenges Nepal confronts and the prospects it holds for the future. By understanding these hurdles and opportunities, Nepal can chart a path forward that ensures inclusive development, social progress, and economic prosperity.

- ***Political Challenges:*** Nepal's political landscape has been marked by instability, frequent changes in government, and challenges in implementing reforms. Political polarization, weak governance structures, and a lack of consensus among political parties often hinder the effective functioning of the state. To address these challenges, Nepal needs to focus on strengthening its democratic institutions, fostering political stability, and promoting inclusive decision-making processes. Encouraging dialogue between different political factions and prioritizing national interests over partisan agendas will be crucial for Nepal's political future.
- ***Economic Development:*** Nepal faces significant economic challenges, including a low GDP growth rate, high unemployment, and a large informal sector. Limited infrastructure, insufficient access to finance, and a lack of skilled labor pose barriers to economic progress. To overcome these challenges, Nepal needs to prioritize investment in infrastructure development, promote entrepreneurship and innovation, and enhance vocational training and skill development programs. Attracting foreign direct investment, promoting export-oriented industries, and diversifying the economy will be vital for Nepal's economic growth and reducing poverty.
- ***Social Inclusion and Inequality:*** Nepal has made strides in reducing poverty and improving social indicators, but challenges in social inclusion and inequality persist. Marginalized communities, including Dalits, ethnic minorities, and rural populations, continue to face discrimination and exclusion from opportunities. Addressing social disparities requires targeted policies and programs that promote inclusivity, ensure equitable access to education, healthcare, and basic services, and empower marginalized

communities. Strengthening social safety nets, promoting affirmative action, and fostering intercultural understanding will be crucial for achieving social harmony and reducing inequality.

- ***Climate Change and Environmental Sustainability:*** Nepal is highly vulnerable to climate change, with rising temperatures, changing rainfall patterns, and increased frequency of natural disasters. Environmental degradation, deforestation, and pollution further exacerbate these challenges. Nepal must prioritize climate change adaptation and mitigation measures, including sustainable land management, afforestation, and renewable energy initiatives. Strengthening environmental governance, promoting sustainable practices in agriculture and tourism, and raising awareness about the importance of conservation will be critical for Nepal's environmental sustainability and resilience.
- ***Infrastructure Development:*** Nepal's infrastructure deficit, particularly in rural and remote areas, hampers its economic growth and social development. Inadequate road networks, unreliable power supply, and limited access to clean water and sanitation facilities pose significant challenges. Addressing infrastructure gaps requires increased investment in transportation, energy, water, and sanitation infrastructure. Public-private partnerships, innovative financing mechanisms, and effective project management will be crucial for Nepal to bridge the infrastructure divide and improve the quality of life for its citizens.
- ***Education and Human Capital Development:*** Despite progress in expanding access to education, Nepal faces challenges in ensuring quality education and developing a skilled workforce. Limited resources, inadequate teacher training, and a mismatch between education and employment opportunities hinder human capital development. To address these challenges, Nepal needs to invest in improving the quality of education, enhancing teacher training programs, and strengthening vocational and technical education. Collaboration between educational institutions, industries, and the government can help align the curriculum with the needs of the job market, fostering a skilled workforce that drives economic growth and innovation.
- ***Governance and Corruption:*** Corruption remains a significant challenge in Nepal, undermining governance, impeding development efforts, and eroding public trust. Nepali society must prioritize transparency, accountability, and the rule of law to combat corruption effectively.

Strengthening anti-corruption mechanisms, promoting a culture of integrity, and ensuring the independence of key institutions, such as the judiciary and anti-corruption bodies, will be critical. By fostering good governance practices and combating corruption at all levels, Nepal can create an enabling environment for sustainable development and attract investment.

- ***Regional Cooperation and Geopolitical Dynamics:*** Nepal's geographical position between two regional powerhouses, India and China, presents both opportunities and challenges. Nepal must navigate geopolitical dynamics while leveraging regional cooperation to its advantage. Strengthening diplomatic ties, enhancing trade and connectivity, and promoting cross-border collaboration can unlock significant economic benefits for Nepal. Maintaining a balanced approach and engaging with neighboring countries based on mutual respect and shared interests will be crucial for Nepal's regional engagement.
- ***Technology and Digital Divide:*** Nepal faces a significant digital divide, with limited access to technology and internet connectivity, particularly in rural areas. Harnessing the power of technology can accelerate Nepal's development across sectors, including education, healthcare, agriculture, and e-governance. To bridge the digital divide, Nepal needs to invest in expanding connectivity infrastructure, promoting digital literacy, and creating an enabling environment for innovation and entrepreneurship. Collaboration with the private sector and international partners can support Nepal's efforts to leverage technology for inclusive growth.
- ***Tourism and Cultural Preservation:*** Tourism is a vital sector for Nepal's economy, but it also poses challenges in terms of environmental impact, cultural preservation, and equitable distribution of benefits. Nepal must adopt sustainable tourism practices that prioritize environmental conservation, community engagement, and cultural preservation. Investing in infrastructure, promoting responsible tourism, and ensuring the participation of local communities in decision-making processes can help maximize the positive impacts of tourism while safeguarding Nepal's unique cultural and natural heritage.

Nepal faces a range of challenges as it strives for sustainable development and inclusive growth. However, these challenges also present opportunities for transformative change. By prioritizing political stability, inclusive governance, economic diversification, social inclusion, environmental sustainability, infrastructure development, education, and technological innovation, Nepal can overcome these hurdles and unlock its full potential. Collaboration between the government, civil society, private sector, and international partners will be crucial in addressing these challenges and shaping a prosperous future for Nepal. With strategic planning, effective implementation, and a commitment to inclusive development, Nepal can navigate the complexities of the global landscape and pave the way for a brighter future for its citizens.

"Democracy in Nepal is a river, carving its path through the mountains of adversity."

Assessing the Success and Limitations of Democracy in Nepal

Nepal's transition from a monarchy to a democratic system in 2008 marked a significant milestone in its history. Over the past decade, Nepal has made notable progress in consolidating democratic practices and institutions. However, the journey towards a successful democracy is not without challenges and limitations. This chapter aims to assess the success and limitations of democracy in Nepal, examining key achievements, persistent challenges, and areas for improvement.

Successes in Democratic Consolidation:

- ***Peaceful Transition:*** One of the major successes of democracy in Nepal is the peaceful transition from a decade-long armed conflict to a democratic system. The Comprehensive Peace Agreement signed in 2006 paved the way for political stability and the integration of Maoist combatants into the national army.
- ***Constitutional Framework:*** Nepal adopted a new constitution in 2015, which aimed to establish a federal democratic republic. The constitution enshrines fundamental rights and liberties, provides for inclusive representation, and ensures a separation of powers among the executive, legislative, and judicial branches.
- ***Electoral Processes:*** Nepal has conducted several successful elections at various levels, including local, provincial, and federal. These elections have witnessed high voter turnout, indicating a growing participation of citizens in the democratic process.
- ***Inclusion and Representation:*** The establishment of inclusive institutions and affirmative action policies has aimed to address historical marginalization and promote social inclusion. Women, ethnic minorities, and marginalized groups have gained increased representation in political offices and decision-making bodies.

Persistent Challenges in Nepalese Democracy:

- ***Political Instability:*** Nepal has experienced frequent changes in government, leading to political instability. This instability has resulted from a fragmented political landscape, coalition governments, and difficulties in consensus-building among political parties.

- ***Corruption and Governance:*** Corruption remains a significant challenge, affecting various sectors and eroding public trust in democratic institutions. Weak governance, lack of accountability, and bureaucratic inefficiencies hinder the effective functioning of democratic processes.
- ***Socio-economic Disparities:*** Despite progress, Nepal faces persistent socio-economic disparities, particularly in rural and marginalized communities. Poverty, lack of basic services, and unequal distribution of resources pose challenges to the inclusivity and sustainability of democracy.
- ***Security Concerns:*** The presence of armed groups, regional conflicts, and border issues pose security challenges to Nepal's democratic stability. Addressing these concerns requires effective security mechanisms and dialogue among diverse stakeholders.

Strengthening Nepalese Democracy:

- ***Rule of Law and Judicial Independence:*** Strengthening the rule of law and ensuring judicial independence are crucial for safeguarding democratic principles. Enhancing the capacity and effectiveness of the judiciary, addressing judicial backlog, and promoting access to justice are essential steps.
- ***Civic Education and Awareness:*** Promoting civic education and raising awareness about democratic values, rights, and responsibilities among the population can foster active citizen participation. Emphasizing democratic values in educational curricula and civil society initiatives can contribute to long-term democratic sustainability.
- ***Anti-corruption Measures:*** Tackling corruption requires a comprehensive approach, including robust anti-corruption laws, transparent governance practices, and effective enforcement mechanisms. Strengthening institutions such as the Anti-Corruption Commission and promoting a culture of integrity are critical in this regard.
- ***Inclusive Development:*** Ensuring equitable development and addressing socio-economic disparities are vital for a thriving

democracy. Policies and programs should focus on poverty alleviation, rural development, job creation, and access to basic services, particularly in marginalized areas. Inclusive economic growth can contribute to social cohesion and strengthen democratic institutions.

- ***Political Stability and Consensus-Building:*** Enhancing political stability requires fostering a culture of consensus-building and dialogue among political parties. Encouraging collaboration, reducing polarization, and promoting a shared vision for the country can contribute to a stable and effective democratic system.
- ***Strengthening Civil Society:*** Civil society organizations play a crucial role in promoting democratic values, advocating for human rights, and holding the government accountable. Creating an enabling environment for civil society activities, ensuring their independence, and facilitating their engagement in policy-making processes can strengthen democratic governance.

International Support and Cooperation:

International actors have a role to play in supporting Nepal's democratic consolidation. Bilateral partners, regional organizations, and international institutions can provide technical assistance, capacity-building support, and financial resources to strengthen democratic institutions, promote good governance, and address socio-economic challenges. However, it is essential to strike a balance between external support and safeguarding Nepal's sovereignty to ensure that international assistance aligns with national priorities.

Lessons from Nepal's Democratic Transition:

Nepal's democratic transition offers valuable lessons for other countries undergoing similar processes. These lessons can help guide their efforts towards building successful and sustainable democracies. Some key lessons include:

- ***Inclusivity and Social Justice:*** Nepal's focus on inclusivity and social justice has been crucial in addressing historical marginalization and promoting equal representation. Emphasizing the rights and participation of marginalized groups can contribute to a more inclusive democracy.

- ***Peaceful Conflict Resolution:*** Nepal's successful transition from armed conflict to a peaceful democratic system highlights the importance of dialogue, negotiation, and reconciliation in resolving conflicts. A commitment to non-violence and peaceful means of conflict resolution is essential for democratic stability.
- ***Constitution-Making Process:*** The constitution-making process in Nepal serves as a lesson in navigating complex political dynamics and ensuring broad-based participation. Engaging diverse stakeholders, promoting dialogue, and accommodating diverse perspectives are crucial in achieving a constitution that reflects the aspirations of the people.
- ***Balancing External Support:*** Nepal's experience highlights the need for balancing external support and safeguarding national sovereignty. While international assistance is valuable, it is essential to ensure that it aligns with national priorities and does not compromise the country's autonomy.
- ***Strengthening Democratic Institutions:*** The importance of strong democratic institutions cannot be overstated. Building the capacity, independence, and effectiveness of institutions such as the judiciary, electoral bodies, and anti-corruption agencies is crucial for upholding democratic principles and ensuring accountability.
- ***Civic Engagement and Awareness:*** Promoting civic education and fostering active citizen participation are vital for a thriving democracy. Enhancing awareness of rights, responsibilities, and democratic values among the population can empower citizens to actively engage in the democratic process.

The Way Forward:

To overcome the limitations and further strengthen democracy in Nepal, concerted efforts are required from various stakeholders. Some key recommendations include:

- ***Political Stability and Consensus-Building:*** Political parties should prioritize national interests over partisan considerations and work towards consensus-building. Encouraging collaboration, reducing polarization, and promoting a shared vision for the country can contribute to political stability.

- ***Accountability and Anti-corruption Measures:*** Strengthening accountability mechanisms, promoting transparency, and tackling corruption are crucial for building public trust in democratic institutions. Effective enforcement of anti-corruption laws and the establishment of independent oversight bodies can play a significant role in this regard.
- ***Inclusive Development:*** Policies and programs should prioritize inclusive development, focusing on poverty alleviation, job creation, and access to basic services. By addressing socio-economic disparities, Nepal can ensure that the benefits of democracy are widely shared.
- ***Strengthening Civil Society:*** Civil society organizations should be empowered and supported to play an active role in promoting democratic values, advocating for human rights, and holding the government accountable. The government should create an enabling environment for civil society activities and ensure their independence.
- ***International Support:*** The international community should continue providing technical and financial support to Nepal's democratic consolidation efforts. Assistance should be aligned with national priorities and be mindful of promoting self-reliance and sovereignty.

Assessing the success and limitations of democracy in Nepal reveals both achievements and challenges in the country's democratic journey. While Nepal has made significant progress in democratic consolidation, persistent challenges such as political instability, corruption, socio-economic disparities, and security concerns remain. By addressing these challenges through strengthened institutions, inclusive development, civic engagement, and international support, Nepal can overcome its limitations and continue on the path towards a successful and sustainable democracy.

Nepal's experience provides valuable lessons for other countries undergoing democratic transitions. The emphasis on inclusivity, peaceful conflict resolution, and a participatory constitution-making process can serve as guiding principles for countries grappling with similar challenges. Additionally, the importance of balancing external support with national sovereignty, strengthening democratic institutions, and promoting civic engagement should be taken into consideration.

Moving forward, Nepal should focus on fostering political stability through consensus-building and accountability. Efforts to combat corruption and promote transparency will be crucial in building public trust in democratic institutions. Prioritizing inclusive development and addressing socio-economic disparities will ensure that the benefits of democracy reach all segments of society. Furthermore, empowering civil society and creating an enabling environment for their activities will enhance democratic governance and citizen participation.

The international community should continue to support Nepal's democratic consolidation through technical assistance, capacity-building, and targeted funding. However, it is essential to respect Nepal's sovereignty and align support with its national priorities.

While Nepal has made significant strides in its democratic transition, challenges persist. By learning from its successes and limitations, Nepal can chart a path towards a more robust and inclusive democracy. With political stability, accountability, inclusive development, and active civic engagement, Nepal can overcome its challenges and continue to strengthen its democratic institutions for the betterment of its people.

"Nepal's democratic journey is a bridge connecting its past to a future where freedom reigns."

---

13. POTENTIAL OF A GORKHA SOLDIER

"Democracy in Nepal creates a system where leaders are accountable to the citizens and can be held responsible for their actions"

Nepal as a Republic: An Indian Soldier's Perspective

Nestled in the embrace of the majestic Himalayas, Nepal has captivated the world with its rich cultural heritage, breathtaking landscapes, and the resilience of its people. In 2008, Nepal made a historic transition from a constitutional monarchy to a federal democratic republic, marking a significant turning point in its history. As an Indian soldier who has had the privilege of serving in military wing of Indian embassy at Kathmandu. I would like to provide an overview of Nepal's transformation into a republic and shed light on its journey towards democracy, progress, and stability.

- ***Historical Context:*** Nepal's history is steeped in tradition and monarchy, with a legacy that dates back centuries. However, it was in 2006 that Nepal witnessed a momentous event known as the People's Movement, also referred to as the Nepal Revolution. The movement was a culmination of years of political, social, and economic grievances, demanding greater democratic freedoms and an end to the absolute monarchy that had ruled the country for generations.
- ***Transition to a Republic:*** The People's Movement led to a comprehensive peace agreement between the government and the Maoist rebels, promising to address the demands for a more inclusive political system. Following this, the first Constituent Assembly was formed in 2008, tasked with drafting a new constitution and deciding the fate of the monarchy. The assembly declared Nepal as a federal democratic republic, effectively ending the reign of the monarchy and establishing a new era for the country.
- ***Democratic Progress and Challenges:*** The transition to a republic marked a significant step towards democratization in Nepal. The country embraced a multi-party system, granting citizens the right to vote and participate in political processes. The Constituent Assembly, subsequently replaced by the Federal Parliament, played a crucial role in shaping Nepal's future by drafting and promulgating the new constitution in 2015.

However, Nepal's journey towards democracy has not been without challenges. The country faced numerous hurdles, including political instability, constitutional disputes, and struggles in implementing federalism effectively. Ethnic and regional tensions, as well as socio-economic disparities, have posed challenges to the country's unity and stability. Nonetheless, Nepal's commitment to democratic values remains unwavering, with ongoing efforts to address these challenges and strengthen democratic institutions.

- ***Inclusive Governance and Social Transformation:*** One of the significant achievements of Nepal's republic has been the pursuit of inclusive governance and social transformation. Marginalized communities, such as Dalits, women, and ethnic minorities, have gained greater representation in political offices and decision-making processes. The new constitution guarantees equal rights and opportunities for all citizens, promoting social justice and equity.

Furthermore, Nepal has made significant strides in areas such as education, healthcare, and infrastructure development. Efforts have been made to improve access to quality education, particularly in rural areas, empowering the youth with knowledge and skills for a brighter future. The government has also prioritized healthcare reforms, aiming to provide affordable and accessible healthcare services to all Nepalese citizens.

- ***Tourism and Economic Potential:*** Nepal's transition to a republic has also had a positive impact on its tourism and economic sectors. The country's natural beauty, including the towering Mount Everest and lush landscapes, continues to attract adventure enthusiasts and nature lovers from around the globe. The tourism industry plays a vital role in generating revenue, creating employment opportunities, and fostering cultural exchange.

Moreover, Nepal's strategic location between two emerging economies, India and China, presents immense economic potential. As a republic, Nepal has actively pursued economic reforms, encouraging foreign direct investment and promoting trade relations with neighboring countries and the international community. Efforts have been made to diversify the economy beyond agriculture and harness sectors such as hydropower, manufacturing, and information technology. These initiatives aim to stimulate economic growth, reduce poverty, and improve the overall standard of living for the Nepalese people.

- ***Security and Defense Cooperation:*** As an Indian soldier who has had the honor of working closely with the Nepalese Govt., I must mention the strong security and defense cooperation between India and Nepal. The two countries share a unique bond and a long history of military collaboration. Bilateral exercises, joint training programs, and exchange visits between the armed forces of India and Nepal have contributed to enhancing the security environment and fostering mutual trust.

Nepal's commitment to maintaining peace and stability in the region is commendable. The Nepalese Army plays a vital role in safeguarding national sovereignty, protecting the country's borders, and supporting disaster relief operations. The professionalism, discipline, and bravery exhibited by the Nepalese soldiers are truly inspiring and reflect their dedication towards ensuring the safety and well-being of the Nepalese people.

- ***Social Harmony and Cultural Diversity:*** Nepal's transition to a republic has also highlighted the country's rich cultural diversity and the importance of social harmony. As a melting pot of various ethnicities, languages, and religions, Nepal has embraced its multicultural fabric and nurtured a spirit of unity in diversity. Festivals like Dashain, Tihar, and Teej bring people from different communities together, fostering a sense of shared heritage and traditions.

The promotion and preservation of cultural heritage sites, such as the Kathmandu Valley's UNESCO World Heritage sites, have been a priority for the government. These sites not only attract tourists but also serve as a reminder of Nepal's glorious past and its commitment to cultural heritage conservation.

Nepal's transition to a republic has been a remarkable journey, marking a significant milestone in the country's history. While challenges persist, Nepal has made commendable progress in consolidating its democratic institutions, promoting social inclusion, and pursuing economic growth. The country's commitment to upholding democratic values, fostering social harmony, and preserving its rich cultural heritage is truly admirable.

"In every democratic stride, Nepal's people march towards a future crafted by their aspirations."

The Contribution of Nepalese Citizens in Foreign Armies: A Global Perspective

Nepalese citizens have a long-standing tradition of serving in foreign armies, utilizing their skills, bravery, and dedication to contribute to the defense forces of various nations. With a rich history of martial traditions and a reputation for resilience and loyalty, Nepalese soldiers have been sought after by several countries around the world. This chapter aims to explore the significant contributions made by Nepalese citizens in foreign armies, highlighting the countries that have recruited them and the reasons behind their recruitment.

- ***The Gurkhas in the British Army:*** Perhaps the most well-known example of Nepalese citizens serving in foreign armies is the Gurkhas in the British Army. Dating back to the early 19th century, the recruitment of Gurkhas began during the British colonial era in India. The Gurkhas established their legacy of bravery and discipline during various conflicts, including the two World Wars, the Falklands War, and numerous peacekeeping missions worldwide. Their distinguished service has earned them a reputation as fearsome warriors and loyal soldiers.
- ***The Gurkhas in the Indian Army:*** Apart from the British Army, Nepalese citizens have also made substantial contributions to the Indian Army. The Gurkha regiments in the Indian Army, like their British counterparts, have a long history of service. The Gurkha soldiers have been an integral part of the Indian Army, participating in both internal security operations and external conflicts. Their remarkable courage and military prowess have been widely acknowledged, making them a valuable asset to the Indian defense forces.
- ***Gurkhas in the Singapore Police Force:*** Singapore is another country that has recruited Nepalese citizens, particularly in the Singapore Police Force. The Gurkha Contingent, established in 1949, is responsible for providing armed protection to key installations and VIPs in Singapore. Highly trained in combat and security operations, the Gurkhas in the Singapore Police Force maintain the reputation of their predecessors, showcasing their unwavering dedication and professionalism.
- ***Gurkhas in the Malaysian Armed Forces:*** Malaysia has a significant number of Nepalese citizens serving in its armed forces. The Gurkha Regiment in the Malaysian Armed Forces is composed of skilled soldiers who

primarily undertake security duties. Their roles range from guarding key installations to participating in counter-terrorism operations. The Gurkhas in Malaysia have demonstrated their capabilities in maintaining law and order, thereby contributing to the nation's security.

- ***Gurkhas in the Brunei Armed Forces:*** Nepalese citizens have also found opportunities to serve in the Brunei Armed Forces. Brunei's Gurkha Reserve Unit, established in 1949, has been an essential component of the country's defense strategy. The Gurkhas in Brunei undertake a variety of roles, including combat operations, peacekeeping missions, and ceremonial duties. Their presence in the armed forces of Brunei reflects the ongoing historical ties between Nepal and Brunei.
- ***Gurkhas in the Indian Paramilitary Forces:*** In addition to the Indian Army, Nepalese citizens have made notable contributions to the Indian Paramilitary Forces. Organizations such as the Sashastra Seema Bal (SSB) and the Indo-Tibetan Border Police (ITBP) have actively recruited Gurkha personnel. These forces are responsible for border security, anti-insurgency operations, and maintaining internal stability. The Gurkhas' inclusion in these paramilitary forces further highlights their crucial role in safeguarding India's borders and maintaining internal security.
- ***Gurkhas in the United Nations Peacekeeping Missions:*** Nepal has a long history of contributing troops to United Nations peacekeeping missions, and Gurkha soldiers have been an integral part of these deployments. Nepalese citizens have served in UN missions worldwide, including countries like Lebanon, South Sudan, Congo, and Liberia. Their professionalism, discipline, and ability to adapt to challenging environments have earned them recognition and respect within the international community.
- ***Gurkhas in the Middle East:*** In recent years, there has been an increasing presence of Nepalese citizens in the armed forces of several Middle Eastern countries. Nations like Qatar, Bahrain, and the United Arab Emirates have recruited Nepalese individuals for their security forces. These individuals play vital roles in maintaining internal security, protecting critical infrastructure, and supporting defense operations.
- ***Gurkhas in the United States Army:*** While relatively smaller in numbers compared to other countries, Nepalese citizens have also made contributions to the United States Army. The U.S. Army has recruited individuals from Nepal, recognizing their military skills and dedication. These individuals typically serve in various roles, including combat units, logistics, and support services.

- ***Reasons for Recruiting Nepalese Citizens:*** The recruitment of Nepalese citizens in foreign armies can be attributed to several factors. First, Nepal has a long history of martial traditions, with a culture that values bravery, loyalty, and discipline. The reputation of Gurkha soldiers, built over centuries, has made them highly sought after by many nations.

Second, Nepalese citizens often possess physical and mental attributes that are desirable in military personnel, such as strength, endurance, and adaptability. They are known for their ability to perform well in challenging terrain and adverse weather conditions.

Furthermore, the recruitment of Nepalese citizens is often driven by economic factors. Many individuals from Nepal join foreign armies as a means to secure better livelihoods for themselves and their families. The income and benefits provided by foreign armies can significantly improve their socio-economic status.

- ***Impact on Nepal:*** The involvement of Nepalese citizens in foreign armies has had a significant impact on Nepal as well. First and foremost, the remittances sent back by these individuals play a crucial role in the country's economy. The income earned by Nepalese soldiers abroad often exceeds what they could earn within Nepal, providing financial stability to their families and contributing to the overall economic growth of the nation.

Additionally, the experiences gained by Nepalese citizens serving in foreign armies bring back valuable skills and knowledge that can be applied within Nepal. These individuals often receive extensive training in various aspects of military operations, leadership, and technical expertise. When they return to their homeland, they can contribute to the development of Nepal's own security forces, sharing their expertise and enhancing the capabilities of the national defense.

Furthermore, the international recognition garnered by Nepalese soldiers for their bravery and professionalism helps raise the profile of Nepal on the global stage. The reputation of Gurkha soldiers, in particular, has become synonymous with excellence in military service. This recognition can open doors for diplomatic and economic opportunities for Nepal, as countries value the strong ties and positive associations linked with Nepalese citizens.

- ***Challenges and Controversies:*** Despite the significant contributions and positive impact, the recruitment of Nepalese citizens in foreign armies has not been without challenges and controversies. One of the primary concerns is related to the welfare and rights of these individuals. Issues such as proper compensation, adequate working conditions, and access to healthcare and social benefits have been raised in some instances. It is crucial for the countries employing Nepalese citizens to ensure that they are treated fairly and provided with the necessary support and protection.

Another area of concern is the potential brain drain effect. As skilled and capable individuals leave Nepal to join foreign armies, there is a loss of talent within the country. This can have implications for various sectors, including the domestic security forces, where the absence of experienced personnel might hinder the development and effectiveness of the national defense.

Lastly, there have been debates surrounding the ethics of recruiting soldiers from economically disadvantaged countries like Nepal. Critics argue that such recruitment practices exploit vulnerable individuals who may have limited options for employment. It is essential for the recruiting countries to ensure that the recruitment process is fair, transparent, and respectful of the rights and dignity of the individuals involved.

The contributions of Nepalese citizens in foreign armies are a testament to their bravery, discipline, and dedication. From serving in the British and Indian armies to joining the armed forces of countries across the globe, Nepalese soldiers have left an indelible mark. Their involvement has not only benefited the receiving nations but has also had a significant impact on Nepal, contributing to the economy, sharing expertise, and enhancing the country's international standing. However, it is crucial to address the challenges and controversies associated with the recruitment process to ensure the fair treatment and well-being of Nepalese citizens serving in foreign armies.

"Democracy in Nepal is the sun rising on the horizon, dispelling the darkness of autocracy."

Nepal Government's Decision to Restrict Citizens Joining Indian Armed Forces Amidst Agniveer Scheme Introduction

The relationship between Nepal and India has been historically intertwined, marked by cultural, social, and economic ties. These two neighboring nations have shared a close bond for centuries. Among the various aspects of bilateral relations, one significant aspect has been the involvement of Nepalese citizens in the Indian Armed Forces. However, in recent times, the government of Nepal made a decision to restrict its citizens from joining the Indian Armed Forces after India introduced the Agniveer scheme. This chapter aims to delve into the reasons behind the Nepalese government's decision, the implications of the Agniveer scheme, and the potential impact on the bilateral relationship between Nepal and India.

- ***Historical Context of Nepalese Citizens in Indian Armed Forces:*** Nepal and India have a long-standing tradition of cooperation in the defense sector. The Gurkha soldiers from Nepal have a rich history of serving in the Indian Armed Forces, dating back to the early 19th century. Over the years, thousands of brave Nepalese citizens have joined various branches of the Indian Army, earning a reputation for their valor, loyalty, and dedication. This practice has not only strengthened the military ties between both nations but has also contributed to the socio-economic development of Nepal through remittances.
- ***The Agniveer Scheme: An Overview:*** The Agniveer scheme, introduced by the Indian government, aimed to streamline the recruitment process for foreign nationals in the Indian Armed Forces. It sought to attract talented individuals from neighboring countries, including Nepal, who could contribute to India's defense capabilities. Under this scheme, foreign nationals would be eligible for direct recruitment without having to go through the existing process of joining the Indian Army. The Agniveer scheme was perceived as a means to bolster India's military strength while forging closer ties with neighboring countries.
- ***Concerns and Reasons behind Nepal's Decision:*** The decision of the Nepal government to restrict its citizens from joining the Indian Armed

Forces after the introduction of the Agniveer scheme was met with surprise and speculation. Several factors contributed to this decision:

- *National Security and Sovereignty:* The Nepalese government expressed concerns about safeguarding its national security and sovereignty. Allowing its citizens to directly join the Indian Armed Forces under the Agniveer scheme could potentially compromise Nepal's ability to maintain an independent defense policy. Nepal's geopolitical position, nestled between India and China, necessitates a cautious approach to military cooperation with its neighbors.
- *Economic Implications:* The recruitment of Nepalese citizens in the Indian Armed Forces has been a significant source of remittances for Nepal. The restriction on joining the Indian Army could impact the livelihoods of many Nepalese families who rely on the income earned by their family members serving in the Indian Armed Forces. The government may have considered the economic implications of such a decision.
- *Strengthening Internal Security:* Nepal has been grappling with internal security challenges, including ethnic tensions and cross-border criminal activities. The government's decision to restrict citizens from joining foreign armed forces might be a strategy to retain skilled personnel within the country to address internal security concerns effectively.

• ***Implications on Bilateral Relations:*** The restriction on Nepalese citizens joining the Indian Armed Forces has the potential to impact the bilateral relationship between Nepal and India. Both nations will need to navigate this decision carefully to ensure that it does not strain their overall relationship. The following implications may arise:

- *Diplomatic Dialogue:* The implementation of the Agniveer scheme and Nepal's response necessitate open and transparent diplomatic dialogue between the two nations. It is crucial for both sides to address each other's concerns, clarify intentions, and explore alternative avenues of cooperation to maintain a healthy bilateral relationship.
- *Economic Cooperation:* With the restriction on Nepalese citizens joining the Indian Armed Forces, both countries might need to explore alternative avenues for economic cooperation. This could involve diversifying economic ties, strengthening trade relations, and

promoting investments in sectors that benefit both nations. Emphasizing economic cooperation can help mitigate the potential economic impact caused by the decision.

- *Defense Cooperation:* While the restriction on Nepalese citizens joining the Indian Armed Forces affects defense cooperation to some extent, it does not necessarily have to undermine the overall defense ties between Nepal and India. Both countries can explore other areas of collaboration, such as joint military exercises, intelligence sharing, and capacity-building programs, to maintain a robust defense partnership.
- *Cultural and People-to-People Exchanges:* Cultural and people-to-people exchanges have been the bedrock of the Nepal-India relationship. It is crucial to preserve and strengthen these ties, despite the decision regarding military recruitment. Promoting cultural exchanges, educational collaborations, tourism, and promoting mutual understanding can help bridge any potential gaps caused by the restriction.

The decision of the Nepal government to restrict its citizens from joining the Indian Armed Forces after the introduction of the Agniveer scheme reflects concerns about national security, sovereignty, and internal stability. While this decision may impact the historical tradition of Nepalese citizens serving in the Indian Army, both Nepal and India must engage in open dialogue to ensure that their bilateral relationship remains strong and unaffected. By focusing on alternative areas of cooperation, economic ties, defense collaboration, and cultural exchanges, both nations can navigate this situation while preserving the spirit of friendship and collaboration that has defined their relationship for centuries.

"From feudalism to freedom: Nepal's democracy is the triumph of the people over oppression."

---

14. AUTHOR'S EXPERIMENTS WITH NEPAL

"Democracy in Nepal encourages dialogue and collaboration among citizens, fostering a culture of open communication and mutual respect"

Memories of Service at the Indian Embassy Kathmandu, Military Wing (1989-1993)

This chapter delves into the personal experiences and memories of serving at the Indian Embassy Kathmandu, Military Wing, from May 1989 to May 1993. During this period, Nepal faced a blockade of entry points by India, which had a significant impact on daily life and transportation. The author had the opportunity to travel extensively throughout Nepal, organizing health camps, and disbursing pensions to retired Nepalese soldiers. Additionally, the author worked closely with three ambassadors, several dignitaries, and military attaches, leaving a lasting impression of a fulfilling and eventful tenure.

- ***Arrival in Kathmandu and the Blockade:*** Upon arrival in Kathmandu, the author recalls witnessing a unique sight—only CD number cars plying on the roads due to the blockade imposed by India. This blockade had resulted in limited access to essential supplies and goods, significantly impacting the daily lives of the Nepalese people. The author experienced firsthand the challenges faced by the local population during this period.
- ***Disbursement of Pensions and Organization of Health Camps:*** During the tenure at the Indian Embassy Kathmandu, the author's responsibilities included the disbursement of pensions to retired Nepalese soldiers and organizing health camps across various districts and zones of Nepal. These initiatives aimed to provide support and assistance to retired soldiers and contribute to their well-being. The author vividly recalls the experiences of traveling to different regions of Nepal, interacting with retired soldiers, and witnessing the impact of these initiatives on their lives.
- ***Interaction with Ambassadors and Dignitaries:*** The author had the privilege of serving under three ambassadors at the Indian Embassy Kathmandu: Sh. A.R. Deo, Lt. Gen. S.K. Sinha, and Prof. Bimal Prasad. These esteemed diplomats provided guidance, leadership, and mentorship during the author's tenure. The author also recounts the memorable visits of notable personalities such as General S.F. Rodrigues, Prime Minister Sh. P.V. Narasimha Rao, and Foreign Secretary Sh. J.N. Dixit. Additionally, the author had the honor of hosting and accompanying Nepalese Prime Ministers

Sh. K.P. Bhattarai and Sh. G.P. Koirala during their visits to the offices/institutions of India located in Nepal.

- ***Permanent Pension Camps and DSBs:*** The Indian Embassy Kathmandu, Military Wing, operated three permanent pension camps: PPO Dharan, PPO Pokhara, and PPO Kathmandu. These camps provided a centralized location for pension-related matters and facilitated efficient processes. The author reflects on the significance of these camps and the positive impact they had on retired soldiers and their families. Additionally, there were 14 District Soldier Boards (DSBs) established to address the needs of retired soldiers across various districts of Nepal.
- ***Memorable Military Attaches:*** The author served under two military attaches, Col. Arvind Sharma and Col. Richard Kare, both of whom later retired as Lieutenant Generals. The author fondly remembers their leadership, professionalism, and guidance. These military attaches played a crucial role in strengthening the relationship between the Indian Embassy Kathmandu and the Nepalese Armed Forces.

The author's tenure at the Indian Embassy Kathmandu, Military Wing, from 1989 to 1993 was marked by significant experiences, challenges, and accomplishments. Serving during a period of blockade and witnessing the impact on daily life in Nepal provided valuable insights into the resilience and spirit of the Nepalese people. The author's involvement in disbursing pensions and organizing health camps across Nepal allowed for direct interaction with retired soldiers and a deep understanding of their needs and aspirations.

Working under the guidance of three distinguished ambassadors and interacting with notable personalities such as General S.F. Rodrigues, Prime Minister P.V. Narasimha Rao, and Foreign Secretary J.N. Dixit added to the author's professional growth and provided unique opportunities to strengthen the relationship between India and Nepal.

The establishment of permanent pension camps and District Soldier Boards (DSBs) within the embassy campus demonstrated the commitment to providing efficient and centralized services to retired soldiers. These initiatives not only improved the lives of retired soldiers and their families but also contributed to fostering a sense of camaraderie and support within the Nepalese military community.

Lastly, the author's tenure was enriched by the mentorship and leadership of military attaches Col. Arvind Sharma and Col. Richard Kare, who later retired as Lieutenant Generals. Their guidance and professionalism left a lasting impression on the author's career and contributed to the successful execution of responsibilities at the embassy.

Thc author's service at the Indian Embassy Kathmandu, Military Wing, from 1989 to 1993 was characterized by meaningful engagements, memorable experiences, and a deep appreciation for the close relationship between India and Nepal. The opportunity to work closely with Nepalese soldiers, retired personnel, and high-ranking officials solidified the author's commitment to serving and supporting the defense and welfare of both nations.

"Democracy in Nepal is not just a system but a symphony played by the hearts of its citizens."

Supporting the Dignity of Nepalese Domiciled Gorkhas: The Role of Pension Paying Offices and Military Wing Welfare Section

➢ Indian Embassy Kathmandu, Nepal: Welfare of Smiling Soldiers

❖ *DEFENCE WING*

- India has always been proud to have Nepalese as soldiers in her Defence Forces and has made every effort to ensure that they are looked after and cared for in their twilight years.
- The Origin of the Defence Wing in Nepal dates back to the Tripartite Agreement signed between the representatives of the Govt. of UK, India and Nepal on 09 November 1947. The then Nepalese Prime Minister and C-in-C, His Highness Padam SJB Rana agreed to maintain the Gorkha connection with the British Army and the Indian Army. The Indian Army has maintained this Agreement in letter and spirit to this day and Gorkhas from Nepal continue to be recruited into the Indian Army. The Defence Wing under the Defence Attaché, Col Amit Sharma, comprises of the offices of the Defence Attaché, the Welfare Branch (NBGSB), the Military Pension Branch, the Record Office and the ECHS Branch at Kathmandu, and the PPOs at Pokhara and Dharan. The Defence Wing is organised as under: -

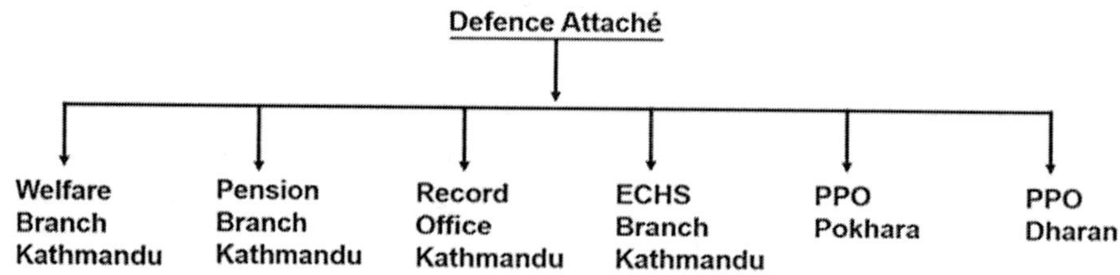

As of now, we have over 1.22 Lakh pensioners residing in Nepal. The Government of India has made every effort to ensure that these pensioners, their families and dependents are looked after in the best possible manner. To ensure this various branch of the Defence Wing are working in sync to fulfill the aspirations of our Nepal Domiciled Gorkha Ex-servicemen community.

The welfare and support provided to Nepalese domiciled Gorkhas who served in the Indian Army and later settled in Nepal after retirement is of paramount importance. During my tenure at the Indian Embassy in Kathmandu from 1989 to 1993, I had the privilege of serving under Col Arvind Sharma (later Lt Gen) & Col Richard Khare (later Lt Gen), Military & Air Attache and witnessing the functioning of the Pension Paying Offices (PPO) in Pokhara and Dharan, as well as the Welfare Section and Record Office under the Military Wing. Led by esteemed individuals, such as Col KS Yadava, Major Anil Kumar Chouhan, Capt JS Sandhu, Capt AR Rehman, Col KJ Singh, Col JB Monis, and Col Barthwal, these establishments played a vital role in providing essential services and support to the retired Gorkha soldiers residing in Nepal. This article aims to shed light on their crucial functions and the impact they had on the lives of those they served.

- ***The Role of Pension Paying Offices (PPO):*** The PPOs in Pokhara and Dharan were instrumental in ensuring the smooth disbursement of pensions to retired Nepalese Gorkha soldiers. Under the command of Col KS Yadava and Major Anil Kumar Chouhan, respectively, these offices acted as a bridge between the Indian Embassy and the retired soldiers. They meticulously handled the administrative tasks, verified pension records, and facilitated timely and accurate payment of pensions, thereby ensuring financial stability and security for the veterans and their families.
- ***The Welfare Section:*** Led by Col KJ Singh, the Welfare Section of the Military Wing played a pivotal role in addressing the diverse needs of the retired Gorkha soldiers. It focused on providing essential services encompassing healthcare, education, vocational training, and social welfare programs. The Welfare Section acted as a liaison between the retired soldiers, various government agencies, and non-governmental organizations, facilitating access to medical facilities, educational opportunities, and other support systems.
- ***The Record Office:*** The Record Office, led by Col JB Monis and later Col Barthwal, played a critical role in maintaining and updating the service records of the retired Gorkha soldiers. This office ensured the accuracy and confidentiality of the soldiers' records, including their years of service, promotions, awards, and entitlements. The diligent work of the Record Office safeguarded the rights and

entitlements of the veterans, ensuring they received the recognition and benefits they rightfully deserved.

- ***Distribution of Duties:*** The Military Attache, in coordination with the commanding officers of the respective establishments, efficiently distributed the duties among the personnel under their command. This streamlined approach ensured the smooth functioning of the PPOs, Welfare Section, and Record Office, allowing them to address the multifaceted needs of the retired Gorkha soldiers effectively. The collaborative efforts of the personnel involved played a crucial role in providing comprehensive support to the veterans and their families.

Ex-Servicemen Contributory Health Scheme (ECHS) Nepal

- ECHS is a flagship welfare scheme of Government of India and the scheme was sanctioned and extended to Nepal for the benefit of Nepal Domiciled Gorkha (NDG) Ex-Servicemen (ESM) and their dependents in Feb 2012.

- The ECHS Branch in the Embassy of India, Kathmandu was established in May 2012, while the three Polyclinics at Kathmandu and Pokhara (Type A) and Dharan (Type B) were established in April 2014. Alongwith the three Polyclinics, the Government of India also sanctioned three Type E Mobile Medical Units (MMUs)

- ECHS caters to the medical care of all NDG ESM pensioners including disabled, family pensioners and their dependents, which includes wife/husband, legitimate children and wholly dependent parents. To be eligible for membership of ECHS, a person must meet following conditions: -

  (a). Individual should have an Ex-serviceman status.

  (b). Individual should be in receipt of Pension / Family Pension / Disability Pension drawn from Controller of Defence Account.

  (c). Unemployed / unmarried son below 25 years of age and unemployed/ unmarried daughter for life can also be the dependents and can avail ECHS facilities.

  (d). The dependents/ dependent parent's income should be less than INR 9,000/- excluding DA.

Impact on Retired Gorkha Soldiers:

The combined efforts of the PPOs, Welfare Section, and Record Office had a profound impact on the lives of the retired Gorkha soldiers in Nepal. The timely disbursement of pensions provided financial stability, allowing the veterans to lead a dignified life after retirement. The welfare programs and support services offered through the Welfare Section improved access to healthcare, education, and vocational training

Enhanced Quality of Life:

The comprehensive support provided by the PPOs, Welfare Section, and Record Office resulted in an enhanced quality of life for the retired Gorkha soldiers. Access to healthcare facilities ensured their well-being, while educational opportunities empowered them and their families. Vocational training programs equipped them with valuable skills, enabling them to pursue alternative livelihoods and contribute to their communities. The holistic approach taken by these establishments aimed to uplift the retired soldiers and improve their overall well-being.

Preservation of Dignity and Recognition:

The diligent efforts of the PPOs and Military Wing establishments not only provided essential services but also played a crucial role in preserving the dignity and recognition of the retired Gorkha soldiers. By ensuring the accurate maintenance of their service records, facilitating timely pension payments, and advocating for their entitlements, these establishments reaffirmed the value and significance of their contributions to the Indian Army. This recognition contributed to the self-esteem and pride of the retired soldiers, fostering a sense of belonging and appreciation.

Overcoming Challenges:

The functioning of the PPOs, Welfare Section, and Record Office was not without its challenges. The sheer volume of retired soldiers, the complexity of administrative procedures, and the evolving needs of the veterans required constant adaptability and resourcefulness. However, the dedication and commitment of the personnel involved, under the leadership of esteemed officers such as Col KS Yadava, Major Anil Kumar Chouhan,

Capt JS Sandhu, Capt AR Rehman, Col KJ Singh, Col JB Monis, and Col Barthwal, ensured that these challenges were met with resilience and efficiency.

Collaborative Efforts and Future Outlook:

The success of the PPOs, Welfare Section, and Record Office was a testament to the collaborative efforts of all personnel involved. The coordination between the Military Attache and the commanding officers, as well as the cooperation with various government agencies and organizations, was crucial in meeting the diverse needs of the retired Gorkha soldiers. Looking ahead, it is essential to build upon the foundations laid by these establishments, further strengthen the support systems, and adapt to the evolving requirements of the veterans and their families.

Gratitude and Appreciation:

The functioning of the Pension Paying Offices in Pokhara and Dharan, along with the Welfare Section and Record Office under the Military Wing of the Indian Embassy in Kathmandu, served as lifelines for the retired Gorkha soldiers in Nepal. The tireless dedication, professionalism, and compassion of the personnel involved made a significant difference in the lives of those they served. The retired soldiers and their families owe a debt of gratitude to Col KS Yadava, Major Anil Kumar Chouhan, Capt JS Sandhu, Capt AR Rehman, Col KJ Singh, Col JB Monis, Col Barthwal, and all the other individuals who contributed to the functioning of these establishments.

Acknowledgment of Contributions:

It is imperative to acknowledge the invaluable contributions of the retired Gorkha soldiers to the Indian Army. Their unwavering dedication, bravery, and sacrifices have greatly contributed to the defense and security of both India and Nepal. The functioning of the PPOs, Welfare Section, and Record Office symbolizes the recognition and appreciation of their service, ensuring that their transition into civilian life is supported and respected.

Continuous Improvement and Adaptation:

As the needs of retired Gorkha soldiers evolve, it is crucial for the PPOs, Welfare Section, and Record Office to continuously improve and adapt their services. Regular assessments, feedback mechanisms, and engagement with the retired soldiers themselves can help identify areas for enhancement.

The utilization of technology and streamlined administrative processes can further streamline and expedite service delivery, ensuring the efficient utilization of resources.

Strengthening Bilateral Relations:

The functioning of these establishments not only serves the retired Gorkha soldiers but also plays a significant role in strengthening the bilateral relations between India and Nepal. The provision of essential services and support demonstrates the commitment of the Indian government to the welfare of its former soldiers residing in Nepal. It fosters a sense of goodwill, trust, and cooperation between the two nations, further deepening their ties.

Collaboration with Non-Governmental Organizations:

In addition to government agencies, collaboration with non-governmental organizations (NGOs) can enhance the support provided to retired Gorkha soldiers. NGOs specializing in healthcare, education, vocational training, and social welfare initiatives can complement the efforts of the PPOs, Welfare Section, and Record Office. Partnerships with NGOs can expand the range of services available and ensure a more comprehensive and holistic approach to supporting the retired soldiers.

Recognition of Personnel:

The personnel serving in the PPOs, Welfare Section, and Record Office deserve recognition and appreciation for their dedication and service. Their commitment to the welfare and well-being of the retired Gorkha soldiers is commendable. Providing training opportunities, career progression prospects, and incentives can motivate and retain skilled personnel, ensuring the continuity and effectiveness of these crucial establishments.

Inspiring Others:

The functioning of the PPOs, Welfare Section, and Record Office can serve as an inspiration for other nations with similar circumstances. It exemplifies how a nation can honor and support its retired soldiers who have dedicated their lives to its defense. Other countries can look to the Indian model and adopt similar structures and mechanisms to ensure the well-being and dignity of their own retired military personnel.

The Pension Paying Offices, Welfare Section, and Record Office under the Military Wing of the Indian Embassy in Kathmandu have played a vital role in providing essential services and support to retired Gorkha soldiers residing in Nepal. Led by esteemed officers and dedicated personnel, these establishments have ensured the timely disbursement of pensions, addressed diverse welfare needs, maintained accurate service records, and preserved the dignity and recognition of the veterans. As we move forward, it is crucial to build upon these foundations, continuously improve services, and strengthen bilateral relations. The tireless efforts of all involved in these establishments serve as a testament to the commitment and appreciation for the contributions of the retired Gorkha soldiers.

"Nepal's journey from monarchy to democracy is a journey from restraint to empowerment."

A Memorable Tenure: Education and Community life at Kendriya Vidyalaya Kathmandu

Embassy postings are often associated with unique experiences and privileges, and my tenure at the Indian Embassy Kathmandu, was no exception. This chapter aims to highlight the exceptional educational opportunities my sons, Navneet Pratap Singh and Navdeep Pratap Singh, received at KV Kathmandu, as well as the vibrant community life we enjoyed during our time there.

• ***The Selection System of Teachers in Kendriya Vidyalaya (KV) Kathmandu:*** Kendriya Vidyalaya (KV) Kathmandu prided itself on maintaining high teaching standards. All teachers, from primary to postgraduate level, underwent a robust selection process before being posted to the school. This ensured that the faculty consisted of highly qualified and dedicated individuals who were passionate about providing quality education to the students.

• ***Academic Excellence:*** At KV Kathmandu, my sons received their primary education in a nurturing and stimulating environment. The school's curriculum followed the guidelines set by the Central Board of Secondary Education (CBSE), ensuring a comprehensive and well-rounded education. The teachers were not only knowledgeable but also employed innovative teaching methods to make learning engaging and enjoyable.

• ***Sports Infrastructure:*** One of the standout features of KV Kathmandu was its sports infrastructure, conveniently located within the embassy complex. The school recognized the importance of physical fitness and provided ample opportunities for students to participate in various sports activities. The well-maintained sports facilities allowed my sons to explore their athletic abilities and fostered a spirit of healthy competition among the students.

• ***Embassy Accommodation:*** As part of the embassy staff, we were provided with a fully furnished three-bedroom house within the embassy complex. This accommodation ensured our comfort and convenience during our stay. The house was equipped with all essential fittings, making it a home away from home for our family.

- ***Community Engagement:*** Living within the embassy complex offered a unique opportunity to build a close-knit community. I actively participated in establishing a children's club within the embassy, which served as a platform for children from various states to interact, engage in cultural exchange, and develop lifelong friendships. Furthermore, I had the privilege of anchoring various embassy programs, which further strengthened my connection with the community.
- ***Cultural Exchange:*** Being in an international setting, KV Kathmandu fostered an environment of cultural diversity and exchange. Students from different nationalities and backgrounds came together, creating a melting pot of ideas, traditions, and perspectives. This exposure broadened my sons' horizons and instilled in them a deep appreciation for different cultures and values.
- ***Parent-Teacher Collaboration:*** KV Kathmandu fostered a strong bond between parents and teachers, promoting a collaborative approach to education. Regular parent-teacher meetings were held to discuss the progress of the students and address any concerns. The teachers were approachable and willing to provide guidance and support, ensuring the holistic development of the students.
- ***Extracurricular Activities:*** Apart from academic pursuits, KV Kathmandu emphasized the importance of extracurricular activities. The school offered a wide range of clubs and societies catering to diverse interests such as music, dance, arts, and science. These activities allowed students to explore their passions and develop their talents beyond the classroom.
- ***Cultural and Festive Celebrations:*** The school actively celebrated various cultural festivals and national events, providing a platform for students to learn about different traditions and customs. These celebrations not only enriched the students' cultural knowledge but also fostered a sense of unity and inclusivity among the diverse student body.
- ***Educational Excursions:*** KV Kathmandu organized educational excursions to places of historical, cultural, and natural significance. These field trips were not only educational but also offered students the opportunity to explore the rich heritage and natural beauty of Nepal. Such excursions expanded their horizons and brought their classroom learning to life.
- ***Focus on Values and Discipline:*** KV Kathmandu placed a strong emphasis on inculcating moral values and discipline in its students. Regular value education classes and character-building activities were integrated into the curriculum, ensuring the holistic development of the students. This focus

on values helped shape students into responsible and compassionate individuals.

- ***Alumni Network:*** KV Kathmandu boasted a robust alumni network that served as a valuable resource for current students. Alumni often returned to share their experiences, provide guidance, and inspire the younger generation. This network created a sense of continuity and pride among the students, fostering a strong bond with the school even after graduating.

My family's experience at Kendriya Vidyalaya Kathmandu inside the Indian embassy complex was nothing short of extraordinary. The school's commitment to academic excellence, coupled with its focus on sports, extracurricular activities, cultural exchange, and values, provided my sons with a well-rounded education. The supportive and engaging environment, combined with the strong parent-teacher collaboration, contributed to their overall growth and development. Our tenure at KV Kathmandu will always hold a special place in our hearts as a time filled with invaluable experiences, lifelong friendships, and cherished memories.

"The pages of Nepal's history are rewritten with the ink of democracy, authored by the people."

The Remarkable Qualities of the Nepalese: A Testament to their Character and Dedication

In any work environment, the qualities and characteristics of the individuals we interact with significantly impact our experience. Throughout my four-year tenure at the embassy, I had the privilege of working closely with Nepalese individuals who held positions as helpers, peons, drivers, and safaiwalas. Their honesty, straightforwardness, loyalty, simplicity, bravery, toughness, spirit of sacrifice, devotion, and submissive qualities left an indelible impression on me. This chapter explores the exceptional attributes of the Nepalese people, their unwavering commitment to perfection, and the profound impact they had on my professional journey.

- ***Honesty and Straightforwardness:*** One of the most striking qualities exhibited by the Nepalese individuals I worked with was their unwavering honesty and straightforwardness. They possessed a remarkable sense of integrity, always choosing truth and transparency over deceit and manipulation. This attribute fostered an atmosphere of trust and reliability within the workplace, leading to more efficient communication and collaboration.
- ***Loyalty and Devotion:*** Loyalty is a rare quality that is highly admired and cherished. The Nepalese workers showcased unwavering loyalty towards their work, superiors, and colleagues. They displayed a deep sense of dedication and devotion, consistently going above and beyond their assigned responsibilities to ensure the smooth functioning of the embassy. Their commitment to their duties was truly commendable and fostered a strong sense of camaraderie within the team.
- ***Simplicity and Humility:*** The simplicity and humility exhibited by the Nepalese individuals were truly refreshing. Despite holding positions that might be considered menial by some, they approached their work with a sense of dignity and pride. Their modesty and lack of pretense created an environment free from ego clashes and power struggles, allowing for a harmonious and productive workplace.
- ***Bravery and Toughness:*** In addition to their humility, the Nepalese workers also displayed remarkable bravery and toughness in the face of challenges. Their resilience and determination were evident in their ability to

overcome obstacles and adapt to difficult circumstances. Whether it was working long hours, braving inclement weather, or navigating unfamiliar territories, they approached every task with unwavering courage and fortitude.

- ***Spirit of Sacrifice and Devotion:*** The spirit of sacrifice and devotion exhibited by the Nepalese workers was truly awe-inspiring. They willingly put the needs of the embassy and their colleagues before their own, often sacrificing personal time and comfort for the greater good. Their selflessness and dedication created a sense of unity and purpose within the team, fostering an environment conducive to achieving shared goals.
- ***Submissive Qualities and Attitude towards Perfection:*** The submissive qualities displayed by the Nepalese individuals were not signs of weakness but rather a testament to their commitment to excellence. They approached their tasks with meticulous attention to detail and a desire for perfection. This attitude towards their work ensured that every task was completed to the best of their abilities, leaving no room for complacency or mediocrity.
- ***Cherishing the Association:*** Throughout my four-year tenure at the embassy, the Nepalese workers became an integral part of my professional journey. Their exceptional qualities and unwavering commitment left a lasting impact on me. The bond we shared, built on trust, respect and mutual admiration, enriched my experience and made it truly memorable. Their presence in my team was not just limited to their job roles; it extended to being a source of inspiration, support, and friendship.
- ***The Impact on Team Dynamics:*** The inclusion of Nepalese individuals in my team brought about a positive transformation in team dynamics. Their exemplary qualities set a high standard for professionalism, integrity, and work ethic. Their dedication and commitment motivated others to strive for excellence and go the extra mile in their own roles. The strong sense of unity and collaboration fostered by the Nepalese workers contributed to increased productivity and a harmonious work environment.
- ***Cultural Exchange and Learning:*** Working closely with the Nepalese individuals provided me with a unique opportunity for cultural exchange and learning. I gained insights into their rich traditions, values, and ways of life. This exchange of ideas and perspectives broadened my horizons and enriched my understanding of diverse cultures. It also enhanced my ability to work effectively in a multicultural environment and appreciate the strengths that each individual brings to the table.

- ***Lessons in Perseverance and Resilience:*** The Nepalese workers exemplified the virtues of perseverance and resilience in the face of adversity. Their ability to overcome challenges with unwavering determination taught me valuable lessons about resilience and the importance of a positive mindset. Their stories of personal struggles and triumphs served as a reminder that no obstacle is insurmountable with the right attitude and perseverance.
- ***Mutual Respect and Gratitude:*** The mutual respect and gratitude shared between myself and the Nepalese workers formed the foundation of our strong bond. I deeply appreciated their contributions and the impact they had on the success of our team. Likewise, they expressed gratitude for the opportunities and support they received in their roles. This mutual respect created an atmosphere of appreciation and acknowledgment, further strengthening our association.
- ***Sustaining the Nepalese Presence:*** Given the remarkable qualities and contributions of the Nepalese individuals, it is only natural to desire their continued presence in any team or organization. Their work ethic, loyalty, and dedication are assets that can greatly enhance the productivity and effectiveness of any workplace. Recognizing and nurturing their talents and providing opportunities for growth and development will not only benefit the individuals but also contribute to the overall success of the organization.

The Nepalese individuals I had the privilege of working with at the embassy embodied a remarkable set of qualities that left a lasting impression on me. Their honesty, straightforwardness, loyalty, simplicity, bravery, toughness, spirit of sacrifice, devotion, and submissive qualities set them apart as exceptional individuals. Their unwavering commitment to perfection and the impact they had on team dynamics and workplace culture were invaluable. I am forever grateful for the association I had with them and the lessons I learned from their exemplary character. Moving forward, I believe that embracing and cherishing the Nepalese presence in any team will undoubtedly lead to a stronger, more cohesive, and successful collective endeavor.

"As the monarchy fades into history, Nepal's democracy rises like the morning sun, bright and promising."

Embracing the Nepali Language: A Journey of Cultural Connection and Personal Growth

Language has the remarkable ability to bridge gaps, foster connections, and deepen our understanding of diverse cultures. My experience at the embassy provided me with a unique opportunity to immerse myself in the Nepali language, thanks to the guidance and support of our Nepalese staff. Over time, I not only became a fluent speaker but also ventured into scriptwriting, crafting lectures for esteemed individuals such as the Military Attaché and other dignitaries. This chapter delves into my journey of learning Nepali, the impact it had on my work and interactions, and the enduring connection I feel whenever I come across someone who speaks the language.

- ***The Power of Language in Cultural Exchange:*** Language serves as a powerful tool for cultural exchange, allowing individuals to connect on a deeper level. Learning Nepali opened doors to a rich cultural heritage, traditions, and values that were previously inaccessible to me. By delving into the language, I gained insights into the Nepalese way of life, their history, and their unique worldview. This linguistic journey provided a foundation for a more profound appreciation and understanding of Nepali culture.
- ***The Role of Nepalese Staff in Language Acquisition:*** The supportive environment created by our Nepalese staff played a pivotal role in my language acquisition journey. Their patience, encouragement, and willingness to teach me Nepali were instrumental in my progress. Their eagerness to share their language and culture exemplified their sense of community and their desire to foster cross-cultural understanding.
- ***Becoming Fluent in Nepali:*** Through consistent practice and immersion in the language, I gradually became a fluent speaker of Nepali. The process involved not only learning vocabulary and grammar but also embracing the nuances of pronunciation and cultural context. Regular conversations with Nepalese colleagues and utilizing Nepali in everyday interactions further solidified my language skills.
- ***Venturing into Scriptwriting:*** As my proficiency in Nepali grew, I sought opportunities to apply my language skills in a professional capacity. This led me to venture into scriptwriting for the embassy, particularly for lectures

delivered by the Military Attaché and other dignitaries. Crafting lecture scripts in Nepali allowed me to combine my language proficiency with my writing skills, contributing to effective communication and conveying messages with cultural sensitivity.

- ***The Impact on Work and Interactions:*** The ability to speak Nepali had a transformative impact on my work and interactions within the embassy. It enabled me to engage more effectively with Nepalese colleagues, forging stronger connections and fostering a sense of camaraderie. Clear communication in their native language not only enhanced efficiency but also demonstrated respect for their culture and language.
- ***Cultural Sensitivity and Connection:*** Speaking Nepali not only facilitated smoother interactions but also deepened cultural sensitivity. Understanding the subtleties of the language allowed me to navigate social situations with greater finesse and respect. It fostered a sense of connection and camaraderie, as I was able to engage in conversations and exchange pleasantries in Nepali, instantly bridging the cultural gap.
- ***The Joy of Language Preservation:*** Language preservation is a vital aspect of cultural heritage. By actively learning and speaking Nepali, I contributed to the preservation and promotion of the language. This endeavor went beyond personal growth, serving as a testament to my appreciation for the richness and diversity of languages worldwide.
- ***Nepali Language as a Gateway to Opportunities:*** The acquisition of Nepali language skills opened up a myriad of opportunities both within and beyond the embassy. It allowed me to connect with a broader network of individuals, including Nepali diplomats, scholars, and community members. The ability to communicate in their native language created a sense of trust and familiarity, facilitating collaborations and fostering new avenues for professional growth.
- ***Language as a Bridge between Cultures:*** Language acts as a bridge, connecting people from different cultures and fostering understanding. Speaking Nepali not only enabled me to communicate with Nepalese individuals but also deepened my understanding of their perspectives, customs, and traditions. It created a platform for meaningful dialogue and cultural exchange, paving the way for mutual respect and appreciation.
- ***The Enduring Connection to Nepali:*** Even after leaving the embassy, my connection to the Nepali language remains strong. Whenever I come across someone who speaks Nepali or have the opportunity to interact with Nepalese

individuals, a sense of familiarity and warmth emerges. The language serves as a reminder of the bonds formed and the cultural experiences shared during my time at the embassy.

- ***Personal Growth and Cross-Cultural Competence:*** The journey of learning Nepali not only enhanced my linguistic abilities but also fostered personal growth and cross-cultural competence. It expanded my worldview, challenged my assumptions, and nurtured a deep appreciation for diversity. The experience broadened my cultural sensitivity, adaptability, and ability to navigate diverse environments with ease.
- ***Embracing Language Learning in a Globalized World:*** In today's interconnected world, the importance of language learning cannot be overstated. Engaging with languages beyond one's mother tongue demonstrates a commitment to understanding, respect, and inclusivity. My journey of learning Nepali serves as a testament to the value of embracing language learning as a means to bridge cultural gaps, foster connections, and promote global understanding.

The journey of learning Nepali at the embassy was a transformative experience that transcended linguistic boundaries. The support and guidance of the Nepalese staff, coupled with consistent practice and immersion, allowed me to become a fluent speaker. This proficiency in Nepali opened doors to professional opportunities, deepened cultural connections, and facilitated meaningful interactions. The enduring connection I feel whenever I encounter the Nepali language serves as a reminder of the bonds formed and the mutual respect fostered during my time at the embassy. Embracing language learning, like learning Nepali, is a powerful tool for cultural exchange, personal growth, and fostering a more inclusive and interconnected world.

"Democracy in Nepal is a phoenix, soaring above the peaks, a symbol of resilience and rebirth."

Pashupatinath Temple: My Sacred Connection with Lord Shiva

In the heart of Kathmandu, Nepal, stands a revered ancient temple, Pashupatinath, dedicated to Lord Shiva, the divine deity known as "Bhole Shankar." My deep attachment to this temple stems from my upbringing in a village where an ancient shrine of Lord Shiva existed. My reverence for Lord Shiva intensified during my frequent visits to Pashupatinath Temple while serving at the Indian Embassy in Kathmandu for four years. Even after returning to India, my connection to Pashupatinath Temple remains unwavering, as reflected in the names I have bestowed upon my buildings, residences, guest houses, and farmhouses. This chapter delves into the profound spiritual bond I share with Pashupatinath Temple, the impact it has had on my life, and the enduring legacy it has inspired.

- ***The Influence of the Village Shrine:*** Growing up in a village with an ancient shrine of Lord Shiva, I was exposed to the spiritual significance and teachings associated with this divine deity from an early age. The rituals, stories, and devotional practices surrounding Lord Shiva nurtured a deep sense of respect and reverence within me.
- ***Discovering Pashupatinath Temple:*** During my tenure at the Indian Embassy in Kathmandu, I had the privilege of visiting Pashupatinath Temple regularly. This sacred pilgrimage site, nestled on the banks of the Bagmati River, captivated me with its awe-inspiring architecture, rich cultural heritage, and profound spiritual atmosphere.
- ***Spiritual Awakening at Pashupatinath Temple:*** With each visit to Pashupatinath Temple, my spiritual connection with Lord Shiva deepened. The divine energy permeating the temple complex, the rhythmic chants, and the devoutness of the pilgrims created an ambiance of serenity and transcendence. I found solace in the presence of Lord Shiva and experienced a profound sense of inner peace and spiritual awakening.
- ***The Significance of Lord Shiva in Hinduism:*** Lord Shiva, one of the principal deities in Hinduism, symbolizes destruction, transformation, and the eternal cycle of creation. His divine attributes of being the destroyer of evil, the embodiment of cosmic energy, and the supreme yogi resonated

deeply with me. I was drawn to Lord Shiva's embodiment of simplicity, renunciation, and spiritual enlightenment.

- ***The Impact of Pashupatinath Temple on Personal and Professional Life:*** The spiritual experiences and tranquility I found at Pashupatinath Temple had a profound impact on both my personal and professional life. The temple's serene environment provided a sanctuary for introspection, clarity, and rejuvenation. It served as a source of inspiration and guidance during challenging times, enabling me to navigate life's complexities with grace and determination.
- ***Carrying the Spirit of Pashupatinath to India:*** Upon returning to India, my attachment to Pashupatinath Temple remained unwavering. To honor and preserve the spiritual legacy of Lord Shiva, I named my buildings, residences, guest houses, and farmhouses after significant aspects associated with Lord Shiva. This act serves as a constant reminder of the sacred connection I share with Pashupatinath Temple and the enduring principles of Lord Shiva that guide.

"From the crown's command to the people's choice, Nepal's democracy is the voice of the masses."

The Significance of Pashupatinath Temple in Kathmandu: A Sacred Hindu Shrine

Nestled along the banks of the holy Bagmati River, the Pashupatinath Temple stands as a symbol of religious and cultural heritage in the heart of Kathmandu, Nepal. Believed to be one of the most sacred Hindu temples dedicated to Lord Shiva, Pashupatinath attracts devotees from far and wide, who come seeking spiritual solace, blessings, and a connection with the divine. This chapter explores the historical, cultural, and religious significance of the Pashupatinath Temple, delving into its control and the role of pujaris in its religious practices.

- ***Historical and Cultural Significance:*** The origin of the Pashupatinath Temple is shrouded in legends and mythology. According to Hindu scriptures, the temple's history dates back thousands of years, with mentions in ancient texts like the Puranas and the Mahabharata. The temple's location holds immense significance as it is believed to be the spot where Lord Shiva took the form of Pashupati (Lord of Animals) and performed his divine cosmic dance, known as the Tandava.

Over the centuries, Pashupatinath has developed into a center of religious and cultural activities. It has served as a focal point for various festivals, including the Maha Shivaratri, Teej, and Bala Chaturdashi, attracting devotees who engage in elaborate rituals, prayers, and offerings. The temple's architecture reflects a blend of Nepalese pagoda and Indian Shikhara styles, showcasing intricate wood carvings, gilded roofs, and sacred imagery.

- ***Control of the Pashupatinath Temple:*** The Pashupatinath Temple is managed and controlled by the Pashupati Area Development Trust (PADT), a governmental body established in 1996. The PADT is responsible for the overall administration, maintenance, and development of the temple premises. Its primary objective is to ensure the preservation of the temple's cultural and religious heritage while facilitating the smooth conduct of rituals and providing necessary facilities for devotees.

The PADT functions under the Ministry of Culture, Tourism, and Civil Aviation, and its board comprises government-appointed members, including religious scholars, administrators, and representatives from various stakeholder groups. The trust regulates the temple's affairs, manages its finances, and oversees the appointment of pujaris (priests) and other temple staff.

- ***The Role of Pujaris:*** Pujaris hold a pivotal role in the religious practices and rituals conducted at the Pashupatinath Temple. They are responsible for conducting daily worship, performing sacred ceremonies, and facilitating the engagement of devotees with Lord Pashupatinath. Pujaris are considered as the intermediaries between the divine and the devotees, guiding them in their spiritual journey and offering blessings and prayers on their behalf.

The appointment of pujaris is a rigorous process overseen by the PADT. Candidates are selected based on their knowledge of Hindu scriptures, spiritual discipline, and dedication to serving the temple and its visitors. Once appointed, pujaris undergo training to enhance their understanding of rituals, mantras, and the traditions associated with Pashupatinath. They are expected to maintain utmost purity, observe religious customs, and adhere to strict codes of conduct.

Pujaris are entrusted with the responsibility of performing daily puja and offering prayers to Lord Pashupatinath. They conduct various rituals, including the abhishekam (sacred bath), aarti (devotional ceremony with lamps), and the recitation of Vedic hymns. These rituals create an atmosphere of divine reverence and allow devotees to connect with the spiritual energy of the temple.

Pujaris also play a crucial role during festivals and special occasions at Pashupatinath. They lead the elaborate ceremonies, coordinate the participation of devotees, and ensure the smooth flow of rituals. Their presence and guidance provide a sense of sanctity and bring devotees closer to the divine presence of Lord Pashupatinath.

The pujaris of Pashupatinath are highly respected and revered within the local community and among devotees. Their knowledge and expertise in Hindu scriptures and rituals make them valuable sources of spiritual guidance and wisdom. They often offer counsel and support to devotees, addressing their concerns, and providing solace in times of distress.

- ***Challenges and Controversies:*** Despite its immense religious and cultural significance, the Pashupatinath Temple has faced various challenges and controversies over the years. One of the primary concerns has been the conservation of the temple's heritage structures and the surrounding environment. The increasing number of visitors, coupled with inadequate infrastructure and waste management systems, has put a strain on the temple premises and the Bagmati River, leading to pollution and degradation.

Another issue that has sparked debates and controversies is the question of access and inclusion within the temple. Traditionally, women and non-Hindus were restricted from entering certain areas of the temple complex. However, in recent years, efforts have been made to promote inclusivity, allowing people from all backgrounds and faiths to visit and experience the spiritual ambiance of Pashupatinath.

There have also been instances of financial mismanagement and allegations of corruption within the management of the temple. These concerns have prompted calls for greater transparency, accountability, and good governance in the administration of Pashupatinath.

- ***Preservation and Future Development:*** Recognizing the importance of preserving the cultural and religious heritage of Pashupatinath, the Nepalese government and the Pashupati Area Development Trust have taken steps to address the challenges and ensure its long-term sustainability. Conservation projects have been initiated to restore and maintain the temple's architectural structures, including the pagoda roofs, intricate wood carvings, and sacred statues.

Efforts are also underway to improve infrastructure, waste management systems, and the overall visitor experience. The construction of new pathways, renovation of ghats (steps leading to the river), and the establishment of visitor centers aim to enhance the accessibility and aesthetics of the temple premises.

Additionally, initiatives have been launched to promote cultural and educational activities within the temple complex. The PADT organizes seminars, workshops, and exhibitions that showcase the rich cultural heritage of Pashupatinath, fostering a deeper understanding and appreciation among visitors.

The Pashupatinath Temple stands as a testament to Nepal's rich religious and cultural heritage. Its significance as a sacred Hindu shrine, dedicated to Lord Pashupatinath, attracts millions of devotees and visitors each year. The temple's control by the Pashupati Area Development Trust and the role of pujaris in conducting rituals and facilitating spiritual experiences are vital aspects of its functioning.

As Nepal navigates the challenges of preserving its cultural and religious heritage, efforts must continue to ensure the conservation and sustainable development of the Pashupatinath Temple. This includes addressing issues of environmental degradation, waste management, and infrastructure improvement. The promotion of inclusivity and accessibility within the temple complex is also crucial, allowing people from diverse backgrounds to experience the spiritual ambiance and cultural significance of Pashupatinath.

Transparency, accountability, and good governance should remain at the forefront of the temple's administration. Measures to combat financial mismanagement and corruption will help build trust among devotees and stakeholders. Regular audits, increased transparency in financial transactions, and strict adherence to ethical standards will contribute to the efficient and responsible management of the temple's resources.

Furthermore, cooperation between the government, the Pashupati Area Development Trust, and local communities is vital for the sustainable preservation and development of Pashupatinath. Engaging local stakeholders in decision-making processes, seeking their input, and involving them in heritage conservation activities will create a sense of ownership and ensure the temple's long-term sustainability.

Education and awareness programs can play a significant role in promoting the cultural and historical significance of Pashupatinath. By disseminating knowledge about the temple's history, rituals, and spiritual significance, both among visitors and the local community, a deeper appreciation and understanding of Pashupatinath's heritage can be fostered. This can be achieved through the establishment of visitor centers, the organization of cultural events, and the inclusion of educational components in the temple experience.

The Pashupatinath Temple in Kathmandu holds immense historical, cultural, and religious significance. Its control by the Pashupati Area Development Trust and the role of pujaris in conducting rituals and guiding devotees are integral to its functioning. However, challenges such as environmental degradation, inclusivity, and governance need to be addressed to ensure the sustainable preservation and development of this sacred Hindu shrine. By fostering collaboration, promoting transparency, and engaging in educational initiatives, Pashupatinath can continue to inspire and provide spiritual solace for generations to come.

"Nepal's democratic spirit is like a river, flowing with the force of the people's will."

Embracing Nepal: Unveiling a Journey of Discovery and Connection

Nepal, a land of majestic mountains, vibrant cultures, and spiritual richness, has always held a special place in my heart. The idea of writing a detailed book on Nepal emerged from a deep longing to share the profound experiences and insights gained during my time exploring this remarkable country. In this chapter, I will delve into the origins of this idea and elaborate on the purpose behind crafting a comprehensive narrative that celebrates Nepal's beauty, history, and people.

- ***A Serendipitous Encounter:*** The seed of inspiration for my book on Nepal was planted during a chance encounter. A friend's vivid storytelling of their trekking adventure in the Everest region left me captivated and filled with an insatiable curiosity. The tales of breathtaking landscapes, warm hospitality, and the spiritual aura that enveloped every step of their journey ignited a flame within me. I yearned to experience Nepal's magic firsthand.
- ***A Journey of Discovery:*** As I embarked on my maiden voyage to Nepal, I quickly realized that this was no ordinary adventure. Nepal's allure lies in its ability to awaken the senses and provoke profound introspection. From the bustling streets of Kathmandu to the serene tranquility of monasteries in the Himalayas, every corner of Nepal offered a unique tapestry of experiences.
- ***Immersion in Cultural Riches:*** One of the primary motivations behind writing a detailed book on Nepal was to celebrate and preserve the rich cultural heritage of this nation. Nepal's diverse ethnic groups and their vibrant traditions form an integral part of its identity. Through my book, I aim to shed light on the rituals, festivals, and customs that shape Nepal's social fabric, allowing readers to gain a deeper understanding of the country's soul.
- ***The Majesty of Nature:*** Nepal's awe-inspiring natural landscapes are nothing short of a masterpiece. The towering Himalayan peaks, including Mount Everest, the world's highest mountain, and the serene beauty of the Annapurna region, leave an indelible mark on the hearts of those fortunate enough to witness them. Through vivid descriptions and personal anecdotes, I hope to transport readers to these breathtaking vistas, evoking a sense of wonder and appreciation for Nepal's ecological treasures.

- ***A Spiritual Odyssey:*** Nepal's spiritual heritage is deeply intertwined with its cultural tapestry. As I explored ancient temples, Buddhist monasteries, and sacred pilgrimage sites, I felt a profound connection to the spiritual energy that permeates the country. I intend to delve into the philosophies, practices, and spiritual beliefs that are intrinsic to Nepal's way of life, inviting readers to embark on a transformative journey of self-discovery and enlightenment.
- ***The People of Nepal:*** The heart and soul of Nepal reside in its people. Warm, welcoming, and resilient, Nepalis possess an innate ability to find joy and contentment in the simplest of things. By sharing the stories of the individuals, I encountered during my travels, I hope to provide readers with an intimate portrait of the Nepali people's strength, resilience, and unwavering spirit.
- ***A Call to Action:*** Beyond the narrative of my personal adventures, my book on Nepal aims to inspire readers to explore the world, embrace diverse cultures, and foster a greater sense of global citizenship. I firmly believe that travel, whether physical or mental, has the power to broaden perspectives, foster empathy, and nurture a deeper appreciation for the world we inhabit. Through my experiences in Nepal, I hope to ignite a spark within readers, encouraging them to embark on their own transformative journeys of discovery.
- ***Preserving Nepal's Heritage:*** Writing a detailed book on Nepal also serves the purpose of contributing to the preservation of Nepal's rich heritage. As the world becomes increasingly interconnected, cultural traditions and practices face the risk of fading away. By documenting and sharing the stories, rituals, and practices that define Nepal's cultural landscape, I hope to create an enduring record that can be cherished by future generations.
- ***Encouraging Sustainable Tourism:*** Tourism is a double-edged sword. While it has the potential to bring economic growth and cultural exchange, it can also strain fragile ecosystems and disrupt local communities. In my book, I emphasize the importance of responsible and sustainable tourism practices. By highlighting eco-friendly initiatives, community-based tourism projects, and ethical travel choices, I aim to inspire readers to be conscious travelers who leave a positive impact on Nepal and its people.
- ***Bridging the Gap:*** Nepal, like many other developing countries, faces challenges such as poverty, lack of access to education, and limited healthcare resources. Through my book, I aim to shed light on these issues, raising awareness and encouraging readers to support grassroots organizations and

initiatives that strive to make a difference in Nepal. By bridging the gap between readers and the needs of local communities, I hope to foster a sense of global solidarity and inspire acts of compassion and generosity.

Writing a detailed book on Nepal is not just a personal endeavor; it is a labor of love and a tribute to the remarkable country that has touched my soul. Through vivid storytelling, cultural exploration, and a call to action, I aim to transport readers to the heart of Nepal, immersing them in its beauty, spirituality, and rich heritage. Beyond the pages, I hope to inspire a new generation of travelers and advocates who will cherish, protect, and celebrate the wonders of Nepal for years to come. May this book be a catalyst for meaningful connections, transformative experiences, and a deeper appreciation of the world we share.

"The monarchy's abdication marks the birth of Nepal's democracy, a child of the people's aspirations."

The Legacy of Nepalese Domiciled Gurkhas and the Need for Inclusivity in Armed Forces

The history of the Nepalese Domiciled Gurkhas (NDG) is one of unparalleled bravery, sacrifice, and loyalty. For decades, these formidable soldiers have served in various armed forces around the world, including India, the United Kingdom, and other nations. However, recent developments in Nepal have led to a disruption in the recruitment of NDG into foreign armed forces, including the Indian Army. This has sparked concerns about the future of NDG recruitment and the impact it could have on their long-standing legacy. Additionally, the potential recruitment of NDG by other countries, including Russia, Ukraine, and even China, raises questions about the geopolitical implications of this shift. This article seeks to explore the historical significance of NDG, the current challenges they face, and the need for a reevaluation of recruitment policies to ensure inclusivity and fairness.

- ***Historical Legacy of the Nepalese Domiciled Gurkhas:*** The legacy of the Nepalese Domiciled Gurkhas dates back to the early 19th century when the British East India Company recognized their exceptional combat skills and valor during the Anglo-Nepalese War. Impressed by their bravery, the British sought to recruit Gurkha soldiers into their own ranks, leading to the formation of the famed Gurkha regiments in the British Indian Army. Since then, NDG have earned a reputation as some of the most skilled and dedicated soldiers, known for their unwavering loyalty and fearlessness in the face of adversity.

Throughout numerous conflicts and peacekeeping operations, NDG have distinguished themselves through acts of heroism and sacrifice, earning the respect and admiration of their fellow soldiers and commanding officers. Their contributions to various military endeavors, including conflicts with Pakistan and China, as well as peacekeeping missions in Sri Lanka, have been instrumental in upholding peace and security in the region.

- ***Challenges Faced by Nepalese Domiciled Gurkhas:*** Despite their storied history and invaluable service, Nepalese Domiciled Gurkhas are currently facing a critical juncture as the Nepalese government has imposed restrictions on their recruitment into foreign armed forces, citing a violation of the 1947 tripartite agreement. This decision has not only disrupted the longstanding tradition of NDG recruitment but has also raised concerns about the impact on the livelihoods and aspirations of prospective Gurkha recruits.

The inability of Nepalese citizens to join armed forces as agniveers has not only stirred discontent within the NDG community but has also prompted international repercussions. Reports of NDG considering offers from other countries, including Russia, Ukraine, and even China, have underscored the urgency of addressing the challenges faced by the NDG community. Furthermore, the potential induction of NDG into the armed forces of nations other than India raises geopolitical implications and warrants careful consideration.

- ***The Need for Inclusivity and Fairness:*** The current predicament facing the Nepalese Domiciled Gurkhas calls for a reevaluation of recruitment policies and a renewed commitment to inclusivity and fairness. The legacy of the NDG, rooted in unwavering dedication and valor, deserves to be upheld and honored through equitable opportunities for service in various armed forces.

India, given its historical ties with the NDG and the significant contributions of Gurkha soldiers to its armed forces, holds a responsibility to address the challenges faced by the NDG community. The interruption of NDG recruitment into the Indian Army not only risks a loss of invaluable talent and expertise but also undermines the longstanding partnership between India and Nepal in the realm of defense and security.

It is imperative for India to engage in diplomatic dialogue with Nepal to seek an amicable resolution that respects the aspirations of Nepalese Domiciled Gurkhas while upholding the spirit of the 1947 tripartite agreement. This entails fostering a collaborative approach that acknowledges the historical significance of the Gurkha regiments and the enduring bond between the two nations. By recognizing the contributions and sacrifices of NDG and working towards a mutually beneficial arrangement, India can reaffirm its commitment to honoring the legacy of the Nepalese Domiciled Gurkhas.

Furthermore, the potential recruitment of NDG by other nations, including Russia, Ukraine, and China, underscores the need for a proactive and concerted effort to address the challenges faced by the NDG community. The prospect of NDG serving in the armed forces of countries beyond their traditional affiliations poses complex geopolitical implications, necessitating a thoughtful and strategic response from all stakeholders involved.

In addition to diplomatic engagement, it is essential for India to prioritize the welfare and interests of Nepalese Domiciled Gurkhas by exploring avenues for collaboration and dialogue. This may involve facilitating discussions with the Nepalese government, engaging in confidence-building measures, and advocating for the preservation of the rich legacy of the NDG within the framework of mutually beneficial agreements.

Moreover, the potential induction of NDG into the armed forces of other nations highlights the importance of fostering a sense of belonging and opportunity within their own countries. Efforts to address the grievances of the NDG community and explore avenues for their meaningful participation in the armed forces can contribute to fostering a climate of inclusivity and empowerment. By recognizing the talents and potential of NDG and creating pathways for their professional growth and fulfillment within their homeland, nations can strengthen the social fabric and uphold principles of equity and justice.

The legacy of the Nepalese Domiciled Gurkhas is a testament to the enduring spirit of courage, loyalty, and sacrifice. Their contributions to various armed forces and their unwavering commitment to upholding peace and security have left an indelible mark on the annals of military history. However, the current challenges facing the NDG community demand thoughtful consideration and proactive engagement to ensure their continued inclusion and recognition.

As India and Nepal navigate the complexities surrounding the recruitment of Nepalese Domiciled Gurkhas, there is an opportunity to reaffirm the bonds of friendship and mutual respect. By acknowledging the historical legacy of the NDG and working towards a collaborative and equitable solution, both nations can uphold the values of partnership and solidarity.

Furthermore, the potential recruitment of NDG by other nations underscores the imperative of addressing the grievances and aspirations of the NDG community. Through diplomatic engagement, advocacy for inclusivity, and a commitment to fairness, nations can honor the legacy of the Nepalese Domiciled Gurkhas and pave the way for a future defined by unity, opportunity, and mutual respect. The valor and dedication of the Nepalese Domiciled Gurkhas merit the highest regard, and it is incumbent upon all stakeholders to uphold their legacy and ensure their rightful place in the annals of military service and honor.

Downsizing and Ultimate Phasing Out Nepalese Domiciled Gurkhas Becoming a Reality

On December 11, 2023, Nepal's Prime Minister Pushpa Kamal Dahal Prachanda admitted that, "Their citizens are not only serving the Russian Army but also reportedly serving in the Ukranian Army". Nepal has urged Russia to stop their recruitment – almost 200 Nepali citizens have joined the Russian Army under dubious circumstances and six Nepalis have reportedly been killed – and to investigate the number of Nepalis fighting for Ukraine. Some have also joined the French Foreign Legion; such is the adverse effect of Nepal apparently rejecting Agniveer.

Not a single NDG has been recruited or become an Agniveer for nearly four years. Nepal has not communicated any reason for not subscribing to the Agniveer project. The Tripartite Treaty of 1947 governed Gorkha recruitment from Nepal by the British and Indian Armies. In June 2022, India announced the Agnipath scheme without consulting Nepal. Gorkhas are recognised as great warriors around the world and were key to the British empire that extended from Honduras to Hong Kong. In 2014, prime minister Modi praised the Gorkhas for shedding their blood for protecting the territorial integrity of India. For India, Gorkhas joining Indian Army is much more that 'recruitment'. It represents the strategic bonding between India and Nepal.

Nepal's Congress led government in 2022 passed on the decision on Agniveer to the new Maoist-led government which said it was seeking political consensus – diplomatic euphemism for rejecting Agniveer. In Nepal, public view on the scheme is divided. Most find it to be deeply flawed but their bottom line is firmly centered on pensionary benefits. The generous One Rank, One Pension

(OROP) has transformed the quality of life of the ex-servicemen. The minority view – "something (Agniveer) is better than nothing" highlights the need of job-seekers even if it for four years sans pension. But politics has trumped strategic and financial factors.

In last year's elections, Communist parties – CPN UML, CPN Maoist and CPN Socialist – captured 68% of the vote. The Maoists' 40-point demand in 1990 prior to the civil war demanded abrogation of foreign recruitment especially in Indian Army. No government in the coalition era – that has become inevitable under the new constitution – can oppose Communist thinking, especially on Agniveer. The hope that under the power-sharing agreement, after one year, the Nepali Congress-led coalition will accept Agniveer is unrealistic.

India, for now, is determined not to budge from Agniveer . Two reasons are offered – first, the government wants to end Gorkha recruitment as there is sufficient male recruitable population (MRP) in India. The more compelling reason is the Modi government's policy of dismantling colonial legacy of recruitment of foreign soldiers. The real reason though is financial – salary and pension costs.

Agniveer is designed to reduce the strength of the Army and cut pensions. The latter alone in 2021-22 accounted for Rs 1.21 lakh crore which was more than allotment for modernisation. Agniveer is the rank prefix of a soldier and is the lowest rank in PBOR (Personnel Below Officer Rank). This is a new rank and tenable by Agniveers.

Nepal is conveying to India that Agniveer is breach of Tripartite Agreement of 1947 and consensus is required between original signatories to change terms of engagement; and in order to accept Agniveer, the ruling government is seeking political consensus. The future of the Gorkha Brigade and its 38 battalions is bleak given the inflexible positions of both countries.

Last year, after returning from Nepal, following his appointment as honorary General of Nepal Army, Chief of Army Staff, General Manoj Pandey said this on Gorkha recruitment: "If they don't decide soon their vacancies will be given to others". As there has been no recruitment for four years, a shortfall in Gorkha regiment is being made up by Kumaonis, Garhwalis and now Nagas while other tribes are being considered. General Pande is also mulling over reducing Gorkha battalions. Indian Domiciled Gorkhas who constitute 40% of recruitment are not a match for NDGs. In 2017, 6/1 Gorkha Rifles was raised comprising 100% IDGs. It has become difficult now to preserve 6/1 GR's IDG sanctity and content as few IDGs meet the qualitative requirements (QRs) even after lowering standards and fewer are available. So the plan to fill up NDG shortfall with IDGs is a non-starter.

A Soldier's View

Nepal Rising: Journey from Monarchy to Democracy

The transition of Nepal from a monarchy to a democracy stands as a significant milestone in the nation's history. The author an eyewitness to this transformative period, having served in the Military Wing of Nepal from May 1989 to May 1993, have had a front-row seat to the dramatic changes that unfolded during this time. In this concluding note, the author would like to reflect on Nepal's transition, the challenges it faced, and the hopes and aspirations that accompanied this historic journey.

- ***The Monarchy's Reign:*** For centuries, Nepal was ruled by a monarchy, with power concentrated in the hands of a few. The monarchy played a central role in shaping the country's political landscape, but as time progressed, the need for change became increasingly apparent. The autocratic nature of the regime stifled progress, limited individual freedoms, and impeded the nation's development.
- ***Winds of Change:*** In the late 1980s, Nepal experienced a wave of political activism and demands for democracy. People from all walks of life, including students, intellectuals, and civil society organizations, rallied together, demanding political reform and a voice in the governance of their country. The winds of change were blowing, and Nepal stood on the precipice of a historic transformation.
- ***The Role of the Military:*** The author as a member of the Military Wing of Indian Embassy in Nepal during this period, witnessed firsthand the delicate balance between upholding order and safeguarding the rights of the people. The Nepalese Army found itself facing a unique challenge—being the guardian of a system that was on the verge of change. It required a delicate approach to ensure stability while respecting the aspirations of the populace. The role contribution & help being extended to Nepalese domiciled Gorkhas residing in Nepal by military wing of Indian Embassy Kathmandu have been elobrately described for understanding the scope & surmises by the readers.
- ***People's Movement and the Birth of Democracy:*** The people's movement of 1990 proved to be a turning point in Nepal's history. The widespread protests and demonstrations compelled the monarchy to bow to the demands of the people. King Birendra announced sweeping reforms, including the

establishment of a multiparty democracy and the formation of a new government. The country rejoiced as the dawn of a new era emerged.

- ***Challenges and Roadblocks:*** The transition from monarchy to democracy was not without its challenges. Nepal faced political instability, economic hardships, and social divisions. The process of building democratic institutions, ensuring the rule of law, and fostering a culture of inclusivity required immense effort and perseverance. The scars of the past lingered, but the determination to overcome them was unwavering.
- ***Consolidating Democratic Gains:*** In the years that followed, Nepal embarked on a journey of consolidating its democratic gains. Constitutional reforms were undertaken, elections were held, and efforts were made to empower marginalized communities. The voices of the people, once suppressed, gained strength and resonance. The nation slowly but steadily moved towards a more inclusive and participatory system of governance.
- ***Lessons Learned:*** The transition of Nepal from monarchy to democracy holds valuable lessons for nations around the world. It highlights the importance of people's participation, the need for inclusive governance, and the recognition that no system is immune to change. The Nepalese experience demonstrates that peaceful protests, dialogue, and a commitment to democratic principles can pave the way for a brighter future.
- ***The Role of International Community:*** During Nepal's transition, the support and engagement of the international community played a crucial role. The encouragement, guidance, and assistance provided by various nations, international organizations, and stakeholders contributed to the successful establishment of a democratic framework in Nepal. This collaboration underlines the significance of global solidarity in promoting democratic values and fostering positive change.
- ***The Path Ahead:*** While Nepal has made significant strides in its democratic journey, there are still challenges to overcome. Ensuring the inclusivity of marginalized groups, addressing economic disparities, and strengthening democratic institutions remain critical tasks. It is essential for the political leadership, civil society, and citizens to work hand in hand to nurture and protect the democratic principles that have been hard-won.
- ***Hope for the Future:*** As the author reflects on Nepal's transition, is filled with hope for the future. The resilience and determination of the Nepalese people, coupled with their rich cultural heritage and spirit of unity, serve as a strong foundation for a vibrant and prosperous democratic nation. The lessons

learned from the past can guide the nation towards a future characterized by peace, stability, and progress.

The transition of Nepal from monarchy to democracy stands as a testament to the power of the people and their unwavering commitment to change. As an eyewitness to this historic period, the author has seen the resilience and determination of the Nepalese people in their pursuit of better future. While the path ahead may still be laden with obstacles, the spirit of democracy has taken root in the hearts of the citizens. Nepal's journey serves as an inspiration, reminding us that change is possible and the collective will of a nation can shape its destiny.

The Nepal Govt. has adopted the model of Indian democracy in totality. Indian experts on constitutional matters have helped the Govt. of Nepal in not only drafting the constitution, but also supported whole heartedly in its implementation, monitoring & subsequent changes/ amendments.

Reference Books

- "The Snow Leopard" by Peter Matthiessen
- "Arresting God in Kathmandu" by Samrat Upadhyay
- "Into Thin Air" by Jon Krakauer
- "Palpasa Café" by Narayan Wagle
- "Kathmandu" by Thomas Bell
- "The Guru of Love" by Samrat Upadhyay
- "The Living Goddess" by Isabella Tree
- "The Kingdom by the Sea: A Journey Around the Coast of Great Britain" by Paul Theroux
- "Mustang: A Lost Tibetan Kingdom" by Michel Peissel
- "Little Princes: One Man's Promise to Bring Home the Lost Children of Nepal" by Conor Grennan
- "The Glass Palace" by Amitav Ghosh
- "The Gurkhas: The Inside Story of the World's Most Feared Soldiers" by Chris Bellamy
- "A Season in Heaven: True Tales from the Road to Kathmandu" edited by David Tomory
- "Annapurna: A Woman's Place" by Arlene Blum
- "The Shadow of the Silk Road" by Colin Thubron
- "The Kingdom of Nepal" by Toni Hagen
- "Nepal: A Travel Survival Kit" by Lonely Planet
- "The Hidden Life of Trees: What They Feel, How They Communicate—Discoveries from a Secret World" by Peter Wohlleben
- "Tiger for Breakfast: The Story of Boris of Kathmandu" by Michel Peissel
- "Nepal: A Short History of Its Geography, Culture, and Politics" by Shishir Kumar Panda
- "The Inheritance of Loss" by Kiran Desai
- "The Bullet and the Ballot Box: The Story of Nepal's Maoist Revolution" by Aditya Adhikari
- "Forget Kathmandu: An Elegy for Democracy" by Manjushree Thapa

- "Nepal: A Journey to the Kingdom of Mustang" by André Alexander
- "The Nepal Chronicles: Marriage, Mountains, and Momos in the Highest Place on Earth" by Dan Szczesny
- "Himalaya" by Michael Palin
- "Nepal - Culture Smart!: The Essential Guide to Customs & Culture" by Tessa Feller
- "A Step Away from Paradise: The True Story of a Tibetan Lama's Journey to a Land of Immortality" by Thomas K. Shor
- "The Sacred Thread: A True Story of Becoming a Mother and Finding a Family—Half a World Away" by Adrienne Arieff
- "From Heaven Lake: Travels Through Sinkiang and Tibet" by Vikram Seth
- "Nepal: Nation-State in the Wilderness" by Mahendra Lawoti
- "The People's War in Nepal: Left Perspectives" edited by Sherry L. Ortner and Nicholas B. Dirks
- "Democracy in Nepal: Challenges and Opportunities" edited by K. Y. Home and Prakash A. Raj
- "The Maoist Insurgency in Nepal: Revolution in the Twenty-First Century" by Mahendra Lawoti and Anup Kumar Pahari
- "Nepal in Transition: From People's War to Fragile Peace" edited by Sebastian von Einsiedel and David M. Malone
- "Democracy and the Politics of Electoral System Choice: Engineering Electoral Dominance in Nepal" by Andrew Reynolds
- "Federalism in Nepal: Journey Towards Building an Inclusive Democratic Nation" edited by Lok Raj Baral and Jivanta Schottli
- "The Politics of Nepal: Persistence and Change in an Asian Monarchy" by Leo E. Rose
- "Nepal's Failed Development: Reflections on the Mission and Its Malcontents" by Michael Hutt
- "Democratization in South Asia: Nepal and Bhutan in Comparative Perspective" by Mahendra Lawoti and Susan Hangen
- "Nepal: Transition to Democratic Republic: An Uncertain Journey" edited by Lok Raj Baral and Yug Raj Pandey
- "Democratization in Nepal: A Political History of Nepal (1950-2008)" by Mahendra Lawoti

- "Political Development in Nepal: A Study of Post-Colonial State Building" by Khadga K. Singh
- "Nepal's Peace Process: Governance, Identity, and Well-being" edited by Bishnu Raj Upreti and Krishna Hachhethu
- "Democratization and Identity: Regimes and Ethnicity in East and Southeast Asia" edited by K. S. Jomo and Joel S. Kahn
- "The Nepal Nexus: An Inside Account of the Maoists, the Durbar, and India" by Sudheer Sharma
- "Democracy and Development in Nepal: The Role of the United Nations" by Bishnu Raj Upreti
- "Democratization in South Asia: Lessons from American Institutions" edited by Sumit Ganguly and Larry Diamond
- "The Quest for Democracy in Nepal: A Study on Political Parties, Elections, and Political Participation" by Hari Bansh Jha
- "Nepal Between Marx and Market: The Politics of Reinventing the State" by Robin Vooys.
- "India-Nepal Relations: Historical, Cultural and Political Perspectives" edited by Mahendra P. Lama and Anshuman Behera
- "India-Nepal Relations: Changing Contours" edited by S.D. Muni and Yubaraj Sangroula
- "India and Nepal: Treaty Relations" by K.R. Singh
- "Nepal-India Open Borders: Problems and Prospects" by Purusottam Oja
- "Nepal-India Relations: Documents, 1947-2007" edited by S.D. Muni and S.M. Michael
- "Nepal and India: A Historical Perspective" by Niranjan S. Sastry
- "India and Nepal: Aspects of Interdependent Relations" by K.R. Singh
- "Nepal-India Relations: Issues and Challenges" edited by Alok Kumar Gupta
- "Nepal's Relations with India and China: Documents, 1947-1995" edited by S.D. Muni and S.M. Michael
- "India-Nepal Relations: The Challenge Ahead" edited by S.D. Muni and Nishchal N. Pandey
- "India and Nepal: Political Aspects" by K.R. Singh

- "Nepal-India Relations: Emerging Scenario and Challenges" edited by Jivesh Jha
- "India and Nepal: A Changing Relationship" by S.D. Muni
- "Nepal-India Relations: Options and Opportunities" edited by B.C. Upreti and R.B. Thapa
- "India, Nepal, and the Kingdom in the Clouds" by Pratyoush Onta
- "Nepal-India Relations: Treaty, Trade, and Transit" edited by Dev Raj Dahal
- "India-Nepal Relations: New Vistas" edited by S.D. Muni and R.K. Mishra
- "Nepal-India Relations: A Historical Analysis" by S. Chalise
- "India and Nepal: Treaty Relations and Diplomatic History" by S.K. Gupta
- "India-Nepal Relations: Historical, Cultural and Political Perspectives" edited by K. Warikoo.

Dr TC Rao as LO (Liaison Officer) to Shri PV Narsimha Rao, PM of India during visit to Nepal

Dr TC Rao with Shri Shivraj Patil, Home Minister of India, Prof Bimal Prasad Former Ambassador to Nepal & Col. (Later Lt. Gen.) Richard Khare, Ex - Military Intelligence Chief & Major Sanjeev Kumar AMA (Welfare) during visit to Nepal

Dr TC Rao with Gen SF Rodrigues, COAS Indian Army during visit to Nepal

Dr TC Rao is with Shri GP Koirala, PM of Nepal

Dr & Mrs TC Rao with Dr. Ram Baran Yadav, President of Nepal

Dr TC Rao with Shri GP Koirala, PM of Nepal